T0301264

A Research Agenda for Social Finance

Elgar Research Agendas outline the future of research in a given area. Leading scholars are given the space to explore their subject in provocative ways, and map out the potential directions of travel. They are relevant but also visionary.

Forward-looking and innovative, Elgar Research Agendas are an essential resource for PhD students, scholars and anybody who wants to be at the forefront of research.

Titles in the series include:

A Research Agenda for Knowledge Management and Analytics
Edited by Jay Liebowitz

A Research Agenda for Heritage Tourism
Edited by Maria Gravari-Barbas

A Research Agenda for Border Studies
Edited by James W. Scott

A Research Agenda for Sales
Edited by Fernando Jaramillo and Jay Prakash Mulki

A Research Agenda for Employee Engagement in a Changing World of Work
Edited by John P. Meyer and Benjamin Schneider

A Research Agenda for the Entrepreneurial University
Edited by Ulla Hytti

A Research Agenda for Place Branding
Edited by Dominic Medway, Gary Warnaby and John Byrom

A Research Agenda for Social Finance
Edited by Othmar M. Lehner

A Research Agenda
for Social Finance

Edited by

OTHMAR M. LEHNER

*Professor and Director, Centre for Accounting,
Finance and Governance, Hanken School of Economics, Finland*

Elgar Research Agendas

 Edward **Elgar**
PUBLISHING

Cheltenham, UK • Northampton, MA, USA

Published by
Edward Elgar Publishing Limited
The Lypiatts
15 Lansdown Road
Cheltenham
Glos GL50 2JA
UK

Edward Elgar Publishing, Inc.
William Pratt House
9 Dewey Court
Northampton
Massachusetts 01060
USA

A catalogue record for this book
is available from the British Library

Library of Congress Control Number: 2021933290

This book is available electronically in the **Elgar**online
Economics subject collection
http://dx.doi.org/10.4337/9781789907964

ISBN 978 1 78990 795 7 (cased)
ISBN 978 1 78990 796 4 (eBook)

Printed and bound by CPI Group (UK) Ltd, Croydon, CR0 4YY

Contents

Figures

Tables

Contributors

Eleonora Broccardo, Associate Professor of Banking and Finance, Department of Economics and Management, University of Trento, Italy.
  ORCID: 0000-0002-5338-1420

Sandro Cabral, Professor of Strategy and Public Management, Insper, Brazil.
  ORCID: 0000-0002-8663-2441

Ericka Costa, Associate Professor of Accounting, Department of Economics and Management, University of Trento, Italy.
  ORCID: 0000-0003-4387-8908

Elizabeth Embry, PhD Candidate, Strategy, Entrepreneurship and Operations, Leeds School of Business, University of Colorado, United States.
  ORCID: 0000-0001-6889-669X

Vanina A. Farber, elea Professor of Social Innovation, IMD Business School, Switzerland.
  ORCID: 0000-0002-6798-9103

Luciana C. de M. Ferreira, Professor of Organizational Behavior, Fundação Dom Cabral, Brazil.
  ORCID: 0000-0002-2670-700X

Andrea Girardi, PhD Student at Marco Biagi Department of Economics, University of Modena & Reggio Emilia, Italy.
  ORCID: 0000-0002-1589-7565

Jessica Jones, Assistant Professor of Management and Entrepreneurship, Haslam School of Business, University of Tennessee, United States.
  ORCID: 0000-0003-3582-3632

J. Howard Kucher, Associate Professor of Social Innovation, The University of Maryland, Baltimore, United States.
  ORCID: 0000-0002-1312-4956

Sergio G. Lazzarini, Chafi Haddad Professor of Management, Insper, Brazil.
ORCID: 0000-0001-8191-1241

Othmar M. Lehner, Professor and Director, Centre for Accounting, Finance and Governance, Hanken School of Economics, Helsinki, Finland.
ORCID: 0000-0002-3317-9604

Maria Mazzuca, Associate Professor of Banking and Finance, Department of Business Administration and Law, University of Calabria, Italy.
ORCID: 0000-0003-1275-3002

Tongyu Meng, PhD Candidate, Department of Management and International Business, The University of Auckland Business School, New Zealand.
ORCID: 0000-0003-3893-3286

Jamie Newth, Lecturer, Department of Management and International Business, The University of Auckland Business School, New Zealand.
ORCID: 0000-0002-9619-3753

Caterina Pesci, Assistant Professor of Accounting, Department of Economics and Management, University of Trento, Italy.
ORCID: 0000-0001-9409-6389

Leandro S. Pongeluppe, PhD Candidate in Strategic Management, Rotman School of Management, University of Toronto, Canada.
ORCID: 0000-0001-6195-4455

Julia M. Puaschunder, Department of Economics, The New School for Social Research and Graduate School of Arts and Sciences, Columbia University, United States.
ORCID: 0000-0003-1977-1545

Patrick Reichert, Postdoctoral Research Fellow at elea Center for Social Innovation, IMD Business School, Switzerland.
ORCID: 0000-0003-4057-0289

Angelica Rotondaro, Alimi Impact Ventures and Research Associate, Center for Organizational Studies (CORS), University of São Paulo, Brazil.
ORCID: 0000-0001-8191-1241

Olaf Weber, Professor and University Research Chair in Sustainable Finance, School of Environment, Enterprise and Development (SEED), University of Waterloo, Canada.
ORCID: 0000-0001-6602-0459

Introduction to *A Research Agenda for Social Finance*

Othmar M. Lehner

Introduction

Social ventures, tackling social as well as environmental problems with hybrid business models, often function as non-governmental actors that pursue a predominantly social or environmental mission through their economic activity (Bertl, 2016; Geobey, Westley and Weber, 2012; Nicholls, 2010a; Weber, 2014). Lehner (2013) remarks that traditional means of finance may be inadequate for starting and sustaining such ventures due to their inherent abnormal risk premiums (Zerbib, 2019). Impact investing is one aspect of the newly emerged social finance sector (Bertl, 2016; Brandstetter and Lehner, 2015; Lehner, Harrer and Quast, 2019) that addresses this inadequacy and has gained importance since the term was first coined by the Rockefeller Foundation in 2007 (Harji and Jackson, 2012, 2018). Wood, Thornley and Grace (2013) assume that institutional impact investors can act as agents who are able to catalyze further investments in social ventures by legitimizing the industry. According to Lehner, Harrer and Quast (2018), however, the social impact investment market still appears to be in its infancy, with institutions lacking an understanding of its new and innovative hybrid business models (Kroeger and Weber, 2014; Lehner and Weber, 2020) and the necessary dyadic focus on socially driven investees, intermediaries and investors from various backgrounds, leading to complex negotiations. The resulting 'liability of newness' is intensified by a lack of terminological clarity as well as by a shortage of track records of successful high-quality impact investment opportunities (Nicholls, 2018; O'Donohoe et al., 2010) and imposes various constraints concerning access to resources.

Literature from fields such as social entrepreneurship and public management already deal extensively with the many faces of social ventures and the 'blended' value focus as a result of the hybrid business models (Gundry et al., 2011; Lehner, 2011; Nicholls, 2009). However, looking at the investors' side – when it comes to informed decision making about individual investments and the building of a portfolio of such ventures – little is actually known about the types and rationale of social investors apart from anecdotal case studies (Brandstetter and Lehner, 2015; Daggers and Nicholls, 2017; Nicholls, 2009).

One example, the 'social risk' – ranging from reputational or cluster risks to opportunity risks of not reaching the desired social goals and impacts (Pintelon et al., 2013) – has been neglected in academic discourse so far (Reeder et al., 2015). In addition, current metrics and models such as the social return on investment (SROI) lack fundamental thoughts on the long-term covariance of social projects from both the financial and the social sides in larger portfolios (Arvidson et al., 2013; Brandstetter and Lehner, 2015; Jackson, 2013).

Specific idiosyncratic factors of the 'social and hybrid sphere' additionally make the use of traditional financial instruments to address these issues complex and difficult (Hehenberger, Mair and Metz, 2019; Lehner et al., 2019; Nicholls, 2018; Tekula and Andersen, 2019). Such factors may be, for example: non-linear risk/reward logics, non-normal risk distributions and/or policy-based supply constraints as identified in impact investment funds and intermediaries. In addition, instruments such as social impact bonds are typically outside the scope of traditional investors and fail to be understood purely in financial terms (Jackson, 2013; Lehner et al., 2018; Warner, 2013).

Yet, as increasing numbers of institutions providing social finance and impact investments emerge, and early talks (O'Donohoe et al., 2010) even try to delineate impact investments as a specific asset class, it becomes clear that in order to professionalize the market and enable efficient social impact portfolio allocations, suitable metrics and models need to be developed (Brandstetter and Lehner, 2015; Geobey et al., 2012; Moore, Westley and Brodhead, 2012; Richardson, 2011). Such metrics should ideally support managers and fiduciaries of public and private social funds, charities and foundations in their rational decision making, while counting in all relevant factors of both spheres, the financial and the social, to proliferate social innovations (Jackson, 2013; Moore, Westley and Nicholls, 2012).

Acceptance of such models, however, can only be achieved when the underlying metrics are based on solid empirical foundations and are subsequently validated in practice for robustness (Daggers and Nicholls, 2017; Nicholls,

2018). Needless to say, these instruments need to be reasonably easy to use and display great adaptability to the individual needs of the various types of social investors and financial intermediaries.

It has so far become clear that in order to understand the field of social finance or impact investing, researchers need to look at it from various angles and employ interdisciplinary approaches, and, in consequence, in the list of references below there are articles from journals of various disciplines, including entrepreneurship and entrepreneurial finance, accounting, finance, management and ethics. Thus, this *Research Agenda for Social Finance* will provide guidance to aspiring researchers both in terms of improving the understanding of the layout of our field and in finding research questions and suitable methodologies to begin their own endeavors. The book is divided into ten chapters, which the authors themselves introduce in the following paragraphs by providing short summaries.

Overview of the book

Chapter 1: Exploring impact investing's emergence in the philanthropic sector, *Jessica Jones and Elizabeth Embry*

This chapter focuses on the integration of impact investing practices by the philanthropic sector. Different from other funders involved in impact investing, philanthropic organizations place a higher priority on allocating capital towards their social mission rather than capturing economic value. As these organizations have been relatively overlooked by management scholars, we provide an overview of the philanthropic sector, specifically introducing how different philanthropic organizations receive and allocate their capital. We then present how philanthropic organizations have become involved in impact investing and describe research at this intersection. Finally, we propose a research agenda that examines the nexus of philanthropy and impact investing at the individual, organizational and institutional levels of analysis. In doing so, we show how the philanthropic sector is critical, yet understudied as a funder utilizing impact investing practices.

Chapter 2: A ladder to nowhere? A research agenda for funding social enterprise, *J. Howard Kucher*

The burgeoning study of social entrepreneurship has fostered substantial inquiry into means and methods for growing a social enterprise (Lumpkin and Bacq, 2019; Santos, Pache and Birkholz, 2015; Wry and York, 2017), with a growing preference for a hybrid entity as the common construct for these ventures (Battilana and Dorado, 2010; Rawhouser, Cummings and Crane, 2015). Responding to numerous calls for additional exploration of the financing of social enterprise (Austin, Stevenson and Wei-Skillern, 2006; Lyons and Kickul, 2013; Nicholls, 2010b), this chapter identifies some critical gaps in the literature and suggests some areas for further exploration that may be useful for developing a more structured and predictable process for funding these hybrid entities.

Chapter 3: Financing a sustainable planet: research agenda for impact investing in the renewable energy sector from an identity based view, Tongyu Meng and Jamie Newth

This chapter offers three theoretical lenses through which to investigate the impact investing field, where institutional logics, stakeholder management theory and sensemaking are all interconnected through the concept of identity. An institutional logics perspective opens up research avenues for the hybridity of blended institutional logics, legitimacy and institutional work by which individuals, groups and organizations evaluate their everyday activities and organize those activities. Stakeholder management theory and the stakeholder salience framework help managers to identify and prioritize stakeholder groups. Further to this point, we offer a behavioral perspective to examine how investors navigate and shape their institutional contexts and what motivates them to do so through ethical sensemaking. This chapter contributes to the environment-focused impact investing literature by offering an overview of the development of the field and a focus on some of the key theoretical anchors upon which a research agenda can build.

Chapter 4: Market infrastructure for social ventures, Vanina A. Farber and Patrick Reichert

The hybrid mission of social ventures enables access to a wide range of financial resources, which range from pure subsidy or philanthropic contributions to fully commercial private investment. In many cases, the temporal evolution of the funding mix for social ventures creates an apparently inconsistent business lifecycle: social start-ups must rely on public and private donors, but mature social ventures often strive for independence from donative resources. In this chapter we provide a conceptualization on the market infrastructure for social ventures. We first examine the two-sided nature of social ventures (matching financial/social goals of investors and the pricing of their products/ services to balance break-even and profit expectations). Then we use a lifecycle view of social ventures to examine potential lines of research inquiry during the evolution from start-up to maturity.

Chapter 5: The best of both worlds? Impact investors and their role in the financial versus social performance debate, *Sergio G. Lazzarini, Sandro Cabral, Leandro S. Pongeluppe, Luciana C. de M. Ferreira and Angelica Rotondaro*

In this chapter, we address how organizations can cope with the tensions involved in the creation of blended economic and social value. Drawing from the literature on organizational complementarities, we employ grounded theory to understand the heterogeneous ways through which impact-oriented investors and entrepreneurs choose organizational attributes promoting an alignment between social and economic goals. We contend that tensions involved in the pursuit of blended value derive from misaligned choices that fail to mitigate potential counter-synergistic effects between these goals. We then identify key attributes whose combination leads to a typology of alternative, self-reinforcing models of blended value creation. By highlighting the importance of complementary choices supporting the creation of blended value, our study advances existing discussions on the challenges faced by organizations seeking multiple – and sometimes conflicting – dimensions of performance.

Chapter 6: Challenges for social impact measurement in the non-profit sector, *Ericka Costa*

This chapter discusses the topic of measuring, accounting, reporting and evaluating impact, with a focus on the non-profit organizations (NPOs). It starts by discussing the limitations of conventional accounting frameworks when applied to NPOs by also considering the increasing pressures NPOs face in terms of funding, particularly after the global financial crisis. Within this context, the chapter presents the current debate around the notion of impact, theory of change and impact measurement and it also discusses major opportunities for further investigation. It explores: (1) the relevance of a standardized approach to social impact measurement; (2) the emergent need to adopt a multiple-stakeholders perspective in social impact measurement; and (3) the current debate around the Sustainable Development Goals (SDGs) and the role of NPOs' social impact measurements within this context. In these concluding remarks, the chapter presents some personal viewpoints and possible challenges regarding social impact measurement.

Chapter 7: At the intersection of financial and non-financial accounting impact measurements, *Caterina Pesci and Andrea Girardi*

Starting from the normative approach of the generally accepted accounting principles (GAAP), the chapter covers the topic of the non-financial impact measurements. The first section is devoted to the objectives and postulates of the GAAP and their possible extension. In the second and third sections, respectively, the most used non-financial impact measurements are explored: Global Reporting Initiative and integrated reporting. The fourth section is devoted to the regulation on non-financial reporting, while the fifth analyses the impact of measurement approaches used in the not-for-profit arena. Finally, the last section recaps the main issues and proposes future trajectories of study at the intersection of financial and non-financial impact measurements.

Chapter 8: The banking sector and the SDGs: interconnections and future directions, *Olaf Weber*

The Sustainable Development Goals (SDGs) define the main goals to achieve sustainable development until 2030. It is estimated that $5–7 trillion will be needed annually until 2030 to achieve the SDGs, with domestic governments providing up to 80 percent of the funding for them. Hence, the SDGs might be an opportunity for the financial industry to further establish sustainability principles and to engage in financing sustainable development. This chapter recommends that future research on the topic should address the analysis of negative impacts of banking on the SDGs; contribute to understanding the net gain of banking on the SDGs; analyze the additionality of SDG finance; help understand financial risk and opportunity of SDG banking for individual SDGs; and explore types of SDG finance products and services.

Chapter 9: Financial sustainability conscientiousness, *Julia M. Puaschunder*

The implementation of sustainability accounts for the most challenging contemporary global governance goals in the trade-off of economic growth versus sustainability. In the bottom-up implementation of sustainability, tax ethics, public–private partnerships (PPPs) and corporate social responsibility (CSR) are discussed. Behavioral insight nudges to steer bottom-up sustainability action include social status manipulations and joint decision-making presentation advantages, which account for a bottom-up democracy in action to ensure natural sustainability. As for the climate injustice of diverse gains and losses around the world from a warming globe, a tax-and-bonds strategy is proposed to alleviate the losses of climate change on the macroeconomic gains of a warmer climate. Strengthening financial social responsibility, social welfare and environmental protection through future-oriented and socially responsible economic market approaches of capitalism in the twenty-first century is aimed at alleviating predictable economic, social and environmental crises to ensure a future sustainable humankind for this generation and the following.

Chapter 10: Social impact bonds: challenges and success, *Eleonora Broccardo and Maria Mazzuca*

In this chapter, we discuss social impact bonds (SIBs) with the objective of enriching the research agenda on social finance. Starting from the emerging challenges in the world of SIBs, we focus on three issues: (1) starting points for developing a theoretical framework for SIBs; (2) characteristics of SIBs that positively contribute to their effectiveness/success; and (3) factors that contribute to the enhancement of SIBs' financial returns. To examine these issues, we first point out the few theoretical contributions to date. Then, using the financial lens, we critically discuss the factors that could affect the SIBs' success and financial returns. With the aim to provide a promising future outlook on SIBs, we suggest some future research questions both from a theoretical and empirical point of view.

***

Before I leave you now to read all these exciting chapters, I would like to express my heartfelt thanks to our project manager, Carina Forstenlechner, for her fantastic support in making this book happen. Thank you, Carina, I truly appreciate all your efforts and work!

The editor and authors sincerely hope this book and research agenda provide much value to scholars, policy makers and interested practitioners in the field alike, and we are looking forward to reading more excellent research in this exciting – and highly relevant – area, based on and inspired by the agenda we present.

References

Arvidson, M., Lyon, F., McKay, S. and Moro, D. (2013). Valuing the social? The nature and controversies of measuring social return on investment (SROI). *Voluntary Sector Review*, 4(1), 3–18.

Austin, J., Stevenson, H. and Wei-Skillern, J. (2006). Social and commercial entrepreneurship: same, different, or both? *Entrepreneurship Theory and Practice*, 30(1), 1–22.

Battilana, J. and Dorado, S. (2010). Building sustainable hybrid organizations: the case of commercial microfinance organizations. *Academy of Management Journal*, 53(6), 1419–40.

Bertl, C. (2016). Environmental finance and impact investing: status quo and future research. *ACRN Oxford Journal of Finance and Risk Perspectives*, 5(2), 75–105.

Brandstetter, L. and Lehner, O.M. (2015). Opening the market for impact investments: the need for adapted portfolio tools. *Entrepreneurship Research Journal*, 5(2), 87–107.

Daggers, J. and Nicholls, A. (2017). Academic research into social investment and impact investing: the status quo and future research. In O.M. Lehner (ed.), *Routledge Handbook of Social and Sustainable Finance* (pp. 68–82). Abingdon: Routledge.

Geobey, S., Westley, F.R. and Weber, O. (2012). Enabling social innovation through developmental social finance. *Journal of Social Entrepreneurship*, 3(2), 151–65.

Gundry, L.K., Kickul, J.R., Griffiths, M.D. and Bacq, S.C. (2011). Creating social change out of nothing: the role of entrepreneurial bricolage in social entrepreneurs' catalytic innovations. *Social and Sustainable Entrepreneurship*, 13, 1–24.

Harji, K. and Jackson, E.T. (2012). *Accelerating Impact: Achievements, Challenges and What's Next in Building the Impact Investing Industry*. New York: The Rockefeller Foundation.

Harji, K. and Jackson, E.T. (2018). Facing challenges, building the field: improving the measurement of the social impact of market-based approaches. *American Journal of Evaluation*, 39(3), 396–401.

Hehenberger, L., Mair, J. and Metz, A. (2019). The assembly of a field ideology: an idea-centric perspective on systemic power in impact investing. *Academy of Management Journal*, 62(6), 1672–704.

Jackson, E.T. (2013). Interrogating the theory of change: evaluating impact investing where it matters most. *Journal of Sustainable Finance and Investment*, 3(2), 95–110.

Kroeger, A. and Weber, C. (2014). Developing a conceptual framework for comparing social value creation. *Academy of Management Review*, 39(4), 513–40.

Lehner, O.M. (2011). Social entrepreneurship perspectives: triangulated approaches to hybridity. Dissertation. *Jyväskylä Studies in Business and Economics*, 111.

Lehner, O.M. (2013). Crowdfunding social ventures: a model and research agenda. *Venture Capital*, 15(4), 289–311.

Lehner, O.M., Harrer, T. and Quast, M. (2018). Legitimacy and discourse in impact investing: searching for the holy grail. *Academy of Management Proceedings*, 2018(1), Article 10935.

Lehner, O.M., Harrer, T. and Quast, M. (2019). Building institutional legitimacy in impact investing. *Journal of Applied Accounting Research*, 20(4), 416–38.

Lehner, O.M. and Weber, C. (2020). Growing up from in-betweeners: alternatives to hybridity in social entrepreneurship research. *Entrepreneurship Research Journal*, 10(3), 1–13.

Lumpkin, G.T. and Bacq, S. (2019). Civic wealth creation: a new view of stakeholder engagement and social impact. *Academy of Management Perspectives*, 33(2), https://doi.org/10.5465/amp.2017.0060.

Lyons, T.S. and Kickul, J.R. (2013). The social enterprise financing landscape: the lay of the land and new research on the horizon. *Entrepreneurship Research Journal*, 3(2), 147–59.

Moore, M.-L., Westley, F.R. and Brodhead, T. (2012). Social finance intermediaries and social innovation. *Journal of Social Entrepreneurship*, 3(2), 184–205.

Moore, M.-L., Westley, F.R. and Nicholls, A. (2012). The social finance and social innovation nexus. *Journal of Social Entrepreneurship*, 3(2), 115–32.

Nicholls, A. (2009). 'We do good things, don't we?': 'blended value accounting' in social entrepreneurship. *Accounting, Organizations and Society*, 34(6–7), 755–69.

Nicholls, A. (2010a). Institutionalizing social entrepreneurship in regulatory space: reporting and disclosure by community interest companies. *Accounting, Organizations and Society*, 35(4), 394–415.

Nicholls, A. (2010b). The legitimacy of social entrepreneurship: reflexive isomorphism in a pre-paradigmatic field. *Entrepreneurship Theory and Practice*, 34(4), 611–33.

Nicholls, A. (2018). A general theory of social impact accounting: materiality, uncertainty and empowerment. *Journal of Social Entrepreneurship*, 9(2), 132–53.

O'Donohoe, N., Leijonhufvud, C. and Saltuk, Y. et al. (2010). *Impact Investments: An Emerging Asset Class*. J.P. Morgan Global Research.

Pintelon, O., Cantillon, B., Van den Bosch, K. and Whelan, C.T. (2013). The social stratification of social risks: the relevance of class for social investment strategies. *Journal of European Social Policy*, 23(1), 52–67.

Rawhouser, H., Cummings, M. and Crane, A. (2015). Benefit corporation legislation and the emergence of a social hybrid category. *California Management Review*, 57(3), 13–35.

Reeder, N., Colantonio, A., Loder, J. and Jones, G.R. (2015). Measuring impact in impact investing: an analysis of the predominant strength that is also its greatest weakness. *Journal of Sustainable Finance and Investment*, 5(3), 136–54.

Richardson, B.J. (2011). From fiduciary *duties* to fiduciary *relationships* for socially responsible investing: responding to the will of beneficiaries. *Journal of Sustainable Finance and Investment*, 1(1), 5–19.

Santos, F., Pache, A.-C. and Birkholz, C. (2015). Making hybrids work: aligning business models and organizational design for social enterprises. *California Management Review*, 57(3), 36–58.

Tekula, R. and Andersen, K. (2019). The role of government, nonprofit, and private facilitation of the impact investing marketplace. *Public Performance and Management Review*, 42(1), 142–61.

Warner, M.E. (2013). Private finance for public goods: social impact bonds. *Journal of Economic Policy Reform*, 16(4), 303–19.

Weber, O. (2014). The financial sector's impact on sustainable development. *Journal of Sustainable Finance and Investment*, 4(1), 1–8.

Wood, D., Thornley, B. and Grace, K. (2013). Institutional impact investing: practice and policy. *Journal of Sustainable Finance and Investment*, 3(2), 75–94.

Wry, T. and York, J.G. (2017). An identity-based approach to social enterprise. *Academy of Management Review*, 42(3), 437–60.

Zerbib, O.D. (2019). The effect of pro-environmental preferences on bond prices: evidence from green bonds. *Journal of Banking and Finance*, 98, 39–60.

1. Exploring impact investing's emergence in the philanthropic sector

Jessica Jones and Elizabeth Embry

Impact investing has received widespread attention in recent years, reaching $502 billion in assets under management in 2019 alone (Mudaliar et al., 2019). Though practiced informally for decades, impact investing did not become formally classified until 2007 (Bugg-Levine and Emerson, 2011). Defined as 'investments made with the intention of generating positive, measurable social and environmental impact alongside a financial return' (Global Impact Investing Network [GIIN], 2019, p. ii), impact investing has gained recognition and adoption across finance, government and philanthropic sectors (Agrawal and Hockerts, 2019). Some describe impact investing as the practice of 'philanthropic objectives with mainstream financial decision making' (Höchstädter and Scheck, 2015, p. 449). Growing global adoption across private and public organizations points to the importance of the phenomenon and the need to understand it, especially as it is utilized alongside other funding strategies (Mudaliar and Dithrich, 2019).

Although it is a multi-sector practice, definitions of impact investing have provided little distinction between how different funders from different sectors uniquely incorporate impact investing within their current practices to achieve their organization's mission. Many funding organizations in the finance sector have adopted the practice due to the purported opportunity for investors to achieve social returns without compromising the benefits of financial returns (Gregory, 2016; Mudaliar and Dithrich, 2019). However, for organizations in the philanthropic sector, the notion of creating funding mechanisms to generate financial return alongside their charitable purpose presents a paradigm shift (Bell, 2013). Thus, it is not surprising that while the pool of capital devoted to impacting investing has rapidly increased, the philanthropic sector has been slower to adopt this funding practice (Emerson, 2018). Of the $502 billion in assets allocated towards impact investments, less than 3 percent of those dollars come from organizations in the philanthropic sector (Mudaliar and Dithrich, 2019).

Defined as individuals, organizations and branches of corporations dedicated to engaging in charitable or philanthropic activities for humanitarian and environmental purposes (Payton and Moody, 2008), the philanthropic sector has historically been resistant to the notion of generating a financial return on their activities (Balboni and Berenbach, 2014; Moody, 2008). However, the rise of impact investing practices is timely for the philanthropic sector, as it has evolved in recent years in response to critiques purporting charitable giving as unsustainable and ineffective at addressing long-term, systemic social issues (Rath and Schuyt, 2014; Roundy, Holzhauer and Dai, 2017). Despite the low dollar amount allocated towards impact investment in the philanthropic sector thus far, philanthropic organizations are uniquely positioned to influence the growing phenomenon (Porter and Kramer, 1999; Tekula and Shah, 2016).

This chapter aims to shed light on emerging questions that rest at the intersection of philanthropy and impact investing. To help advance this necessary conversation, this chapter is organized as follows. First, we describe the evolution of impact investing, its purported appeal to and involvement of the philanthropic sector. We then unpack characteristics of the philanthropic sector, specifically focused on philanthropic organizations and the unique features that distinguish them from other types of funders who have adopted impact investing practices. In this discussion, we shed light on the shift in the philanthropic sector from being described and treated as simply charity, to the evolving ways its social mission and funding strategies can be utilized to address systemic societal issues.

By unpacking the complexity of the philanthropic sector, scholars and practitioners can more fully capture how the practice of impact investing can be adopted by philanthropic organizations, and with what challenges. As impact investing is an emerging phenomenon, especially within the philanthropic sector, it is important to engage scholars at the micro and macro levels across diverse fields, such as management, organizational behavior, strategy, entrepreneurship, economics and finance, to gain a more comprehensive perspective. To aid this exploration, we present future research questions at the individual, organizational and institutional levels of analysis. Ultimately, this chapter facilitates more exploration around the intersection of philanthropy and impact investing, pointing to questions that may explain impact investing's purported appeal yet slow adoption by the philanthropic sector and existing future opportunities for growth and impact on the pressing social and environmental issues.

Aligned opportunities: impact investing and the philanthropic sector

Impact investing, the practice of directly creating positive, measurable social and environmental impact alongside a financial return, stemmed from a series of events that called society to rethink long-term outcomes of financial markets. Socially responsible investing and corporate social responsibility (Battilana and Dorado, 2010; Santos, Pache and Birkholz, 2015) were becoming well-accepted practices when the United States' financial crisis took place in 2008. The concept of impact investing formally emerged a year earlier from a group of institutional investors and philanthropists, including The Rockefeller Foundation, Acumen Fund, and B Lab (Bugg-Levine and Emerson, 2011). This group then formed the GIIN as a non-profit convening body to facilitate knowledge exchange, build infrastructure and develop research to accelerate the development of a coherent impact investing movement that was cross-disciplinary and amenable across multiple sectors (Höchstädter and Scheck, 2015).

Built from the assumption that there is not enough charitable and governmental capital to meet increasingly pervasive social and environmental challenges, impact investing aims to fill this gap by engaging multiple sectors to focus on the purpose of generating positive impact and change. What makes impact investing unique is the claimed paradigm shift away from the belief that financial and social returns should be mutually exclusive (Emerson, 2003). Impact investing certainly purports many benefits and has generated optimism for the philanthropic sector's ability to meet both social and financial demands (Bolis and West, 2017). However, it is important to fully understand the characteristics and norms of the philanthropic sector in order to understand its relatively low adoption rate of impact investing in comparison to the finance and government sectors (Koh, Karamchandani and Katz, 2012).

The philanthropic sector has been and continues to be well positioned to incorporate a practice like impact investing, given its own evolution. For decades, the philanthropic sector demonstrated the incorporation of impact investing characteristics, such as monitoring and searching for long-term funding recipients (Agrawal and Hockerts, 2019; Brest and Born, 2013). As early as the 1960s, private foundation leaders such as John D. Rockefeller began incorporating accountability and investment approaches in how they engaged with their funding recipients (Arrillaga-Andreessen and Hoyt, 2004; Cobb, 2002). Subsequently, other philanthropic organizations began adopting financing approaches used in the private market. For example, the Center for

Venture Philanthropy in Silicon Valley spearheaded the use of venture philanthropy, a practice by funders that encourages high engagement, accountability and exit strategies for their non-profit funding recipients (Moody, 2008).

Because of limited financial resources for grant making, the philanthropic sector has a 'tremendous appetite for innovations to improve effectiveness and sustainability, including those [innovations] that seek to direct the power of private markets' (Koh et al., 2012, p. 7). Practices such as responsible investing and mission-related investing allow philanthropic organizations to align their donor dollars with investments that affect their social mission (Hebb, 2013; Roundy et al., 2017). In addition, program-related investing allows philanthropic organizations to improve upon traditional grant making by adopting techniques used by venture capital firms that advanced the accountability and move towards financial sustainability for their recipients (Letts, Ryan and Grossman, 1997). Each of these practices can be considered a form of impact investing as the term integrates a spectrum of financial strategies used to achieve their philanthropic goals. Specific strategies range from the engagement of more traditional grants to include financial considerations, to the inclusion of social reporting in traditional investments, with more balanced approaches in between (Hebb, 2013; Höchstädter and Scheck, 2015).

Under the umbrella of impact investing, each of these financial strategies has been designed in a way that improves the effectiveness of philanthropic dollars. It is quite surprising then, that relatively few philanthropic organizations are adopting impact investing practices. This chapter lays the groundwork for exploring this puzzle: if impact investing is meant to be adopted across multiple sectors, why are so few from the philanthropic sector engaging in the practice?

In order to answer this question, a deep dive into the philanthropic sector is essential. Current literature in management, strategy, economics and finance oversimplifies the philanthropic sector by mostly discussing philanthropy as an arm of corporate giving (e.g., Brown, Helland and Smith, 2006; Saiia, Carroll and Buchholtz, 2003), or labeling it as only direct, charitable activity (e.g., Cain, Dana and Newman, 2014; Jeong and Kim, 2019). A more in-depth overview that describes how philanthropic organizations within the sector are structured, receive funding and allocate their dollars is necessary to then address the intersection of the sector and impact investing.

The philanthropic sector: uncomplicating organizational structures and strategies

The origins of philanthropy come from the root word 'phil', meaning 'love of mankind' (Merriam-Webster, n.d.). Philanthropic activity aims to serve a public good, usually through private means (Wood and Hagerman, 2010). For the purposes of clarity in this chapter, we will separate direct charitable giving from philanthropic practices, which is the focus. Direct charitable giving occurs when an individual provides money or in-kind gifts to independent causes or solicitations without a formalized agenda or plan for their giving (Wright, 2001). In contrast, philanthropic practices are the intentional giving of funds to identified individuals and organizations to fulfill a specific mission and designated strategy (Wright, 2001). Philanthropic giving, from here on referred to as philanthropy, often comes from individual or corporate wealth. Philanthropic organizations are established to facilitate the giving of those funds to individuals and organizations, typically non-profits, working to make a positive impact on a social or environmental cause. Further, the practice of establishing philanthropic organizations enables the separation of an individual or organization's philanthropic work from their primary business in both activity and legal manners.

While grouped into the same sector, there are many different types of organizations that comprise the philanthropic sector. We briefly describe the most common types of philanthropic organizations and explain the differences in organizational form, how they engage in philanthropic activity, and how they fund those activities. This list is not meant to be exhaustive as there are many variations within the descriptions that follow. Rather, we describe the diversity of organizational forms and funding mechanisms in the philanthropic sector. In doing so, we demonstrate the importance of these nuances in exploring the emergence of impact investing within the philanthropic sector.

Philanthropic organizational forms

Public charities

Public charities are organizations that raise money from the public to support organizations and individuals working to achieve the charity's goals. Public charities are funded by individuals, corporations and some foundations, and their primary method of giving is through traditional grants (Brown and Metter, 2019). Given that their funds are established through a diverse set of donors, these organizations are not classified as a foundation (Sansing, 2010). Public charities are established as non-profits and typically have an operating endowment; however, unlike foundations, they are required to have leaders and board members that represent the public that is being served (Calabrese and Ely, 2017). One of the most well-known public charities is United Way.[1]

Private foundations

Private foundations are non-profit, non-governmental organizations that are typically funded from a single source: individual, family or corporation. These foundations are established as either charitable trusts or non-profit Internal Revenue Service (IRS) section 501(c)(3) corporations, and thus tax-exempt in the United States. To maintain their status, private foundations are legally required to disperse at least 5 percent of their endowment's income each year (Wexler and Fei, 2019). Private foundations are classified as either operating or non operating. An operating private foundation utilizes their funding themselves to reach their charitable goals, and may offer a few grants to related organizations. Primary examples of operating private foundations are museums, research groups and think tanks (Sansing, 2010). A non-operating private foundation disperses their funds to other organizations who are working in the areas of the foundation's missions and goals (Sansing and Yetman, 2006). Non-operating private foundations are the most common type of private foundation, and can be further classified by their funding source.

Corporate foundations

Corporate foundations are established primarily through the funds of a for-profit business. These company-sponsored foundations are independent organizations but retain close ties to their donor corporation. Many corporate foundations have a mission to give back to the communities where their employees are located, support philanthropic concerns of their customers or to strengthen their brand. Additionally, corporate foundations can be used to provide employee matching grants or administer scholarship programs for employees' families or customers. According to the Giving USA Foundation, there are more than 2600 corporate foundations in the United States whose grant making in 2018 totaled $6.88 billion, up 6.5 percent from the previous year (Brown and Metter, 2019). Well-known examples of corporate foundations include the Ford Motor Company Fund[2] and the Coca-Cola Foundation.[3]

Family foundations

Family foundations are created through funds given by at least one member or a group of members of a single family, and require that at least one member of that family must continually serve as a leader or board member of the foundation, at all times (Gersick et al., 2004). Typically, family foundations are established to support organizations with missions that align with the family's interests and values. These foundations vary substantially in organizational size, structure and scope of giving, ranging from large international reaches, such as the Bill & Melinda Gates Foundation,[4] to small foundations focused on a single issue or geographic location.

Community foundations

Community foundations are foundations established through a permanent fund created by a group of donors. Typically, a community foundation serves the needs of a specific geographic region (Graddy and Wang, 2009). In addition to giving funds, community foundations also support donors who want to create endowed funds but do not have the means of starting their own independent foundation. There are currently more than 750 community foundations in the United States (Council on Foundations, 2021).

How philanthropic organizations engage in charitable activity

Guided by their mission and goals, there are many different funding mechanisms that philanthropic organizations use to disperse funds to individuals and organizations working to advance their social or environmental mission. This overview is intended to introduce basic existing practices of philanthropic organizations to illustrate some of the contextual uniqueness prior to discussing their involvement with impact investing practices.

While some philanthropic organizations accept direct solicitations for funding consideration, most have a formal process to receive grant applications. The most common is a request for proposal (RFP) which outlines specifics about the type of funds being offered, eligibility of applicants, required application materials, and timeline for funding and reporting. The following are the most common types of RFPs, typically allocated as a grant (Brown and Metter, 2019):

- Project grants are the most traditional form of grants as funding is given to support a specific program or project for a designated period of time.
- Capacity-building grants allow the recipient organization to increase their abilities or expand their services. These grants are for a process rather than a project.
- Operating fund grants are designated to support overhead costs like staffing and physical infrastructure needs.

- Sponsored research grants provide financial support for scientists and laboratories at universities or research-oriented non-profit organizations. These grants are typically focused around a specific disease, animal species, or novel phenomenon.
- In-kind grants provide non-monetary assistance such as equipment, office space, meeting space, and pro bono personnel. These grants are most often given by corporate foundations.

In addition to these types of grants, some foundations provide their board members and staff members with specific amounts of funds to use at their own discretion to support special causes or ideas they are personally connected with. This type of discretionary grant making can foster new enthusiasm and partnerships, but also run the risk of diverting the focus of the foundation's mission. Similarly, many of the larger foundations offer special cause or emergency funding to offer assistance when there is a critical, short-term need including natural disasters, equipment failure, or civil disturbance.

How philanthropic organizations finance charitable activity

Up to this point we have discussed how philanthropic organizations are established and disperse money to achieve their social mission. In order to disperse this money, philanthropic organizations rely on funders themselves to fund their activities. Public charities rely on the public, often from smaller donors, whereas foundations rely on an individual, community, family, or corporations to provide the funds to establish an endowment (Fidelity Charitable, 2019). An individual or team is then charged with the goal for the endowment to exist in perpetuity in order to annually allocate money in the form of charitable activity.

Structurally then, the majority of philanthropic organizations' assets exist in investments expected to grow at a rate at which they can then distribute a portion annually to individuals and non-profit organizations (Sansing and Yetman, 2006). Private foundations are required to allocate at least 5 percent of their net assets toward charitable purposes annually (Wexler and Fei, 2019). Traditionally, then, philanthropic organizations segregate their investment and philanthropic activities structurally by having some staff manage the investment portfolio to maintain the growth of the foundations' assets and other staff focus on programs related to philanthropic giving, typically in the form of grants (Mintz and Ziegler, 2013). Impact investing is a unique opportunity for both investment and program areas to adopt new practices; we next turn to the ways in which both grant-making and investment strategies have shifted to include impact investing.

Adoption of impact investing by philanthropic organizations

Shifts in traditional grant-making strategies

While there will always be a need for strictly charitable grants that enable organizations to start new initiatives and pilot new solutions, this generates no financial return and requires non-profits and recipients of philanthropic dollars to continue to source funds from their donors. Recently, many non-profit executives discussed how they entered into their work because they were deeply passionate about the cause, but now find themselves constantly chasing funding, piecing together numerous grants to support their staff teams, and trying to keep up with the reporting requirements for each grant received, rather than working to directly implement their solutions (Kanter and Sherman, 2016). Ultimately, achieving a social mission by solely engaging in traditional grant making does not address systemic solutions to deep social concerns. This has led philanthropic organizations to rethink their funding strategies. Questions remain as to how the philanthropic sector can unlock capital that is traditionally given away to be used as recyclable capital. How can philanthropic organizations move to integrate investment behavior with phil-anthropic behavior to promote more sustainable financing and opportunities to address more systemic solutions to social issues?

Impact investing has created a way to provide continued investments over a longer time horizon to support an initiative, and simultaneously also provide some financial return to the philanthropic organization that can be further used to support the mission. Advocates of impact investing have argued that philanthropic organizations can adopt low-risk financial instruments – for example, in the form of a loan rather than a traditional grant – that recycle some capital. This transition towards investment practices is not meant to sub-stitute for all grants, but is an additional step for a recipient to move towards financial sustainability. As discussed, the philanthropic sector is ripe for inno-vation and has been called to 'leverage every single tool and asset and resource at your [philanthropic organization's] disposal to ensure that you have the maximum impact on society that you can possibly have'.[5]

Some philanthropic organizations that have adopted impact investing pro-ceeded with a tiered approach. For example, Blue Meridian Partners,[6] focused on transforming the lives of families and youth, offers initial grants and then has a scaled approach to investing in organizations to ensure their recipients' success with successively larger investments over time. This movement into impact investing ensures that the recipient is positioned to be able to utilize the funding without it overwhelming their programmatic capacity, and also maximizes Blue Meridian's financial return on investment. Similarly, ZOMALAB,[7] which has a specific geographic focus in their funding priorities, has established traditional grants for immediate needs for education and health care, and impact investing for longer-term strategies like energy and water.

Opportunities and challenges of integrating impact investing into philanthropic organizations

Impact investing is appealing to philanthropic organizations for several reasons. First, philanthropic organizations have the capacity to be innovative and influential in a variety of ways. Philanthropic organizations can use impact investing directly as a way to improve accountability and social performance of their recipients, educate and attract other funders to support similar social issues, and advance the state of knowledge through funded research (Jaskyte et al., 2018; Porter and Kramer, 1999). Second, philanthropic organizations typically operate on a longer time horizon than mainstream finance investors, as they are founded with the purpose to exist in perpetuity (Reich, 2019). Third, since the formalization of impact investing, younger leaders, who are more likely to be open to innovation and new practices, have transitioned into executive positions at philanthropic organizations (Van Slyke and Newman, 2006; Wood and Hagerman, 2010).

Despite impact investing's purported appeal, evidence points to a relatively slow adoption rate by philanthropic organizations in comparison to mainstream finance investors. This may be due to the following challenges that philanthropic organizations face in incorporating impact investing practices.

First, as previously discussed, impact investing practices are relatively broad. The challenge for philanthropic organizations may not necessarily be in understanding *why* impact investing can be incorporated, but *how* and *to whom*. It may also be unclear to a philanthropic organization exactly what financial instruments should be adopted to begin impact investing, and how to effectively do so (Koh et al., 2012). Incorporating new funding mechanisms also require different forms of analysis to measure return on investment of funds given. Thus, organizations must have the internal capacity to adopt the new practice, as well as educate their funding recipients and key stakeholders on the differences in practice, expectations and measurement.

Another challenge is that the use of private capital financing instruments clashes with the existing institutional norm of philanthropic giving (Reddy, 2015; Roth, 2020; Roundy et al., 2017). While impact investing purports that generating positive social and environmental impact can be *integrated* into the mission of philanthropic organizations, philanthropy originated by distinguishing itself from the private market (Gripne, Kelley and Merchant, 2016; Onek, 2017). The philanthropic sector has typically separated philanthropic and investment activities, both structurally and cognitively (Gregory, 2016; Hehenberger, Mair and Metz, 2019). Thus, philanthropic organizations may feel that giving and investing are substitutes, rather than complements (Glänzel and Scheuerle, 2016). Additionally, adopting impact investing may be perceived as a shift away from supporting the public good and social needs. This perception comes with the risk of losing legitimacy and support from the philanthropic sector at large if they adopt impact investing practices because, apart from some strong pioneers, it differs from current institutionally accepted norms (e.g., Phillips, Lawrence and Hardy, 2000). Overcoming these challenges requires additional research and education for stakeholders involved at the intersection of impact investing and the philanthropic sector.

Future research

The distinctive features of philanthropic organizations both challenge existing paradigms and creates new research opportunities for understanding its intersection with impact investing. We have noted that philanthropic organizations are comprised of dynamic individuals, are complex regarding their design and structures, and balance multiple institutional norms that often differ. Therefore, we propose research opportunities at the nexus of philanthropic organizations and impact investing at multiple levels of analysis: individual, organizational and institutional. Table 1.1. outlines how each level of analysis is defined, examples of actors and entities that can be studied at that level of analysis, exemplar research questions and corresponding theories. We next elaborate on this table to generate research ideas that may challenge, elaborate and refine theory pertaining to the overlap of philanthropy and impact investing.

Table 1.1   Future research

Level of Analysis	Example Actors and Entities	Example Future Research Concepts	Applicable Theories
Individual level			
Individuals that participate in the philanthropic sector by funding, leading, working for, or being funded by philanthropic organizations	– Individual donors – Founders of philanthropic organizations – Board members – Leaders of philanthropic organizations: fund/investment managers, program managers, other executives – Recipients of funds	– Impacts of imprinting by founders on future decision making – Influence of motivation (prosocial, financial, etc.) on leaders' goals and strategy – Role of an individual's characteristics, experience, and environment on their decisions in creating a philanthropic organization – Changes in organizational culture based on transition of leadership, especially across family generations – Influence of board composition and backgrounds on organizational strategy – Impact of diversity and representation within the philanthropic organization on mission, values and practices	– Imprinting/founder identity – Motivation (e.g., prosocial/altruistic behavior) – Leadership – Team dynamics – Board membership – Diversity and inclusion

Level of Analysis	Example Actors and Entities	Example Future Research Concepts	Applicable Theories
Organizational level			
Organizational strategies, structures and decision-making processes of philanthropic organizations	– Public charities – Private foundations – Community foundations – Family foundations – Corporate foundations – Funding recipient organizations	– Differences in organizational structures within the philanthropic sector – Relationship between organizational culture and innovation/risk tolerance – Distinction between innovative or entrepreneurial philanthropic organizations and more traditional ones in their openness to impact investing – Influence of funding source on organization's culture and business strategy – Navigation and balance of different organizational identities – Structure and accountability of interorganizational relationships between philanthropic organizations and funding recipients	– Organizational culture – Innovation and entrepreneurial action – Organizational design: structure and incentives – Organizational identity – Inter-organizational relationships

Level of Analysis	Example Actors and Entities	Example Future Research Concepts	Applicable Theories
Institutional level			
Exogenous factors that influence philanthropic activity in the charitable sector	– Certification bodies – Intermediary groups – Adjacent sectors: business, finance, government – Infrastructure – Regulatory policies	– Influence of a social movement on paradigm development – Role of certifying bodies and convening groups in the education and broadening of widespread adoption – Examination of the institutional entrepreneurs in the philanthropic sector – Impact of regulatory policies on adoption of impact investing – Exploration of the institutional logics and norms present in the philanthropic sector – Influence of exogenous shocks (pandemics, climate change, financial crisis etc.) on adoption of new strategies	– Social movements – Certification – Institutional entrepreneurship – Institutional theory and logics – Environmental shocks and institutional arrangements

Individual level

Individuals who establish, lead, are employed by, and are funded by philanthropic organizations vary in their motivations, values and identities. Thus, there is a need for scholars to examine the adoption of impact investing by philanthropic organizations at the individual level. While our focus in presenting a possible research agenda is largely focused on founders and leaders of philanthropic organizations, it is important to note that recipients of funding are also impacted by the adoption of impact investing and should be considered in future research endeavors.

It is well established that founders' characteristics shape initial firm characteristics, policies and practices (Boeker, 1989). This imprinting effect, the characteristics that reflect prominent organizational features that persist over time (Marquis and Tilcsik, 2013), will differ depending on the unique individuals and their environments. For example, wealthy individuals who create private foundations in later stages of their lives may approach their organizations differently from individuals forming community foundations, based on the influence of their different situations and contexts. Further, future research examining organizational behaviors may also explore how organizational characteristics are imprinted by the founders and their behaviors at the time of formation.

Research on imprinting has also explored how early-career experiences impact the trajectory of one's career (Azoulay, Fons-Rosen and Graff Zivin, 2019; Tilcsik, 2013). How might early-career experiences influence individuals who form philanthropic organizations? Perhaps some individuals may be more prosocially motivated, whereas others may be more financially motivated (Batson and Powell, 2003; Grant and Berry, 2011; Shepherd, 2015). Exploration of such differences may explain the openness to practices like impact investing. This brings to light questions about how prior individual experiences influence organizational decision making.

While the link between founders' leadership styles and characteristics embodied in the organizational culture is well established (Bird, 1988; Schein, 1983), research suggests that leadership linked to innovation deserves much greater attention (Borins, 2002). This context may be useful to explore how founders' leadership characteristics influence the willingness for philanthropic organizations to explore new practices and take risks, including the adoption of impact investing practices. Then to take this research one step further, philanthropic organizations typically last across generations, which opens up questions of leadership transition to a new generation of family members or hired executives. Therefore, attention and comparison of original founders and current leadership of philanthropic organizations may also generate interesting insights related to leadership and motivation. Questions can also explore whether differences in leadership characteristics lead to openness for new strategies, such as integrating impact investing.

Other individuals within the organization are also likely to influence whether and how impact investing is integrated. In addition to members of the management team, board members of philanthropic organizations play a significant role in organizational decision making and support (e.g., Cha and Abebe, 2016; Lungeanu and Ward, 2012). In this context, board members from business backgrounds may exude the expertise and knowledge necessary to incorporate the requisite financial mechanisms for impact investing. At the same time, board members from public sector backgrounds may influence the resistance or hesitancy of adopting impact investing. Exploring board members' backgrounds and their interactions may generate important nuances to how new practices are negotiated and instantiated.

Finally, research is needed to explore the role and impact of diversity, equity and inclusion across the leadership, employees, board and funding recipients (Coffey and Wang, 1998; Wagner, 2016). Whether the founder and leadership of the philanthropic organization represent or belong to the population that is directly experiencing the social issue of the organization likely impacts how funding is allocated. Does the board have personal experiences that give voice to the needs of the community being served (Serafeim, 2018; Wry and Haugh, 2018)? These questions influence decisions being made by the philanthropic organization, and the knowledge of what funding strategies best serve their funding recipients. Research is needed to understand how the composition and intention of diversity across the leadership influence the mission, issues and practices of the foundation.

Organizational level

An additional contribution of this chapter is that it highlights intricacies among and within philanthropic organizations. While all philanthropic organizations share the common goal of creating positive social and environmental impact, more research is needed to disentangle the influences of organizational design and structure on the involvement of impact investing activities. This research requires scholars at the organizational level to explore the organizational strategies, structures, and decision-making processes of philanthropic organizations.

Existing research largely assumes that organizations within the same sector (e.g., philanthropy) share common characteristics (e.g., Aldrich and Fiol, 1994; Carroll and Hannan, 2004; DiMaggio and Powell, 1983); however, our work here demonstrates that is not the case. Different philanthropic organizations have different funding structures and requirements, which is linked to other characteristics such as motivation and risk tolerance. Instead of grouping all philanthropic organizations together, there are opportunities to identify nuances across organizations and thus explore the role of these differences in adopting and implementing impact investment practices (Sanders and Tuschke, 2007; Waldron, Fisher and Pfarrer, 2016). Future work should shed light on both the rationale behind and the consequences of these nuanced structures across philanthropic organizations. For example, does organizational structure create or hinder opportunities for innovation? Further, what structural conditions influence the level of motivation and risk tolerance needed for adopting new financing strategies?

Organizational culture is another important consideration as it impacts internal strategy and operations, and helps define the organization to its stakeholders (Hatch and Schultz, 1997; Markus and Kitayama, 1991). In philanthropic organizations, the mission, the scope of social issues supported and the internal operations influence organizational culture (Payton and Moody, 2008; Schein, 1983). Questions about culture are pertinent in this context because certain cultures not only help audiences to make sense of what an organization is, but also how organizations may engage in the integration of impact investing. For example, entrepreneurial organizations may demonstrate more interest in adopting impact investing than legacy-focused organizational cultures because of their innovative culture (Cortimiglia, Ghezzi and Frank, 2016; Guth and Ginsberg, 1990). Corporate business cultures that influence corporate foundations may align more closely with the principles of impact investing, leading to a higher likelihood of designing riskier impact-investing funds. Research can be used to create a deeper understanding of how different organizational cultures influence or are in turn influenced by the funding strategies adopted.

Additionally, organizational identity, those organizational characteristics that are central, enduring and distinctive (Albert and Whetten, 1985; Pratt et al., 2016), create an interesting set of unexplored opportunities and challenges for philanthropic organizations. While it is well known that organizations have multiple identities (Foreman and Whetten, 2002; Pratt, 2016), it is unclear how multiple identities that a philanthropic organization holds will interact with the opportunity to integrate impact investing practices. For example, philanthropic and financial identities exist within every philanthropic organization, but their relative strength may influence the likelihood to adopt impact investing practices. How foundations navigate, balance and make decisions based on their complementing or competing identities is worthy of future attention.

In addition, the interorganizational relationships that philanthropic organizations share with their funding recipients are unique in comparison with other funders who use impact investing strategies. The adoption of impact investing by philanthropic organizations shifts the relationship with their recipients from being solely a beneficiary to becoming both a beneficiary and an investee. While the principal–agent framework is a common characterization of funding relationships between investors and entrepreneurs (De Clercq et al., 2006; Sapienza and Gupta, 1994), whether and how the dyadic relationship between philanthropic organizations and their recipients adopts the tenants of principal agent roles is less understood. Future research asks whether more accountability to recipients via principal agent relationships leads to highly generative financial and social value. When a philanthropic organization adds additional financial instruments in order to achieve its mission, a higher sense of accountability is required to either repay or grow the capital provided to the recipient. Further understanding is needed about how the relationship between philanthropic organizations and recipients shifts when the financial instrument is a grant, loan or other form of impact investment (Glänzel and Scheuerle, 2016; Tekula and Shah, 2016).

At a relational level, scholars studying identity and work relationships can also extend knowledge about the mechanisms driving charitable, financial and hybrid relationships between philanthropic organizations and their recipients (e.g., Heaphy et al., 2018; Sluss and Ashforth, 2007). Examining this relationship leads to several interesting questions. What combinations of relationships between philanthropic organizations and funding recipients are possible, and how do these relationships evolve over time? Scholars studying identity (Ashforth, Rogers and Corley, 2011; Ashforth, Schinoff and Brickson, 2020; Barney et al., 1998) and power dynamics (Hehenberger et al., 2019) can further expand on the funder–recipient relationship across philanthropic organizations, or compare philanthropic organizations to other impact investing funders.

Institutional level

The previous sections presented opportunities for exploring the intersection of philanthropic organizations and impact investing at individual and organizational levels. It is also important to examine how philanthropic organizations are embedded in particular contexts that carry different institutional norms and expectations. Institutional-level analysis should explore different forces that influence the philanthropic sectors' integration of impact investing, such as the targeted social issue (e.g., health or housing), larger membership organization (e.g., Foundations and Donors Interested in Catholic Activities – FADICA), or geographic location (e.g., North America or Africa). Philanthropy is often positioned within the culture and/or region where their funding recipients are located. While this chapter takes the perspective of philanthropic organizations based in the United States, it is important to consider the cultural, political and regulatory influences in different environments. Theorizing the intersection of philanthropic organizations and impact investing is incomplete without an examination of how complex institutional environments impact organizational decisions.

One major trend within the impact investing movement is the focus on paradigm consensus, both in what impact investing is and how it should be measured (Costa and Pesci, 2016; Rawhouser, Cummings and Newbert, 2019). Although discussions about the specific definitions of impact investing, socially responsible investing and venture philanthropy are stimulating (see Agrawal and Hockerts, 2019; Trelstad, 2016 for reviews), it is also important to further refine our understanding of how the overall movement of impact investing is emerging in diverse sectors. For example, how does non-market strategy play a role in the integration of impact investing? What role do powerful actors have in influencing the paradigm development, and with what consequences? The GIIN emerged and formally coined the term impact investing in 2007 (Emerson, 2018). Fruitful research could direct scholars to understand potential pitfalls and opportunities that can be learned by the creation of a convening group that is relevant to organizations in multiple sectors, such as financial, government and philanthropic sectors. Scholars could study the GIIN as an intermediary, alongside other educational bodies or convening groups, and build from knowledge about convening processes across sectors (e.g., Mair and Hehenberger, 2014).

Further, institutional norms from one sector (e.g., philanthropy) may be a barrier to adopting norms of impact investing that are being established by another sector (e.g., financial or government). For example, the regulatory environment of philanthropy in the United States is high, whereby practices are driven by the desire to maintain the philanthropic organization's non-profit, tax-exempt status (Daly, 2008). Researchers could test the relationships between regulatory agencies (such as the IRS in the United States), by examining policy implementation and practice adoption. Other research could examine where specific actors, such as Blue Meridian, serve as institutional entrepreneurs (Tracey, Phillips and Jarvis, 2011) and their ability to broaden impact investing practices accepted within the philanthropic sector.

Understanding how philanthropic organizations not only practice impact investing but also become pioneers for others to follow will be important contributions to both academic and practitioner audiences.

Another practitioner-driven question is how philanthropic organizations straddle both market and charitable orientations in a way that serves both mission and sustainability of the organization. Our academic knowledge about how philanthropic organizations carry certain institutional logics, the shared beliefs that legitimize the value of specific goals and interests (Thornton, Ocasio and Lounsbury, 2012), can be used to explain the integration of impact investing into the philanthropic sector. The philanthropic sector may have a set of institutional logics built from charitable norms, whereas impact investing involves a logic that puts financial logic as a core value alongside a charitable logic. How philanthropic organizations engage in the institutional work (Gawer and Phillips, 2013) of integrating impact investing practices and shift how different institutional logics are accepted within the philanthropic sector remains an open question. Certain philanthropic organizations, such as The Rockefeller Foundation,[8] are well known and carry the characteristics of institutional entrepreneurs, actors who leverage resources to create new or transform existing institutions (Battilana, Leca and Boxenbaum, 2009; DiMaggio and Powell, 1983; Garud, Gehman and Giuliani, 2015). They can actively utilize their power within the philanthropic sector to promote impact investing but also to challenge the prevailing institutional logics. How and with what consequences are these changes possible remain important scholarly questions.

As institutions change, another question this context may shed light on is how the philanthropic sector adopts new practices yet remains core to its origins. In other words, how will the philanthropic sector stay true to its core mission of generating financial support to address social and environmental concerns, while also navigating the integration of new practices that require considerations outside of their core mission? Process-focused studies (Langley et al., 2013) that examine multiple actors over time may be able to examine how collaborating across institutions may help to answer why some actors are positioned well to adopt certain practices while others are not.

Finally, the institutional level of analysis also examines factors exogeneous to the organization or individual. Exogeneous shocks can be fast moving, such as pandemics that shock the global economy and society at rampant rates, or slower and more incremental, such as climate change or economic turmoil. While these shocks alter the way in which all institutions operate, they also escalate the social need as they strain existing social safety nets. These factors may amplify or suppress the momentum to adopt new practices like impact investing that emphasize a social and environmental return alongside a financial one. Learning from historic shocks, such as the US financial crisis that began in 2007 or the COVID-19 pandemic beginning in 2020, may help uncover the mechanisms for understanding when and how organizations may turn away from prior practices and look towards impact investments or vice versa.

Conclusion

As private markets increasingly address social and environmental issues, there is a growing call for the philanthropic sector to innovate and evolve alongside other funders, particularly in the practice of impact investing (Moody, 2008). While impact investing purports to be a funding strategy to help philanthropic organizations meet societal needs in a more fiscally sustainable manner, relatively few philanthropic organizations are engaging in these practices. It is important for scholars to study the intersection of philanthropy and impact investing to understand what opportunities and barriers exist at this nexus. This chapter provides an overview of the philanthropic sector and describes opportunities and challenges in integrating impact investing practices. In doing so, we illustrate nuanced differences in organizations that comprise the philanthropic sector, and present opportunities for future research at the intersection of philanthropy and impact investing. We see an opportunity for scholars across different levels of analysis to continue the path towards theoretically meaningful knowledge that addresses the current and changing reality of the financial and philanthropic landscapes.

Notes

1. See https://www.unitedway.org/; accessed 16 January 2021.
2. See https://www.fordfund.org/; accessed 16 January 2021.
3. See   https://www.coca-colacompany.com/shared-future/coca-cola-foundation/; accessed 16 January 2021.
4. See https://www.gatesfoundation.org/; accessed 16 January 2021.
5. Informal interview, foundation executive director, 2015.
6. See ttps://www.bluemeridian.org/; accessed 16 January 2021.
7. See https://zomalab.com/; accessed 16 January 2021.
8. See https://www.rockefellerfoundation.org; accessed 16 January 2021.

References

Agrawal, A. and Hockerts, K. (2019). Impact investing: review and research agenda. *Journal of Small Business and Entrepreneurship*, 1–29, https://doi.org/10.1080/08276331.2018.1551457.

Albert, S. and Whetten, D.A. (1985). Organizational identity. *Research in Organizational Behavior*, 7, 263–95.

Aldrich, H.E. and Fiol, C.M. (1994). Fools rush in? The institutional context of industry creation. *Academy of Management Review*, 19(4), 645–70.

Arrillaga-Andreessen, L. and Hoyt, D. (2004). Venture philanthropy summit overview. *Stanford Business School Case Studies, No. SI-73*.

Ashforth, B.E., Rogers, K.M. and Corley, K.G. (2011). Identity in organizations: exploring cross-level dynamics. *Organization Science*, 22(5), 1144–56.

Ashforth, B.E., Schinoff, B.S. and Brickson, S.L. (2020). My company is friendly, 'mine's a rebel': anthropomorphism and shifting organizational identity from 'what' to 'who'. *Academy of Management Review*, 45(1), 29–57.

Azoulay, P., Fons-Rosen, C. and Graff Zivin, J.S. (2019). Does science advance one funeral at a time? *American Economic Review*, 109(8), 2889–920.

Balboni, E. and Berenbach, S. (2014). Fixed income securities. In L.M. Salamon (ed.), *New Frontiers of Philanthropy: A Guide to the New Tools and New Actors That Are Reshaping Global Philanthropy and Social Investing* (pp. 341–65). New York: Oxford University Press.

Barney, J.B., Bunderson, J.S. and Foreman et al. (1998). A strategy conversation on the topic of organization identity. In D.A. Whetten and P.C. Godfrey (eds), *Identity in Organizations: Building Theory Through Conversations* (pp. 99–168). Thousand Oaks, CA: SAGE.

Batson, C.D. and Powell, A.A. (2003). Altruism and prosocial behavior. In T. Millon and J. Lerner (eds), *Handbook of Psychology: Personality and Social Psychology, Vol. 5* (pp. 282–387). Hoboken, NJ: John Wiley & Sons.

Battilana, J. and Dorado, S. (2010). Building sustainable hybrid organizations: the case of commercial microfinance organizations. *Academy of Management Journal*, 53(6), 1419–40.

Battilana, J., Leca, B. and Boxenbaum, E. (2009). How actors change institutions: towards a theory of institutional entrepreneurship. *Academy of Management Annals*, 3(1), 65–107.

Bell, A. (2013, 30 July). Why impact investing is an emerging paradigm shift in philanthropy. *Forbes*. Accessed 15 January 2021 at https://www.forbes.com/sites/skollworldforum/2013/07/30/why-impact-investing-is-an-emerging-paradigm-shift-in-philanthropy/?sh=5f8174372aaa.

Bird, B. (1988). Implementing entrepreneurial ideas: the case for intention. *Academy of Management Review*, 13(3), 442–53.

Boeker, W. (1989). Strategic change: the effects of founding and history. *Academy of Management Journal*, 32(3), 489–515.

Bolis, M. and West, C. (2017). Marginalized returns. *Stanford Social Innovation Review*, 15(4), 55–7.

Borins, S. (2002). Leadership and innovation in the public sector. *Leadership & Organization Development Journal*, 23(8), 467–75.

Brest, P. and Born, K. (2013, 14 August). Unpacking the impact in impact investing. *Stanford Social Innovation Review*. Accessed 15 January 2021 at https://ssir.org/up_for_debate/article/impact_investing.

Brown, M. and Metter, R. (2019). *Giving USA 2019: The Annual Report on Philanthropy for the Year 2018*. Chicago, IL: Giving USA Foundation.
Brown, W.O., Helland, E. and Smith, J.K. (2006). Corporate philanthropic practices. *Journal of Corporate Finance*, 12(5), 855–77.
Bugg-Levine, A. and Emerson, J. (2011). Impact investing: transforming how we make money while making a difference. *Innovations: Technology, Governance, Globalization*, 6(3), 9–18.
Cain, D.M., Dana, J. and Newman, G.E. (2014). Giving versus giving in. *The Academy of Management Annals*, 8(1), 505–33.
Calabrese, T.D. and Ely, T.L. (2017). Understanding and measuring endowment in public charities. *Nonprofit and Voluntary Sector Quarterly*, 46(4), 859–73.
Carroll, G.R. and Hannan, M.T. (2004). *The Demography of Corporations and Industries*. Princeton, NJ: Princeton University Press.
Cha, W. and Abebe, M.A. (2016). Board of directors and industry determinants of corporate philanthropy. *Leadership & Organization Development Journal*, 37(5), 672–88.
Cobb, N.K. (2002). The new philanthropy: its impact on funding arts and culture. *The Journal of Arts Management, Law, and Society*, 32(2), 125–43.
Coffey, B.S. and Wang, J. (1998). Board diversity and managerial control as predictors of corporate social performance. *Journal of Business Ethics*, 17(14), 1595–603.
Cortimiglia, M.N., Ghezzi, A. and Frank, A.G. (2016). Business model innovation and strategy making nexus: evidence from a cross-industry mixed-methods study. *R&D Management*, 46(3), 414–32.
Costa, E. and Pesci, C. (2016). Social impact measurement: why do stakeholders matter? *Sustainability Accounting, Management and Policy Journal*, 7(1), 99–124.
Council on Foundations (2021). Community foundations. Accessed 16 January 2021 at https://www.cof.org/foundation-type/community-foundations-taxonomy.
Daly, S. (2008). Institutional innovation in philanthropy: community foundations in the UK. *VOLUNTAS: International Journal of Voluntary and Nonprofit Organizations*, 19(3), 219–41.
De Clercq, D., Fried, V.H., Lehtonen, O. and Sapienza, H.J. (2006). An entrepreneur's guide to the venture capital galaxy. *Academy of Management Perspectives*, 20(3), 90–112.
DiMaggio, P.J. and Powell, W.W. (1983). The iron cage revisited: institutional isomorphism and collective rationality in organizational fields. *American Sociological Review*, 48(2), 147–60.
Emerson, J. (2003). The blended value proposition: integrating social and financial returns. *California Management Review*, 45(4), 35–51.
Emerson, J. (2018). *The Purpose of Capital: Elements of Impact, Financial Flows, and Natural Being*. San Francisco, CA: Blended Value Group Press.
Fidelity Charitable (2019). *2019 Annual Report*. Accessed 16 January 2021 at https://www.fidelitycharitable.org/content/dam/fc-public/docs/annual-reports/2019-annual-report.pdf.
Foreman, P. and Whetten, D.A. (2002). Members' identification with multiple-identity organizations. *Organization Science*, 13(6), 618–35.
Garud, R., Gehman, J. and Giuliani, A.P. (2015). Contextualizing entrepreneurial innovation: a narrative perspective. *IEEE Engineering Management Review*, 43(1), 80–102.
Gawer, A. and Phillips, N. (2013). Institutional work as logics shift: the case of Intel's transformation to platform leader. *Organization Studies*, 34(8), 1035–71.
Gersick, K.E., Stone, D. and Grady, K. et al. (2004). *Generations of Giving: Leadership and Continuity in Family Foundations*. Lanham, MD: Lexington Books.

Glänzel, G. and Scheuerle, T. (2016). Social impact investing in Germany: current impediments from investors' and social entrepreneurs' perspectives. *VOLUNTAS: International Journal of Voluntary and Nonprofit Organizations*, 27(4), 1638–68.

Global Impact Investing Network (GIIN) (2019). *Impact Investing: A Guide to This Dynamic Market*. Accessed 27 April 2020 at https://thegiin.org/assets/documents/GIIN_impact_investing_guide.pdf.

Graddy, E. and Wang, L. (2009). Community foundation development and social capital. *Nonprofit and Voluntary Sector Quarterly*, 38(3), 392–412.

Grant, A.M. and Berry, J.W. (2011). The necessity of others is the mother of invention: intrinsic and prosocial motivations, perspective taking, and creativity. *Academy of Management Journal*, 54(1), 73–96.

Gregory, N. (2016). De-risking impact investing. *World Economics*, 17(2), 143–58.

Gripne, S.L., Kelley, J. and Merchant, K. (2016). Laying the groundwork for a national impact investing marketplace. *The Foundation Review*, 8(5), https://doi.org/10.9707/1944-5660.1341.

Guth, W.D. and Ginsberg, A. (1990). Guest editors' introduction: corporate entrepreneurship. *Strategic Management Journal*, 11, 5–15.

Hatch, M.J. and Schultz, M. (1997). Relations between organizational culture, identity and image. *European Journal of Marketing*, 31(5/6), 356–65.

Heaphy, E.D., Byron, K. and Ballinger, G.A. et al. (2018). Introduction to special topic forum: the changing nature of work relationships. *Academy of Management Review*, 43(4), 558–69.

Hebb, T. (2013). Impact investing and responsible investing: what does it mean? *Journal of Sustainable Finance & Investment*, 3(2), 71–4.

Hehenberger, L., Mair, J. and Metz, A. (2019). The assembly of a field ideology: an idea-centric perspective on systemic power in impact investing. *Academy of Management Journal*, 62(6), 1672–704.

Höchstädter, A.K. and Scheck, B. (2015). What's in a name: an analysis of impact investing understandings by academics and practitioners. *Journal of Business Ethics*, 132(2), 449–75.

Jaskyte, K., Amato, O. and Sperber, R. (2018). Foundations and innovation in the nonprofit sector. *Nonprofit Management and Leadership*, 29(1), 47–64.

Jeong, Y.C. and Kim, T.Y. (2019). Between legitimacy and efficiency: an institutional theory of corporate giving. *Academy of Management Journal*, 62(5), 1583–608.

Kanter, B. and Sherman, A. (2016). *The Happy, Healthy Nonprofit: Strategies for Impact Without Burnout*. Hoboken, NJ: John Wiley & Sons.

Koh, H., Karamchandani, A. and Katz, R. (2012). *From Blueprint to Scale: The Case for Philanthropy in Impact Investing*. Monitor Group.

Langley, A.N.N., Smallman, C., Tsoukas, H. and Van de Ven, A.H. (2013). Process studies of change in organization and management: unveiling temporality, activity, and flow. *Academy of Management Journal*, 56(1), 1–13.

Letts, C.W., Ryan, W. and Grossman, A. (1997). Virtuous capital: what foundations can learn from venture capitalists. *Harvard Business Review*, 75, 36–50.

Lungeanu, R. and Ward, J.L. (2012). A governance-based typology of family foundations: the effect of generation stage and governance structure on family philanthropic activities. *Family Business Review*, 25(4), 409–24.

Mair, J. and Hehenberger, L. (2014). Front-stage and backstage convening: the transition from opposition to mutualistic coexistence in organizational philanthropy. *Academy of Management Journal*, 57(4), 1174–200.

Markus, H.R. and Kitayama, S. (1991). Culture and the self: implications for cognition, emotion, and motivation. *Psychological Review*, 98(2), 224–53.

Marquis, C. and Tilcsik, A. (2013). Imprinting: toward a multilevel theory. *Academy of Management Annals*, 7(1), 195–245.

Merriam-Webster (n.d.). Philanthropy. Accessed June 2020 at https://www.merriam
-webster.com/dictionary/philanthropy.

Mintz, J. and Ziegler, C. (2013). *Mission-Related Investing: Legal and Policy Issues to
Consider Before Investing*. Macarthur Foundation. Accessed 12 February 2020 at
https://www.macfound.org/media/article_pdfs/Mission-Related_Investing.pdf.

Moody, M. (2008). 'Building a culture': the construction and evolution of venture philanthropy as a new organizational field. *Nonprofit and Voluntary Sector Quarterly*, 37(2),
324–52.

Mudaliar, A., Bass, R., Dithrich, H. and Nova, N. (2019). *Annual Impact Investor Survey*.
Global Impact Investing Network (GIIN).

Mudaliar, A. and Dithrich, H. (2019). *Sizing the Impact Investing Market*. Global Impact
Investing Network (GIIN).

Onek, M. (2017, 11 April). Now is the time for foundations to invest for mission and
impact. *Stanford Social Innovation Review*. Accessed 16 January 2021 at https://ssir
.org/articles/entry/now_is_the_time_for_foundations_to_invest_for_mission_and
_impact.

Payton, R.L. and Moody, M.P. (2008). *Understanding Philanthropy: Its Meaning and
Mission*. Bloomington, IN: Indiana University Press.

Phillips, N., Lawrence, T.B. and Hardy, C. (2000). Inter-organizational collaboration and
the dynamics of institutional fields. *Journal of Management Studies*, 37(1), https://doi
.org/10.1111/1467-6486.00171.

Porter, M.E. and Kramer, M.R. (1999). Philanthropy's new agenda: creating value.
Harvard Business Review, 77, 121–31.

Pratt, M.G. (2016). Hybrid and multiple organizational identities. In M.G. Pratt, M.
Schultz, B.E. Ashforth and D. Ravasi (eds), *The Oxford Handbook of Organizational
Identity* (pp. 106–20). Oxford: Oxford University Press.

Pratt, M.G., Schultz, M., Ashforth, B.E. and Ravasi, D. (eds) (2016). Introduction: organi-
zational identity, mapping where we have been, where we are, and where we might go.
In M.G. Pratt, M. Schultz, B.E. Ashforth and D. Ravasi (eds), *The Oxford Handbook of
Organizational Identity* (pp. 1–19). Oxford: Oxford University Press.

Rath, J. and Schuyt, T. (2014). Entrepreneurial philanthropy: an exploratory review. *The
Journal of Wealth Management*, 17(3), 35–46.

Rawhouser, H., Cummings, M. and Newbert, S.L. (2019). Social impact measurement: current approaches and future directions for social entrepreneurship research.
Entrepreneurship Theory and Practice, 43(1), 82–115.

Reddy, C.D. (2015). Social entrepreneurship and venture philanthropy: a conceptual
framework. Paper presented at the SAIMS 27th Annual Conference: Management in
Southern Africa: Change, Challenge and Opportunity, Cape Town, South Africa.

Reich, K. (2019). *What It Really Takes to Influence Funder Practice*. Ford Foundation.
Accessed 16 January 2021 at https://www.fordfoundation.org/media/4915/build
-influence-funder-practice-report-121719.pdf.

Roth, B.N. (2020). Impact investing: a theory of financing social enterprises. *Harvard
Business School Working Paper, No. 20-078*, p. 40.

Roundy, P., Holzhauer, H. and Dai, Y. (2017). Finance or philanthropy? Exploring the
motivations and criteria of impact investors. *Social Responsibility Journal*, 13(3),
https://doi.org/10.1108/SRJ-08-2016-0135.

Saiia, D.H., Carroll, A.B. and Buchholtz, A.K. (2003). Philanthropy as strategy: when
corporate charity 'begins at home'. *Business and Society*, 42(2), 169–201.

Sanders, W.G. and Tuschke, A. (2007). The adoption of institutionally contested organizational practices: the emergence of stock option pay in Germany. *Academy of
Management Journal*, 50(1), 33–56.

Sansing, R. (2010). Distribution policies of private foundations. In B.A. Seaman and D.R. Young (eds), *Handbook of Research on Nonprofit Economics and Management* (pp. 42–58). Cheltenham, UK and Northampton, MA, USA: Edward Elgar Publishing.

Sansing, R. and Yetman, R. (2006). Governing private foundations using the tax law. *Journal of Accounting and Economics*, 41(3), 363–84.

Santos, F., Pache, A.C. and Birkholz, C. (2015). Making hybrids work: aligning business models and organizational design for social enterprises. *California Management Review*, 57(3), 36–58.

Sapienza, H.J. and Gupta, A.K. (1994). Impact of agency risks and task uncertainty on venture capitalist–CEO interaction. *Academy of Management Journal*, 37(6), 1618–32.

Schein, E.H. (1983). The role of the founder in creating organizational culture. *Organizational Dynamics*, 12(1), 13–28.

Serafeim, G. (2018). Investors as stewards of the commons? *Journal of Applied Corporate Finance*, 30(2), 8–17.

Shepherd, D. (2015). Party on! A call for entrepreneurship research that is more interactive, activity based, cognitively hot, compassionate, and prosocial. *Journal of Business Venturing*, 30(4), 489–507.

Sluss, D.M. and Ashforth, B.E. (2007). Relational identity and identification: defining ourselves through work relationships. *Academy of Management Review*, 32(1), 9–32.

Tekula, R. and Shah, A. (2016). Funding social innovation. In O.M. Lehner (ed.), *Routledge Handbook of Social and Sustainable Finance* (pp. 125–36). Abingdon: Routledge.

Thornton, P.H., Ocasio, W. and Lounsbury, M. (2012). *The Institutional Logics Perspective: A New Approach to Culture, Structure, and Process*. Oxford: Oxford University Press.

Tilcsik, A. (2013). Remembrance of things past: individual imprinting in organizations. Doctoral dissertation. Harvard University.

Tracey, P., Phillips, N. and Jarvis, O. (2011). Bridging institutional entrepreneurship and the creation of new organizational forms: a multilevel model. *Organization Science*, 22(1), 60–80.

Trelstad, B. (2016). Making sense of the many kinds of impact investing. *Harvard Business Review*. Accessed 20 November 2018 at https://hbr.org/2016/01/making-sense-of-the-many-kinds-of-impact-investing.

Van Slyke, D.M. and Newman, H.K. (2006). Venture philanthropy and social entrepreneurship in community redevelopment. *Nonprofit Management and Leadership*, 16(3), 345–68.

Wagner, L. (2016). *Diversity and Philanthropy: Expanding the Circle of Giving*: Santa Barbara, CA: ABC-CLIO.

Waldron, T.L., Fisher, G. and Pfarrer, M. (2016). How social entrepreneurs facilitate the adoption of new industry practices. *Journal of Management Studies*, 53(5), 821–45.

Wexler, R. and Fei, R. (2019). Legal explanation of program related investments. Adler & Covin. Accessed 16 January 2021 at https://www.adlercolvin.com/wp-content/themes/adlercolvin/pdf/Legal-Explanation-of-Program-Related-Investments-PRI-Primer.pdf.

Wood, D. and Hagerman, L. (2010). Mission investing and the philanthropic toolbox. *Policy and Society*, 29(3), 257–68.

Wright, K. (2001). Generosity vs. altruism: philanthropy and charity in the United States and United Kingdom. *VOLUNTAS: International Journal of Voluntary and Nonprofit Organizations*, 12(4), 399–416.

Wry, T. and Haugh, H. (2018). Brace for impact: uniting our diverse voices through a social impact frame. *Journal of Business Venturing*, 33(5), 566–74.

2. A ladder to nowhere? A research agenda for funding social enterprise

J. Howard Kucher

Introduction to issues in funding social enterprise

The burgeoning study of social entrepreneurship has fostered substantial inquiry into means and methods for growing a social enterprise (Lumpkin and Bacq, 2019; Santos, Pache and Birkholz, 2015; Wry and York, 2017), with a growing preference for a hybrid entity as the common construct for these ventures (Battilana and Dorado, 2010; Rawhouser, Cummings and Crane, 2015).

Responding to numerous calls for additional exploration of the financing of social enterprise (Austin, Stevenson and Wei-Skillern, 2006; Lyons and Kickul, 2013; Nicholls, 2010), this chapter identifies some critical gaps in the literature and suggests some areas for further exploration that may be useful for developing a more structured and predictable process for funding these hybrid entities.

The process for funding a new commercial venture in the United States involves a well-established series of steps. In seeking to create civic, social and economic value, a social entrepreneur encounters challenges in funding and legal structures that make capital acquisition significantly more challenging. To provide the necessary background for my main point, I will first review the various steps that are typically taken to fund the development of for-profit and nonprofit enterprises. I will then discuss the systems and structures that exist to provide technical assistance as each of these types of ventures grows. I will then review distinctive complexities in both funding and technical assistance that are faced by the social enterprise, as well as a legal and organizational challenge that is unique to this type of firm. Finally, I will suggest some key areas that call for further exploration as we seek to better understand this field and guide these nascent ventures. Additional insight into these questions will enhance the growing body of literature on the development of viable social enterprises and may also help to advance the legitimacy and distinctiveness of social entrepreneurship.

Funding the new venture

The commercial entrepreneur obtains funding from numerous sources, including debt, various types of equity investments, crowdfunding and a limited number of governmental and institutional subsidies (Stangler, Tareque and Morelix, 2016). Regardless of the type of funding, the funder's evaluation of risk and return is focused on the firm's ability to produce enough revenue to meet the obligations and expectations of the funder (Emerson, 2000). Further, the various stages of firm development, the types of capital needed at each stage, and the role that each capital source plays in the growth of the organization are all well established (ibid.).

In the initial concept stage, various versions of 'bootstrapping' are employed (Ryan, 2001). These methods can include investing one's wealth, low-level crowdfunding (e.g., Kickstarter), and the oft-cited 'friends, family and fools' (Vanacker et al., 2011). As the firm begins to grow (and can demonstrate some sort of potential for developing a revenue stream), it attracts the attention of various professional funders. Regardless of the type of investment (debt or equity), the ability to produce the desired return is the primary focus of the underwriting process that the funder uses to evaluate the potential investment (Gompers and Lerner, 2006; Santikian, 2014). Various intermediary organizations have evolved to assist both the investor and the entrepreneur, including a wide range of incubators, co-working spaces and economic development agencies (Rice and Matthews, 1995; Salinger, 2013) and a settled market provides distinct signaling devices to the market participants (Kaplan and Grossman, 2010). Both the funding structures and the support systems align with the growth patterns of the firm in a manner that could be considered longitudinal. This process is technically referred to as a capital formation strategy (Baker, 2011; Sherman, 2005), but colloquially referred to as a capital stack (the term I will use throughout this chapter).

In the traditional nonprofit organization, a similar structure exists, albeit with different goals and objectives. At a macro level, there is an array of income sources, including fees for service, individual donations, and grants from both government sources and private foundations (McKeever, 2015). Further, the fee for service income can be either a direct sale of a product or service or the delivery of services under a subcontract from a government entity (ibid.). To make the matter more complex, the mix of funding sources within a particular organization is highly dependent on the social issue that the enterprise is trying to address (von Schnurbein and Fritz, 2017) as well as the level of risk the entity is willing to entertain (Fischer, Wilsker and Young, 2011). For example, organizations such as hospitals and universities show a high level of fee revenue from service consumers (McKeever, 2015), while human services organizations tend to rely more on charitable donations (Fischer et al., 2011). While giving patterns within the various social sectors tend to fluctuate based on current events and changes in consumer behavior (MacLaughlin, 2015), it is also highly dependent on the interpersonal relationship between the donor and the recipient entity (Khodakarami, Petersen and Venkatesan, 2015). However, there is no expectation in the nonprofit funding model that the funder will ever receive a direct financial return on investment, nor any return of the principle funds invested (Bowman, 2002). Rather, the focus is on building relationships with donors and grant makers to build a consistent and dependable revenue stream (Khodakarami et al., 2015).

Further, to receive charitable funding from grants and gifts, an organization must be able to demonstrate that it has been recognized as a tax-exempt charitable entity by the US Internal Revenue Service under IRS section 501(c)3. This process can take upwards of 180 days, and involve substantial legal fees (Hammerschmidt, 2013), creating a substantive barrier to entry for any new venture seeking to operate in a donor-funded model. Should a nonprofit seek to obtain the market rate financing options that are typically secured by mature firms, the organization must be able to provide some sort of collateral, which is usually more easily done in an equity-based context that is not available to the 501(c)3 (Dees and Anderson, 2003; Lyons and Kickul, 2013).

Having reviewed the traditional funding paths of both for-profit and nonprofit enterprises, I now turn my attention to the systems and networks that exist to help these organizations grow.

Unique challenges in social enterprise

When a firm seeks to produce value across multiple metrics, the funding of the new venture becomes much more complex. Organizational strategies and the choices in funding models that ensue are far murkier.

Strategic complexity

Moizer and Tracey (2010) identify 11 different strategic factors in three general areas (social action, organizational legitimacy and revenue generation) that the fledgling social enterprise must grapple with as it begins to develop its strategic plan. From these factors, three generic strategic options are generated. However, it is recognized that several of these options can be combined and intertwined (ibid.), so there are nine or more different strategic combinations that must be considered. More importantly, each of these options has its own set of implications (both positive and negative), leaving the aspiring social entrepreneur with a wide range of issues to consider.

Santos et al. (2015) identify four typologies of hybrid organizations (market hybrid, bridging hybrid, blending hybrid and coupling hybrid) and then provide thoughts on the organizational structures needed to achieve success within each of the four structures, as well as challenges that may be faced by each typology. Specific recommendations on the means and methods to monitor performance within each typology are also provided (ibid.). While the need to 'assess the situation, learn how to best design...[a] social enterprise and organize for sustainable value' (ibid., p. 56) is recognized, the effort needed to come to these conclusions is left implicit.

Battilana and Lee (2014) examine how the hybrid organization must reconcile multiple organizational identities and multiple institutional logics to arrive at an organizational design that effectively addresses the pursuit of value across more than one metric. Internal tensions arise in trying to create a clear sense of mission and identity as well as in making decisions about the allocation of resources. External tensions are also present in the choice of legal structure, regulatory environment and the acquisition of resources and financial capital. Further, successful navigation of these various challenges may require the entity to make strategic changes in its organizational structure over time (a point I will return to shortly) (ibid.).

Nebulous funding strategies

The funding challenges faced by a social enterprise (Battilana and Lee, 2014) exist primarily because the risk/reward evaluation for funders becomes much more complex (Emerson et al., 2007; Meyskens and Bird, 2015). Further, these needs can vary widely based on the market orientation of the product or service that is intended to generate revenue for the enterprise (Dohrmann, Raith and Siebold, 2015; Martin, 2015).

In the nonprofit social enterprise, early-stage financing is often available through various charitable sources (Emerson et al., 2007), but requires that the firm obtain tax-exempt charitable status under IRS section 501(c)3, with the accompanying time delays discussed previously (Hammerschmidt, 2013). As the organization matures, it may become eligible for more sophisticated forms of funding, but legal restrictions on the distribution of profits limit these solutions to various 'equity equivalents' (Ryan, 2001) and restrict the firm's ability to secure more aggressive equity-based investments (Lyons and Kickul, 2013). In the early stages of a for-profit social enterprise, seed capital may be available through the well-worn 'friends, family and fools' (Emerson et al., 2007) or through various methods of crowdfunding (Colombo, Franzoni and Rossi-Lamastra, 2015). However, the selection of a for-profit model (and the concomitant reductions in net profit caused by the pursuit of social outcomes) can limit the firm's ability to secure philanthropic funding (Dees and Anderson, 2003; Lyons and Kickul, 2013). Siqueira et al. (2018) observe that these early funding decisions can impact the trajectory of the organization for many years to come and that the entrepreneur is often unwilling or unable to shift the organization to a new model when circumstances might suggest that such a shift would be prudent.

In attempting to resolve these issues, numerous hybrid funding concepts have been developed (Kaplan and Grossman, 2010), but the current assortment of solutions are fragmented and complex (Martin, 2011), and require a level of sophistication that the early-stage social entrepreneur has yet to develop. Much of this currently falls under the label of 'venture philanthropy' (Scarlata and Alemany, 2008). Scarlata, Gil and Zacharakis (2012) review a screening process used by these 'philanthropic venture capitalists', listing areas such as human capital, social impact, financial feasibility and organizational structure as factors in the decision to invest. The literature observes that the type of financial instrument varies along with the stage of development of the firm, but a review of 'deals' made shows that the majority of funding (regardless of the growth stage of the enterprise) come from grant-based sources (ibid.).

Several attempts have been made to diagram a viable path for capital acquisition in a social enterprise (Martin, 2011; Ryan, 2001; Scarlata and Alemany, 2008; Scarlata et al., 2012) and various alternative solutions have been proposed (Martin, 2015; Meyskens and Bird, 2015). However, these diagrams ignore a significant tension that the social entrepreneur must resolve (Emerson et al., 2007) – namely, the lack of flexibility that still exists in the deployment of 'social venture capital'. Martin (2015) observes that grant and non-grant funding can be combined in the capitalization of a social enterprise, either simultaneously or sequentially. However, the legal and structural challenges that this 'hybrid financing' strategy implies are left unsaid. Should a nascent social enterprise seek to deploy such a strategy, it would need to convert from one legal structure or organizational model to another, diverting critical resources in the process.

The trade-off

The development of an operating model for a social enterprise takes more thought (and therefore more time) due to the need to balance a greater number of strategic trade-offs (Battilana and Lee, 2014; Moizer and Tracey, 2010; Santos et al., 2015). It is also clear that funding needs can force a venture down a specific path (Siqueira et al., 2018) that may or may not allow the enterprise to access the appropriate form of latter-stage funding (Scarlata et al., 2012). Finally, a successful social venture must be able to implement multiple organizational structures over the life of the entity (Battilana and Lee, 2014). Therefore, it would seem that the many well-intentioned suggestions made as to how to resolve this tension have artificially constrained our aspiring social entrepreneurs, forcing them to make decisions on structure and funding that may prove detrimental down the road.

Current legal solutions

Several attempts have been made to solve this problem by legal means through the development of various hybrid legal structures such as the low-profit limited liability corporation (L3C) and the benefit corporation. Each of these legal structures advances the cause but falls short of the goal, primarily in failing to resolve the tax and liability issues related to the receipt of philanthropic support (Raz, 2012). The development of the social purpose organization statutes in the state of California may partially resolve some of these tensions (ibid.), but the field is far from settled.

Future research suggestions

The concept of hybridity is beginning to take hold as a key theoretical construct in understanding the unique aspects of a social enterprise, both in considering organizational challenges and funding strategies (Battilana and Lee, 2014; Eldar, 2017; Martin, 2011; Santos et al., 2015). However, the current state of debate does not resolve the practical matters that arise in developing these hybrid entities, particularly in the acquisition of strategic capital. Accordingly, additional research is called for to shed light on both theory and practice in this emerging field. The following section outlines some topics that may benefit from further exploration. Since the goal of this agenda is to help advance the growth of social entrepreneurship, it seems reasonable to start with a question about the growth patterns of the hybrid social enterprise.

Organizational lifecycles

Question 1: What is the lifecycle of the social enterprise?
Question 1A: How does the notion of a capital stack interface with that lifecycle?

The stages of growth in a for-profit enterprise have been examined at length (Bhave, 1994; Jawahar and McLaughlin, 2001). Galbraith's (1982) model lines out the stages (proof of concept, initial protype, early sales, growth and maturity) that have become the model for many of the leading texts on business start-ups (Blank, 2013; Cooper, 2011; Kawasaki, 2015). In a similar fashion, Bailey and Grochau (1993) outlined a lifecycle for nonprofit organizations that parallels the phases of growth in a for-profit venture (albeit with slightly different labels). While it is recognized that the social entrepreneur follows some sort of growth pattern, there is concern that the 'competing logics' faced by a hybrid entity may impact the stages of growth in some way (Wry and York, 2017). Gaining a greater understanding of the lifecycle of the social enterprise would clarify how specific types of capital might best be used to further the organization's goals.

Issues in capital acquisition

Question 2: How does bootstrapping affect the social enterprise capital stack?

In the development of a profit-seeking enterprise, the concept of 'bootstrapping' (use of personal assets, loans from family and unpaid labor) is recognized as a common practice for early-stage funding, in part because there is an expectation that these investments will be paid back when the firm turns a profit (Lahm and Little, 2005). When a firm is seeking a broader set of goals (including a concessionary profit expectation), bootstrapping may be less effective as an early-stage funding strategy. On the other hand, the common use of volunteer labor in many socially oriented ventures (Simmons and Emanuele, 2010) may be analogous to the sweat equity invested by a founder in a for-profit firm. While some exploration of the contributions of volunteer labor to the development of nonprofits has been made (Handy, Mook and Quarter, 2008; Simmons and Emanuele, 2010), its effect on a hybrid entity remains an open question. More specifically, greater understanding of the use of volunteers (as well as other bootstrapping techniques) as part of the strategic development of a hybrid entity could enhance the development of these firms.

Question 2A: What is the impact of crowdfunding?

The recent expansion of crowdfunding techniques (where relatively small amounts of money are solicited from a large group of individuals) has become a topic of exploration in the study of commercial entrepreneurship (Mollick, 2014), and also an object of inquiry in nonprofit fundraising (Gleasure and Feller, 2016; Zhou and Ye, 2019). One recent study has compared the behaviors that influence funding success of both for-profit and nonprofit enterprises (Moleskis, Alegre and Canela, 2019) and another has examined how an earned income strategy may impact a nonprofit's ability to raise funds on a crowdfunding platform (Makýšová and Vaceková, 2017). However, the unique structural needs of a hybrid organization and the concomitant need for a flexible organizational structure blur the lines of funder expectations and may limit the use of crowdfunding as a source of early stage capital for hybrid entities. A quantitative study of this blended dynamic and its impact on the ability to acquire crowdfunded capital would be very helpful to the aspiring social entrepreneur as they develop a capital stack strategy.

Question 2B: Is Kiva a special case within the crowdfunding universe?

As one of the largest crowdfunding sites (Moleskis and Canela, 2016), Kiva has become the source of substantial inquiry, and its data has formed the basis of many analytical studies. Although it was introduced and promoted as a peer-to-peer lending platform (Flannery, 2007), Kiva operates through a series of intermediaries who perform the loan underwriting function on behalf of the Kiva lender (Strom, 2009). Kiva itself does not charge an interest rate due to legal restrictions (Schwittay, 2014) but these intermediaries can and do charge interest (Ly and Mason, 2012; Strom, 2009). While higher than the rates offered by commercial lenders, the rates are comparable with other microcredit lenders (Ly and Mason, 2012). The involvement of these inter-mediary firms has caused some reputation loss for Kiva, although it did not seem to have any negative impact on the flow of funds into the organization (Strom, 2009). Kiva is, in fact, a facilitator, not a direct lender (ibid.) and does not manage loan portfolios.

In 2011, Kiva launched a new program in the United States called Kiva Zip. The concept behind this program was that the US market could more readily replicate a pure peer-to-peer model (Singh, 2019). Utilizing a process known as 'character-based lending', Kiva Zip provided a peer-to-peer zero interest lending platform that did not require any collateral or a particular credit score (Said, 2013). However, that project suffered a number of operational difficulties and was recently transformed into a model that operates much more like the original program founded in South Asia (Singh, 2019).

The unique operational issues that exist in the Kiva organization might lead to questions regarding the applicability of Kiva's lending data to the larger universe of crowdfunding platforms for both commercially and socially oriented enterprises. Further, as with crowdfunding in general, the hybrid organization's need for flexibility may further compound the challenges the Kiva model has faced, potentially reducing its effectiveness as a capital source for a hybrid entity. A deeper analysis of the unique attributes of this crowdfunding platform and its generalizability to the study of the funding of hybrid entities would aid in the further analysis of social venture funding.

Question 3: Does the lack of intermediaries affect the social enterprise capital stack?

The world of social enterprise has witnessed an emerging network of so-called social venture capitalists (Lyons and Kickul, 2013) and a broadening array of financial vehicles that are comfortable with transactions that produce a blended value (Clarkin and Cangioni, 2016). A handful of social venture incubators have sprung up in recent years (Casasnovas and Bruno, 2013), but the underlying infrastructure of intermediaries that exists in for-profit entrepreneurship has yet to develop in the social venture context (Brandstetter and Lehner, 2015). This issue is further complicated by the diverse perspectives and identities represented by those who found these hybrid ventures (Wry and York, 2017). While some founders have a reasonable level of competence regarding financial matters (Lee and Battilana, 2013), others come to this work from a more traditional nonprofit perspective (Alter, 2004).

Since the service provider (in the form of legal, accounting or financial service advisory firms) has been shown to be a positive factor in the growth of a for-profit firm (Zhang and Li, 2010), it would seem that such a network might also be useful in the growth of a hybrid entity. A more focused inquiry into how intermediaries might function in the social venture context would be an aid to the development of this sector.

Question 3A: Can venture philanthropy fill this role?

Increased interest in social entrepreneurship has garnered a concomitant shift in the deployment of philanthropic funding and the popularization of venture philanthropy, wherein the tools and techniques of commercial venture capitalists are adapted to the social benefit context (Moody, 2008). Critical to the exploration of this question is the understanding that the commercial venture capitalist takes a very active role in the development of the firms it funds, often taking a seat on the company's board and serving as an active intermediary by making introductions to potential customers, partners and other service providers (Sherman, 2005).

Within the venture philanthropy framework, the traditional focus on the funding activities of charitable foundations is broadened to include a more general role as agents of institutional change, including the development of entrepreneurial talent and convening and combining various support structures to advance the development of specific social enterprises (Moore, Westley and Brodhead, 2012; Quinn, Tompkins-Stange and Meyerson, 2014). There are also some indications that the impact investor may take on a more proactive role in the growth and development of the firms within their portfolio (Roundy, Holzhauer and Dai, 2017). To date, these studies have reported on qualitative examples of the actions of specific funders. A broader panel study of a larger group of the intermediation activities undertaken by venture philanthropists and impact investors might lead to a more normalized set of behaviors that would further strengthen the development of social ventures.

Question 4: Does the blended value proposition affect the amount of capital a social enterprise can attract?

As a hybrid entity, a social enterprise blends elements of the for-profit and nonprofit worlds (Pache and Santos, 2013). These 'competing logics' would then suggest that the appeal to capital is also a blended value proposition. However, each of these worlds uses distinct appeals to capital that may impact the ability of the hybrid organization to attract funding.

The for-profit entity clearly makes its appeal to funders on its ability to return invested capital to the funder, often with a desired premium expressed as a multiple of the initial investment (Sherman, 2005). The nonprofit organization appeals to donors on a more emotional level, where the donor's ability to empathize with the social cause being addressed can have a substantial impact on the amount of money raised (Barman, 2008; Gleasure and Feller, 2016; Khodakarami et al., 2015).

In seeking a blended return on investment, the social enterprise presents a value proposition that asks the investor to concede a portion of the financial return in exchange for the advancement of a specific social cause (Emerson, 2003). While the theoretical frameworks supporting this notion of blended value and concessionary return have been explored (Beugré, 2017; Kroeger and Weber, 2014), the impact on the firm's ability to raise capital calls for a more quantitative study. Smith, Cronley and Barr (2012) examined this issue within a nonprofit context, but further exploration of this question within a hybrid framework would be helpful to the aspiring social entrepreneur as they seek to build their capital stack strategy.

Question 4A: How does empathy affect investors and other funders in a social enterprise?

As mentioned above, the ability to develop an emotional connection to a donor is a critical element of nonprofit fundraising. Since the value proposition being extended to an investor in a hybrid social enterprise specifically asks for a concession on the financial return in exchange for the advancement of a specific social concern, it would seem reasonable to assume that the concession would be more easily made if the investor had a similar empathetic connection to the social cause the hybrid seeks to address.

The effect of empathy on the intentions of the social entrepreneur has been examined in many studies (Bacq and Alt, 2018; Hockerts, 2015; Mair and Noboa, 2006). Empathy as a driving force in donor behavior in funding nonprofits has also been examined at length (Gleasure and Feller, 2016; Khodakarami et al., 2015; Verhaert and Van den Poel, 2011).

One recent study of for-profit entrepreneurship suggests that the level to which the investor identifies with the project can have an effect on the decision to fund the venture (Smith and Bergman, 2020). In the study of social ventures, the identification of an individual investor with a specific cause has been identified as one of the screening tools that is used to make a decision to invest in a specific project (Brest and Born, 2013), and a few small sample surveys suggest that this empathy may impact the social investor (Glänzel and Scheuerle, 2016; Wood, 2012). However, substantive exploration of how an emotional connection to a cause might impact the decision to make an impact investment has yet to be made. Gaining insight into the relationship between empathetic connection to a cause and the behavior of an impact investor would increase the efficiency of the social capital market and improve the likelihood of successful funding transactions.

Conclusion

By definition, hybrid organizations 'combine the organizational forms of both business and charity at their cores' (Battilana and Lee, 2014, p. 397). Accordingly, the means of attracting capital to these ventures must also combine the tools and techniques of funding practices from for-profit and nonprofit contexts. However, the timing and blending of the various layers of capital into a cohesive capital formation strategy has yet to be developed.

The strategic complexities that are inherent to the hybrid entity and the nebulous funding practices currently available to them complicate the ability of these ventures to gain the traction they need to reach their potential. Examining questions regarding organizational lifecycles and the effect of various conditions on the ability of these firms to finance their operations will lead to a greater understanding of the phenomena that drive the funding of these hybrids.

It is entirely possible that there is no consistent practice for funding a social enterprise, and that each venture will need to chart its own course through the myriad options that currently exist. Conversely, it is at least conceivable that a predictable pattern of funding practices could emerge that mirrors the generally accepted capital stack process that exists in the for-profit domain. I hope that the examination of the questions outlined in this chapter will provide much needed clarity in this area, adding to the literature while also aiding the aspiring social entrepreneur to build a better world.

References

Alter, K. (2004). Social enterprise typology. Virtue Ventures LLC. Accessed 21 January 2021 at https://canvas.brown.edu/courses/1073328/files/61028038.

Austin, J., Stevenson, H. and Wei-Skillern, J. (2006). Social and commercial entrepreneurship: same, different, or both? *Entrepreneurship Theory and Practice*, 30(1), 1–22.

Bacq, S. and Alt, E. (2018). Feeling capable and valued: a prosocial perspective on the link between empathy and social entrepreneurial intentions. *Journal of Business Venturing*, 33(3), 333–50.

Bailey, D. and Grochau, K.E. (1993). Aligning leadership needs to the organizational stage of development: applying management theory to nonprofit organizations. *Administration in Social Work*, 17(1), 23–45.

Baker, H.K. (2011). *Capital Structure and Corporate Financing Decisions: Theory, Evidence, and Practice*. Hoboken, NJ: John Wiley & Sons.

Barman, E. (2008). With strings attached: nonprofits and the adoption of donor choice. *Nonprofit and Voluntary Sector Quarterly*, 37(1), 39–56.

Battilana, J. and Dorado, S. (2010). Building sustainable hybrid organizations: the case of commercial microfinance organizations. *Academy of Management Journal*, 53(6), 1419–40.

Battilana, J. and Lee, M. (2014). Advancing research on hybrid organizing – insights from the study of social enterprises. *The Academy of Management Annals*, 8(1), 397–441.

Beugré, C. (2017). *Social Entrepreneurship: Managing the Creation of Social Value*. New York: Routledge.

Bhave, M.P. (1994). A process model of entrepreneurial venture creation. *Journal of Business Venturing*, 9(3), 223–42.

Blank, S. (2013). *The Four Steps to the Epiphany: Successful Strategies for Products That Win*. Hoboken, NJ: John Wiley & Sons.

Bowman, W. (2002). The uniqueness of nonprofit finance and the decision to borrow. *Nonprofit Management and Leadership*, 12(3), 293–311.

Brandstetter, L. and Lehner, O.M. (2015). Opening the market for impact investments: the need for adapted portfolio tools. *Entrepreneurship Research Journal*, 5(2), 87–107.

Brest, P. and Born, K. (2013, 14 August). Unpacking the impact in impact investing. *Stanford Social Innovation Review*.

Casasnovas, G. and Bruno, A.V. (2013). Scaling social ventures. *Journal of Management for Global Sustainability*, 1(2), https://doi.org/10.13185%2FJM2013.01211.

Clarkin, J.E. and Cangioni, C.L. (2016). Impact investing: a primer and review of the literature. *Entrepreneurship Research Journal*, 6(2), 135–73.

Colombo, M.G., Franzoni, C. and Rossi-Lamastra, C. (2015). Internal social capital and the attraction of early contributions in crowdfunding. *Entrepreneurship Theory and Practice*, 39(1), 75–100.

Cooper, R.G. (2011). *Winning at New Products: Creating Value Through Innovation*. New York: Basic Books.

Dees, J.G. and Anderson, B.B. (2003). For-profit social ventures. *International Journal of Entrepreneurship Education*, 2(1), 1–26.

Dohrmann, S., Raith, M. and Siebold, N. (2015). Monetizing social value creation – a business model approach. *Entrepreneurship Research Journal*, 5(2), 127–54.

Eldar, O. (2017). The role of social enterprise and hybrid organizations. *Columbia Business Law Review*, No. 1, 92–194.

Emerson, J. (2000). The nature of returns: a social capital markets inquiry into elements of investment and the blended value proposition. *Social Enterprise Series, No. 17*. Harvard Business School.

Emerson, J. (2003). The blended value proposition: integrating social and financial returns. *California Management Review*, 45(4), 35–51.

Emerson, J., Freundlich, T. and Fruchterman, J. et al. (2007). Nothing ventured, nothing gained: addressing the critical gaps in risk-taking capital for social enterprise. Working paper. SAID Business School, University of Oxford.

Fischer, R.L., Wilsker, A. and Young, D.R. (2011). Exploring the revenue mix of nonprofit organizations: does it relate to publicness? *Nonprofit and Voluntary Sector Quarterly*, 40(4), 662–81.

Flannery, M. (2007). Kiva and the birth of person-to-person microfinance. *Innovations*, 2(1–2), 31–56.

Galbraith, J. (1982). The stages of growth. *The Journal of Business Strategy*, 3(1), 70–79.

Glänzel, G. and Scheuerle, T. (2016). Social impact investing in Germany: current impediments from investors' and social entrepreneurs' perspectives. *VOLUNTAS: International Journal of Voluntary and Nonprofit Organizations*, 27(4), 1638–68.

Gleasure, R. and Feller, J. (2016). Does heart or head rule donor behaviors in charitable crowdfunding markets? *International Journal of Electronic Commerce*, 20(4), 499–524.

Gompers, P.A. and Lerner, J. (2006). *The Venture Capital Cycle*. Cambridge, MA: MIT Press.

Hammerschmidt, P. (2013, 25 October). My application for tax exemption was submitted to the IRS. Why is it taking so long? *Nonprofit Quarterly*, 11(3), 260–80.

Handy, F., Mook, L. and Quarter, J. (2008). The interchangeability of paid staff and volunteers in nonprofit organizations. *Nonprofit and Voluntary Sector Quarterly*, 37(1), 76–92.

Hockerts, K. (2015). The social entrepreneurial antecedents scale (SEAS): a validation study. *Social Enterprise Journal*, 11(3), 260–80.

Jawahar, I. and McLaughlin, G.L. (2001). Toward a descriptive stakeholder theory: an organizational life cycle approach. *Academy of Management Review*, 26(3), 397–414.

Kaplan, R.S. and Grossman, A.S. (2010). The emerging capital market for nonprofits. *Harvard Business Review*, 88(10), 110–18.

Kawasaki, G. (2015). *The Art of the Start 2.0: The Time-Tested, Battle-Hardened Guide for Anyone Starting Anything*. New York: Portfolio/Penguin.

Khodakarami, F., Petersen, J.A. and Venkatesan, R. (2015). Developing donor relationships: the role of the breadth of giving. *Journal of Marketing*, 79(4), 77–93.

Kroeger, A. and Weber, C. (2014). Developing a conceptual framework for comparing social value creation. *Academy of Management Review*, 39(4), 513–40.

Lahm, R. and Little, H. (2005). Bootstrapping business start-ups: entrepreneurship literature, textbooks, and teaching practices versus current business practices. *Journal of Entrepreneurship Education*, 8, 61–73.

Lee, M. and Battilana, J. (2013). How the zebra got its stripes: imprinting of individuals and hybrid social ventures. *Harvard Business School Organizational Behavior Unit Working Paper, No. 14–005*.

Lumpkin, G.T. and Bacq, S. (2019). Civic wealth creation: a new view of stakeholder engagement and social impact. *Academy of Management Perspectives*, 33(2), https://doi.org/10.5465/amp.2017.0060.

Ly, P. and Mason, G. (2012). Individual preferences over development projects: evidence from microlending on Kiva. *VOLUNTAS: International Journal of Voluntary and Nonprofit Organizations*, 23(4), 1036–55.

Lyons, T.S. and Kickul, J.R. (2013). The social enterprise financing landscape: the lay of the land and new research on the horizon. *Entrepreneurship Research Journal*, 3(2), 147–59.

MacLaughlin, S. (2015). *Charitable Giving Report*. Blackbaud Institute. Accessed 5 May 2020 at https://institute.blackbaud.com/asset/2015-charitable-giving-report/.

Mair, J. and Noboa, E. (2006). Social entrepreneurship: how intentions to create a social venture are formed. In J. Mair, J. Robinson and K. Hockerts (eds), *Social Entrepreneurship* (pp. 121–35). Basingstoke: Palgrave Macmillan.

Makýšová, L. and Vaceková, G. (2017). Profitable nonprofits? Reward-based crowdfunding in the Czech Republic. *NISPAcee Journal of Public Administration and Policy*, 10(2), 203–27.

Martin, M. (2011). Understanding the true potential of hybrid financing strategies for social entrepreneurs. *Impact Economy Working Papers, No. 2.*

Martin, M. (2015). Building impact businesses through hybrid financing. *Entrepreneurship Research Journal*, 5(2), 109–26.

McKeever, B.S. (2015, 29 October). The nonprofit sector in brief 2015. Urban Institute. Accessed 22 May 2020 at https://www.urban.org/research/publication/nonprofit -sector-brief-2015-public-charities-giving-and-volunteering.

Meyskens, M. and Bird, L. (2015). Crowdfunding and value creation. *Entrepreneurship Research Journal*, 5(2), 155–66.

Moizer, J. and Tracey, P. (2010). Strategy making in social enterprise: the role of resource allocation and its effects on organizational sustainability. *Systems Research and Behavioral Science*, 27(3), 252–66.

Moleskis, M., Alegre, I. and Canela, M.A. (2019). Crowdfunding entrepreneurial or humanitarian needs? The influence of signals and biases on decisions. *Nonprofit and Voluntary Sector Quarterly*, 48(3), 552–71.

Moleskis, M. and Canela, M.Á. (2016). Crowdfunding success: the case of Kiva.org. *IESE Research Papers, No. D/1137.* IESE Business School.

Mollick, E. (2014). The dynamics of crowdfunding: an exploratory study. *Journal of Business Venturing*, 29(1), 1–16.

Moody, M. (2008). 'Building a culture': the construction and evolution of venture philanthropy as a new organizational field. *Nonprofit and Voluntary Sector Quarterly*, 37(2), 324–52.

Moore, M.-L., Westley, F.R. and Brodhead, T. (2012). Social finance intermediaries and social innovation. *Journal of Social Entrepreneurship*, 3(2), 184–205.

Nicholls, A. (2010). The legitimacy of social entrepreneurship: reflexive isomorphism in a pre-paradigmatic field. *Entrepreneurship Theory and Practice*, 34(4), 611–33.

Pache, A.-C. and Santos, F. (2013). Inside the hybrid organization: selective coupling as a response to competing institutional logics. *Academy of Management Journal*, 56(4), 972–1001.

Quinn, R., Tompkins-Stange, M. and Meyerson, D. (2014). Beyond grantmaking: philanthropic foundations as agents of change and institutional entrepreneurs. *Nonprofit and Voluntary Sector Quarterly*, 43(6), 950–68.

Rawhouser, H., Cummings, M. and Crane, A. (2015). Benefit corporation legislation and the emergence of a social hybrid category. *California Management Review*, 57(3), 13–35.

Raz, K.G. (2012). Toward an improved legal form for social enterprise. *NYU Review Law and Social Change*, 36(2) 283.

Rice, M.P. and Matthews, J.B. (1995). *Growing New Ventures, Creating New Jobs.* Westport, CT: Quorum Books.

Roundy, P., Holzhauer, H. and Dai, Y. (2017). Finance or philanthropy? Exploring the motivations and criteria of impact investors. *Social Responsibility Journal*, 13, 491–512.

Ryan, W.P. (2001). Nonprofit capital: a review of problems and strategies. Rockefeller Foundation and Fannie Mae Foundation. Accessed 21 January 2021 at https://community-wealth.org/sites/clone.community-wealth.org/files/downloads/paper-ryan.pdf.

Said, C. (2013, 10 August). Kiva Zip loans aid low-income U.S. entrepreneurs. *SFGate.com*. Accessed 22 May 2020 at http://www.sfgate.com/news/article/Kiva-Zip-loans-aid-low-income-U-S-entrepreneurs-4723319.php.

Salinger, J.H. (2013). Economic development policies through business incubation and co-working: a study of San Francisco and New York City. Thesis. Columbia University.

Santikian, L. (2014). The ties that bind: bank relationships and small business lending. *Journal of Financial Intermediation*, 23(2), 177–213.

Santos, F., Pache, A.-C. and Birkholz, C. (2015). Making hybrids work: aligning business models and organizational design for social enterprises. *California Management Review*, 57(3), 36–58.

Scarlata, M. and Alemany, L. (2008). Philanthropic venture capital: can the key elements of venture capital be applied successfully to social enterprises? Accessed 21 January 2021 at http://eprints.lse.ac.uk/30880/.

Scarlata, M., Gil, L.A. and Zacharakis, A. (2012). Philanthropic venture capital: venture capital for social entrepreneurs? *Foundations and Trends' in Entrepreneurship*, 8(4), 279–342.

Schwittay, A.F. (2014). Making poverty into a financial problem: from global poverty lines to Kiva.org. *Journal of International Development*, 26(4), 508–19.

Sherman, A.J. (2005). *Raising Capital: Get the Money You Need to Grow Your Business*. New York: AMACOM.

Simmons, W.O. and Emanuele, R. (2010). Are volunteers substitute for paid labor in nonprofit organizations? *Journal of Economics and Business*, 62(1), 65–77.

Singh, J. (2019, 22 August). Kiva's crowdfunding platform transforms into hub for impact investing and financial inclusion. *Stanford Social Innovation Review*.

Siqueira, A.C.O., Guenster, N., Vanacker, T. and Crucke, S. (2018). A longitudinal comparison of capital structure between young for-profit social and commercial enterprises. *Journal of Business Venturing*, 33(2), 225–40.

Smith, B.R. and Bergman, B.J. (2020). The other side of the coin: investor identity and its role in resource provision. *Journal of Business Venturing Insights*, 14(C), Article e00175.

Smith, B.R., Cronley, M.L. and Barr, T.F. (2012). Funding implications of social enterprise: the role of mission consistency, entrepreneurial competence, and attitude toward social enterprise on donor behavior. *Journal of Public Policy and Marketing*, 31(1), 142–57.

Stangler, D., Tareque, I.S. and Morelix, A. (2016). *Trends in Venture Capital, Angel Investments, and Crowdfunding across the Fifty Largest U.S. Metropolitan Areas*. Ewing Marion Kauffman Foundation. Accessed 5 May 2020 at https://www.kauffman.org/what-we-do/research/2016/trends-in-venture-capital-angel-investments-and-crowdfunding.

Strom, S. (2009, 9 November). Confusion on where money lent via Kiva goes. *The New York Times*.

Vanacker, T., Manigart, S., Meuleman, M. and Sels, L. (2011). A longitudinal study on the relationship between financial bootstrapping and new venture growth. *Entrepreneurship and Regional Development*, 23(9–10), 681–705.

Verhaert, G.A. and Van den Poel, D. (2011). Empathy as added value in predicting donation behavior. *Journal of Business Research*, 64(12), 1288–95.

von Schnurbein, G. and Fritz, T.M. (2017). Benefits and drivers of nonprofit revenue concentration. *Nonprofit and Voluntary Sector Quarterly*, 46(5), 922–43.

Wood, S. (2012). Prone to progress: using personality to identify supporters of innovative social entrepreneurship. *Journal of Public Policy and Marketing*, 31(1), 129–41.

Wry, T. and York, J.G. (2017). An identity-based approach to social enterprise. *Academy of Management Review*, 42(3), 437–60.

Zhang, Y. and Li, H. (2010). Innovation search of new ventures in a technology cluster: the role of ties with service intermediaries. *Strategic Management Journal*, 31(1), 88–109.

Zhou, H. and Ye, S. (2019). Legitimacy, worthiness, and social network: an empirical study of the key factors influencing crowdfunding outcomes for nonprofit projects. *VOLUNTAS: International Journal of Voluntary and Nonprofit Organizations*, 30(4), 849–64.

3. Financing a sustainable planet: research agenda for impact investing in the renewable energy sector from an identity-based view

Tongyu Meng and Jamie Newth

Introduction

Climate change, air and water pollution, and other environmental issues are among the most pressing concerns for humanity. These human-induced negative impacts have far-reaching and long-term social implications beyond the harm to the natural environment and ecological balance. Climate change, for example, is highly inequitable, influencing the poorest populations and developing countries the most, who tend to have lower adaptive capacity to climate risks (Campbell-Lendrum and Corvalán, 2007). These complex challenges are driving changes in attitudes and behaviours for various stakeholder groups such as policy makers, firms, non-governmental organizations, social enterprises, communities and the financial market as a whole. Global commitments such as the Sustainable Development Goals and Paris Accord have been initiated to drive governmental leadership and to catalyse action from actors across various sectors to tackle climate change and other environmental issues. But we still have a long way to go to reach the targets we set for ourselves. The development of social finance has the potential to play a crucial role in addressing these challenges by offering sustainable finance solutions to achieve social, environmental, climate and health outcomes. Substantial research in the field of impact investing is required to realize this potential. This chapter reviews the literature of this emerging field from a selection of key theoretical bases and offers a research agenda for future research.

Impact investing is a form of social finance that uses investment tools traditionally belonging to the private sector to bring about social and/or environmental impacts. As a subset of socially responsible investment or ethical investment (Sparkes and Cowton, 2004), it reflects the society's growing consciousness of businesses' social impact and responsibility (Ransome and Sampford, 2010), and the belief that business can go beyond minimizing the harm of its practices to play a key role in addressing social and environmental problems. Impact investing brings purpose into private capital that funds innovative solutions to wicked problems, and the development and growth of businesses that are socially and environmentally sustainable. Not only is new knowledge regarding the policy, strategy, execution, ethics and measurement (among many other things) of impact investing important for development of more sustainable economies, but it also presents a rich and interesting research field. This is because of the confluence of institutional pressures, stakeholder interaction, personal motivations and behavioural factors that enable and constrain the actions of investors, investees, entrepreneurs and policy makers. We start by reviewing the development of impact investing research over the past two decades from a selection of disciplines. Located in management research, the concept of identity is used as a thread to offer research avenues in institutional logics, stakeholder management theory and sensemaking from a behavioural perspective.

Development of impact investing research

Impact investing can be considered as a subset of the broader context of social finance (Daggers and Nicholls, 2016; Mendell and Barbosa, 2013). Research in impact investing is driven by the growing 'impact capital' market development across many countries over the last two decades, with US$239 billion in impact investing assets under management (Mudaliar et al., 2019). Broader concepts with environmental appeal such as circular economics (Zink and Geyer, 2017), low-carbon economy (Bridge et al., 2013), and blue economy (Silver et al., 2015) are gaining momentum among stakeholder groups, leading to growing attention to impact investing as a key financial tool to overcome various environmental challenges and to enable the business models to operationalize these forms of venturing. However, the field of impact investing has yet to be established as an academic paradigm of its own due to its blurred definition and boundaries with fragmented development across disciplines (Daggers and Nicholls, 2016).

Interdisciplinary research in the field of impact investing is common and reflects the interdisciplinarity and blurred boundaries of the impact investing practice. This interdisciplinarity is reflected and enhanced by the lack of consensus on language and terminology use within impact investing research and practice. Various terms referring to similar concepts, including social impact investments (Daggers and Nicholls, 2016), environmental finance (Linnenluecke, Smith and McKnight, 2016), sustainable investment (Talan and Sharma, 2019), green finance with an environmental focus (Azhgaliyeva and Liddle, 2020; Pham, 2016) and blue finance with a focus on ocean conservation and coastal ecosystems (Wabnitz and Blasiak, 2019), are used by both researchers and practitioners. These terms all refer to variations in investment approach and intended impact. For example, in sustainable investment, the integration of environmental, social and governance (ESG) factors in investment decision making is one of the core research areas and has become a mainstream investor practice (Talan and Sharma, 2019). However, in impact investing, most research is derived from sustainable development (Bugg-Levine and Emerson, 2011), social entrepreneurship (Mair, Mayer and Lutz, 2015), sustainable entrepreneurship (Schaltegger and Wagner, 2011; Shepherd and Patzelt, 2011) and social innovation (Moore, Westley and Nicholls, 2012) using institutional theories and concepts in management research.

Impact investing's blurred boundaries are also reflected in the many activities it includes. Impact investing incorporates many areas such as development finance, social enterprise financing, clean-tech investment and renewable energy investment (REI). Despite the blurred boundaries, or perhaps because of them, these sector-specific topics remain largely separate from the main impact investing discourse that has developed within the social entrepreneurship literature. REI, for example, can be approached from various disciplines, but most REI research adopts the perspectives of energy economics and energy policy (Alagappan, Orans and Woo, 2011; Sangroya and Nayak, 2017), natural science in terms of carbon emission and ecology (Hultman et al., 2010) and engineering with attention paid to clean technology resolutions.

Furthermore, the issue is complicated by the various financing tools employed by impact investors. Although impact investing's focus is on impact and financial returns, which are the ends, rather than on instruments, which are the means, the range of financial instruments and asset classes and their innovative deployment is central to the defining characters of impact investing. The investment itself can take the form of debt, equity, cash, or other hybrid finance, and can come from various sectors, including social, private and the public sectors (Nicholls, 2010; Ormiston et al., 2015). There remain many barriers to channelling capital into impact investing that call for further development of a secondary market to increase liquidity, intermediary support to improve the deal flow of investable social ventures, and shifts in institutionalized thinking around shareholder primacy, and bringing institutional investors into impact investing (Mendell and Barbosa, 2013). Finance and public policy researchers have looked at the sources of funds such as venture capital funds, pension funds, sovereign funds and infrastructure funds (Barber, Morse and Yasuda, 2019); and specific types of financing instrument such as bonds, including social impact bonds (Edmiston and Nicholls, 2018; Jackson, 2013), green bonds, blue bonds and the related managerial incentives in bond/financial securities design (Chowdhry, Davies and Waters, 2015). Social impact bonds, for example, are payment-by-results contracts that bring private investment into outcome-based commissioning to fund novel interventions to deliver specific outcomes for a specific stakeholder group (Edmiston and Nicholls, 2018). Green bonds are fixed-income securities aimed at increasing the flow of capital to environmentally beneficial projects (Ehlers and Packer, 2017). Empirical researchers have looked into green bond development in terms of the volatility of the green bond market (Pham, 2016), the yield in comparison with conventional bonds with non-pecuniary motives of the investors (Zerbib, 2019), and the correlation between the green bond and financial markets such as corporate and treasury bond markets (Reboredo, 2018).

As this section has demonstrated, impact investing with an environmental focus such as green finance is interdisciplinary in nature, and is yet to become an established paradigm in management research. The lack of theories that are native to the field creates challenges for researchers looking to meaningfully advance the field. The challenge, therefore, is to move beyond green finance and impact investing merely as an interesting context to consider the theoretical contributions that can be made from researching this context. The specific research questions this field raises and the new knowledge that is required for its development will facilitate our endeavours to achieve global sustainability imperatives. Moreover, this field creates the opportunity to build theoretical bridges to more established fields to understand impact investing phenomena and, ultimately, to use these insights to contribute back to those fields.

Here we identify three research avenues located in business management derived from institutional logics, stakeholder management theory, and sensemaking from an identity-based view in the field of impact investing with an environmental focus. While there are myriad theoretical lenses through which to view this activity, we discuss these three here as they open especially fertile avenues for research and reveal critical research questions for building our fundamental understanding of the drivers and barriers to this important and growing field.

An identity-based approach

Identity is a concept that provides a common thread through our discussion of institutional logics perspective, stakeholder management theory and ethical sensemaking in environmentally driven impact investing. The term 'identity' has considerable variability in its meanings and theoretical conceptualization. Identities refer to the self that is composed of various meanings that people attach to multiple roles (Stryker and Burke, 2000). Identities are widely recognized and meaningful categories and classes that people apply to themselves, with each identity's expected behavioural standards (Wry and York, 2017). The concept of identity combining both social identity theory and identity theory creates an integrated view of the self, with the group, the role and the person as the bases of identity (Stets and Burke, 2000). The self is a group-based concept, where individuals have many identities in distinct networks of relationships in which they occupy positions and play roles. Social roles are expectations attached to positions occupied in networks of relationships where identities are internalized role expectations and meanings (Stryker and Burke, 2000).

Patterns of organizational action are affected by individuals' interpretations and motivations, which are guided by organizational identity (Dutton and Dukerich, 1991). People can manipulate these identities to maximize who they want to be and how they want to be perceived by others, which is also reinforced or constrained by institutional factors. In impact investing, actors often define their identities by their stated social missions, which can be used as legitimization strategies to idealize their identity (Lehner, Harrer and Quast, 2019). Communication gaps between the involved actors are therefore common in impact investing due to the different discursive foci associated with their distinctive identities (ibid.). As multiple identities and communication gaps create tensions and equivocality, sensemaking is used by actors to navigate these. This sensemaking can best be understood in conjunction with the strong guiding influence of institutional logics.

Institutional logics is an inherently cross-level concept that can be applied to individuals, groups, organizations and wider social contexts. Individuals within organizations and organizations themselves have varying identities and subtle variations in their logics. Social identity theory and stakeholder theory are often utilized in identity-based analysis to explain these institutional phenomena. For example, Wry and York (2017) used an identity-based approach linking identity theory, institutional logics and entrepreneurship to explain opportunity recognition in social enterprise creation. In terms of stakeholder theory, organizational identity consists of participants' shared perception of the entity that drives behaviour, which links directly to the mandate of stakeholder theory (Brickson, 2007). Commercial companies are considered to have a combination of an individualistic orientation, a relational orientation and a collectivistic orientation, where the latter two go beyond self-interest to create social value for stakeholders (Brickson, 2005, 2007).

The social categories that people identify with influence their 'self-concept' and behaviours (Smith and Woodworth, 2012), and a single individual or a single organization can have multiple and varied identities. The behaviours associated with a certain identity can come into play when that identity salience is high. Identity salience is the probability that an identity will be activated or invoked in various situations, where higher salience of an identity leads to greater probability of the behaviours according to the expectation attached to a particular identity (Stryker and Burke, 2000). Under different conditions, the group, role and personal identities may reinforce or constrain the self (Stets and Burke, 2000). In the field of impact investing, various actors from different sectors interact with each other; each has different identities influenced by behavioural factors, with inherently hybrid thinking incorporating both social and commercial logics.

Institutional logics

An appreciation of the institutions and the institutional logics that underpin the strategies and decisions of relevant actors is a fundamental line of enquiry for the understanding of impact investors and impact investing markets. This is because impact investing often operates amidst the dynamics unfolding at the complex intersection of various types of organizations, including foundations, private firms, local communities, entrepreneurs and state actors. Institutional logics are socially constructed and historically contingent patterns of material practices and symbolic systems including assumptions, values and beliefs by which individuals and organizations provide meaning to their social reality, organize time and space and reproduce their lives and experiences (Thornton and Ocasio, 1999). In this way they determine both ends and means, engendering categories and motives as the bases for individual and organizational actions (Friedland and Alford, 1991). Actors' behaviours are the manifestations of their embedded institutional logics, while, simultaneously, actors' material practices shape institutional logics (Thornton, Ocasio and Lounsbury, 2015). Therefore institutional logics shape individual preferences, organizational interests and the behaviours to attain those preferences and interests

(Thornton, Lounsbury and Ocasio, 2012), and consequently have a profound impact on the decision-making process in an organization.

An institutional logics perspective emphasizes the mechanisms and the variety of substantive contexts where institutional orders are temporally and contextually dependent (Thornton et al., 2015; Tracey, 2012). Institutional orders are made up by institutional content, of which legitimacy, values and practices are the building blocks (Thornton et al., 2012). Legitimacy is the expectation and perception that the behaviours of an entity in a given social system are desirable or appropriate (Suchman, 1995) and can be defined from three unique epistemological and ontological positions: theorizing legitimacy as a property, an interactive process of social construction via renegotiation of prevalent legitimacy, and a form of perception or evaluation (Suddaby, Bitektine and Haack, 2017). Research has shown there is a strong connection between the social identity of actors and legitimization strategies of organizations (Lehner et al., 2019). One legitimizing strategy employed by organizations that incorporates competing institutional logics is selectively coupling intact elements prescribed by each logic to project legitimacy and propriety to external stakeholders (Pache and Santos, 2013).

Similar to social entrepreneurship, impact investing demonstrates institutional logic hybridity that combines the typically conflicting social welfare and commercial logics (Nicholls, 2010). Multiple institutional logics can coexist, interact and compete for influence, and sometimes no single logic dominates (Friedland and Alford, 1991; Thornton et al., 2015). Such organizational contexts with multiple institutional logics operate in a context of institutional complexity, where some organizations prioritize a single institutional logic and some couple and innovate to balance several institutional logics (Mair et al., 2015). When actors are able to reconcile and exploit competing institutional logics, they enable mechanisms of institutional change (Dimaggio, 1988).

Disruptive institutional change is built by the process of institutional work embedded in individuals' and organizations' day-to-day practices. An institutional work perspective examines 'the practices of individual and collective actors aimed at creating, maintaining, and disrupting institutions', explaining how individual agency influences the institutions and the interactions between actors and institutional structures (Lawrence, Suddaby and Leca, 2011, p. 52). Institutional change, such as the emergence of new organizational forms, happens through forms of institutional work that combines established institutional logics to create a hybrid logic (Tracey, Phillips and Jarvis, 2011). Impact investing is one such example, as it seeks to blend the logics of social and financial value creation into new models of finance. Linking back to legitimacy, the hybrid positions taken by impact investing and social enterprises create legitimization issues. Institutions with hybrid logics put effort into being aligned with stable positions in an existing field while also taking a position that leads to institutional change to gain legitimacy (Granados and Rosli, 2019).

Pertinent to legitimacy and institutional work, organizational identity is defined as the central, distinctive and enduring attributes of an organization's character (Albert and Whetten, 1985; Whetten, 2006). Identities and associated practices are at the core of institutional logics as the linkages to organizational processes (Thornton et al., 2012). Organizational identities can be relatively fluid as well to adapt to changes, where an entity can have multiple and conflicting organizational identities (Gioia, Schultz and Corley, 2000). Actors and organizations with multiple identities can variously align with different institutional logics to make sense of and evaluate their everyday activities. For example, as one type of impact investee, social ventures exhibit dual identities compared with traditional enterprises – namely, an equivalent utilitarian organizational identity that is entrepreneurially oriented, and a greater normative organizational identity that is socially oriented (Moss et al., 2011). The institutional logics perspective, therefore, brings concepts of institutional orders, legitimacy and legitimizing strategies, institutional change based on the process of institutional work and identity formation to the fore, to be examined and further developed in the impact investing context.

Stakeholder management theory

Stakeholder theory originated from Freeman's seminal work (1984) that has acted as a platform for considerable business ethics and corporate social responsibility literature. Subsequent research conducted by Donaldson and Preston (1995) argues that stakeholder theory contains a theory of three different types – namely, descriptive/empirical, instrumental and normative (Donaldson and Preston, 1995; Jones, 1995). Descriptive stakeholder theory presents a model describing how organizations manage or interact with stakeholders while the normative model prescribes how organizations ought to treat their stakeholders, and the instrumental theory links means and ends (Freeman, 1999). Instrumental stakeholder theory was later developed by Jones (1995), who asserts that firms will gain a competitive advantage if they can establish relationships with their stakeholders based on ethical principles (trust, trustworthiness and cooperativeness), which explains why certain behaviours heretofore thought to be irrational or altruistic are, in fact, entirely compatible with economic objectives. The combination of social, environmental and financial objectives makes stakeholder management theory relevant to social entrepreneurship and impact investing research because it provides a lens through which to analyse how and why the pro-social and/ or pro-environmental actions are enabled and/or constrained by institutional contexts through the viewpoint of the stakeholders and their expectations. Here we discuss two research avenues on the locus of stakeholder analysis and the stakeholder salience framework.

Locus of stakeholder analysis

The locus of the original stakeholder management theory is the managers of firms (Mitchell, Agle and Wood, 1997). Much of the emergent academic literature in impact investing focuses on investment logics and investor rationalities, with investors (investment managers) being the locus of analysis (Chowdhry et al., 2015; Lazzarini et al., 2014; Nicholls, 2010) and with other actors often lacking sufficient attention. This has left an opportunity for impact investing researchers to shift the locus of stakeholder analysis to other stakeholder groups to contribute to a more rounded theory. By considering the institutional logics tensions, legitimacy challenges and multiple identities of various stakeholder groups around impact investing from the perspective of each group, we could better elucidate the constraints and opportunities of this phenomenon.

The key actors that could be the locus of stakeholder analysis in the impact investing field include investors, investees, community, the government and the natural environment. These five actors are identified in previous research in impact investing as being active in the field and are all strongly intercon-nected. Some scholars have simply distinguished the actors as investors, intermediaries and investees (Brandstetter and Lehner, 2015), while others empirically identified four archetypes of actors based on their social missions and core activities – namely, social investors, sustainable financers, enablers and impact entrepreneurs (Lehner et al., 2019). Our five-actor approach adds the natural environment and the community to the 'actor list' by expanding the understanding of what constitutes a stakeholder. Investors form the most common locus of analysis in impact investing, where researchers focus on investors' investment rationale and logics (Nicholls, 2010), impact investors' roles, and how they gauge and approach conflicting performance dimensions (Lazzarini et al., 2014). Investees are often studied together with investors (Glänzel and Scheuerle, 2016) or through their relationship to the investors (Agrawal and Hockerts, 2019), where social enterprise and for-purpose busi-ness can be the archetypical organizational form. One promising research avenue is to look at social entrepreneurs in the investee organization. These social and sustainable entrepreneurs present a promising avenue for insight into the issues and challenges on the demand side of impact investment capital (Houtbeckers, 2016). This is because for many instruments, especially equity-based instruments, entrepreneurs are at the heart of the investee, and their focus on the preservation of nature, life support and community presents challenging contexts in which to create value for investors (Hoogendoorn, Van der Zwan and Thurik, 2019; Shepherd and Patzelt, 2011). Why these entrepreneurs seek these prosocial or altruistic ends, how opportunities are found and shaped, and how these propositions elicit capital of various kinds from various sources are examples of the fertile research questions that emerge from this locus of analysis.

The 'community' stakeholder group in impact investing refers to those within physical proximity to the investee's main activities, and those that have similar interests and purposes, or people within a professional group (Dunham, Freeman and Liedtka, 2006). The community can also be the consumers or users of the investee's services and products. Using the field of REI as an example, the literature has investigated energy user participation, such as the role of users in the technology innovation processes (Ornetzeder and Rohracher, 2006), and managing distributed energy resources through demand response by user participation in micro-grids (Nunna and Doolla, 2014). Further research using community as the locus of stakeholder analysis will bring insights to our understanding of impact investing.

The government as policy maker also influences and benefits from impact investing projects. Governments can use policy mechanisms such as feed-in tariffs, establish wholesale funds, quotas, offer subsidies, tax or credit incentives, sales tax exemptions and green certificate schemes as incentives to promote the development of impact investing with an environmental focus. Government has the power to facilitate the legitimization of impact investing by working with investors and entrepreneurs and educating communities. The development of these projects, in turn, helps governments to meet carbon emission goals, promote local economic growth, facilitate the recovery of ecosystems and sustainable use of natural resources, and enhance energy security and supply.

Increasingly, impact investors, social entrepreneurs and environmentally conscious consumers are giving increased salience to the planet, its natural ecosystems and non-human life. For these reasons and due to the moral imperative that is increasingly becoming embedded as a societal value, the natural environment and the non-human life it contains can therefore also assume stakeholder status (Starik, 1995). This position values the natural environment not only for resources it provides and the ways it sustains human activities, but also holds that it has value in its own right as an ecological system independent of society (Driscoll and Starik, 2004). In environmentally focused impact investing, the natural environment is afforded greater salience from managers, and is often represented by an agent to voice its interests and needs. In an advancement on agent representation, some jurisdictions have given features of the natural environment personhood, thereby recognizing them as entities possessing juridical rights. Advocates for the protection of the natural environment consider this a promising tool to protect environmental interests (Gordon, 2018). For example, in New Zealand, the Te Urewera National Park and Whanganui River were given personhood granting them legal rights like other stakeholders, which also reflects the aspirations of Indigenous peoples for the land (Sanders, 2017). We encourage future research to investigate the natural environment as the locus of the stakeholder analysis, which goes beyond taking it as a legitimate stakeholder and will extend our understanding of stakeholder management theory.

Stakeholder salience revisited

Stakeholder salience framework is widely used to predict the level of salience of a stakeholder group on three attributes – namely, power, legitimacy and urgency (Mitchell et al., 1997). The three attributes were later developed into four to include proximity, which are useful tools to understand stakeholder relationships in impact investing (Driscoll and Starik, 2004; Mitchell et al., 1997). Like the link between legitimacy and identity discussed earlier, the concepts of power, urgency and proximity also derive from institutional theories and have identity-related mandates in their meaning and implication. Power is the imposition of an actor's view despite resistance to it (Weber and Henderson, 1947). Urgency means that stakeholder salience is time sensitive and critically important (Mitchell et al., 1997). Proximity indicates both physical distance and conceptual proximity (Driscoll and Starik, 2004). We believe that further development of these concepts and the extension of this framework to include more attributes for both human and non-human stakeholders could strengthen the stakeholder salience model. These may include concepts that are used to assess interactions and relationships among stakeholders, such as connectivity (especially in the context of modern technology) (Dery, Kolb and MacCormick, 2014), multiplicity (Neville and Menguc, 2006) and reciprocity (Fassin, 2012).

Sensemaking from a behavioural perspective

Investment in renewable energy is a key global concern and will continue to be an important focus for the impact investing sector. REI is mostly studied in energy economics by adopting the assumption of full rationality, yet a purely rational techno-economic model of REI cannot explain how decision makers deploy limited resources among competing objectives (Masini and Menichetti, 2012). Much of the utilitarian tradition assumes investors only make rational and self-interested decisions with consideration of risk and financial returns and are affected minimally by other social or cultural factors. From a conventional utilitarian point of view, social or environmental performance is only marginal with respect to financial returns, yet investment decisions are often made within social and cultural norms and constrained by institutional logics. Conventional investors in the private sector with rational consideration of risks and economic returns currently dominate the REI field. Common risks include technology risks such as unstable electricity and immature electricity storage, policy risks, country/context risks and market risks. However, this strand of theory vastly overestimates the efficacy of utility maximization and economic profit-seeking rationale while ignoring the underlying social and institutional influences. The concepts of self-interested and utility-maximizing agents by 'homo economicus' are challenged by many social scientists using social preferences and bounded rationality from a behavioural perspective (Fehr and Fischbacher, 2002; Kahneman, 2003; Simon, 1986). This is especially relevant in impact investing, as it is often underpinned by personal values and moral beliefs and constrained by decision makers' behavioural biases, their context's institutional logics and the expectations and power of influential stakeholders. However, there is a lack of rigorous studies examining non-financial issues in the REI literature, and an emerging stream of RE literature calls for a broader socio-psychological understanding of renewable energy research (Masini and Menichetti, 2012; Safarzynska and Van den Bergh, 2011; West, Bailey and Winter, 2010).

Using a socio-psychological understanding of impact investing, Lee, Adbi and Singh (2020) looked into the behavioural factors that influence social and financial outcomes. Specifically, they looked into how categorical labels suppress investment options and negatively influence decision-making efficacy (Lee et al., 2020). The influence of categorical labels on decision making relates to the concept of identity whereby actors may be motivated to act in accordance with the behavioural standards that reflect the expectation for a particular identity (Wry and York, 2017). Understanding the behavioural factors of impact investing will enable many stakeholders, including policy makers, to leverage the key drivers for impact investing, remove barriers, create appropriate incentives and develop the appropriate legislative environment directing greater capital to the sector (Masini and Menichetti, 2012).

Sensemaking is a useful theoretical perspective from which to understand these behavioural aspects of impact investing with actors' social and environmental concerns. Sensemaking involves creating a coherent account of the world around us by categorizing the things we see, do and feel, and applying patterns to connect this to things we have seen, done and felt before, or anticipate seeing, doing and feeling in the future (Weick, 1995). Actors' embedded understanding of appropriate behaviour and definitions of success are influenced by their identity and the fields in which they operate, or in which they believe they operate.

Within impact investing, equivocality and uncertainty characterize organizational and individual identities, where actors use sensemaking to construct identities and reduce equivocality. If looking at impact investors and investees' decision making and their underlying logics, sensemaking is a useful and interesting way to interpret how they reconcile tensions. Sensemaking involves the ongoing development of plausible situations that rationalize people's behaviours where meanings materialize that inform and constrain identity and behaviours (Weick, 1995; Weick, Sutcliffe and Obstfeld, 2005). Ethical sensemaking happens when cognitively limited decision makers recognize an ethical dilemma and use sensemaking to account for individual, social and environmental constraints (Ness and Connelly, 2017; Thiel et al., 2012).

In the adjacent social entrepreneurship literature, research has explored four forms of organizational sensemaking – namely, contextualized, objectivized, bureaucratized and standardized sensemaking – to make sense of social entrepreneurship as an organizational identity (Grimes, 2010). The concept of identity serves as the core component of the sensemaking process. Similar in impact investing, investor identity is also shaped by the sensemaking process, where investors engage in sensemaking and sensegiving to (re)define their organizational reality about who they are (Smith and Bergman, 2020). Identity formation and construction vary in terms of their complexity and diversity. Thus, sensemaking can be dynamically used to construct, deconstruct and reconstruct organizational identities to be complex or simplified, diverse or homogeneous (Grimes, 2010). Future studies may wish to consider how the sensemaking processes differ between a simplified and diverse identity, or a complex and homogeneous identity.

Avenues for further research

Impact investing research, although embryonic, has anchors in management theory mainstays, as has been discussed through an identity perspective here – institutional logics, stakeholder management theory and sensemaking. Many researchers and practitioners call for a more holistic approach to impact investing to generate value for all stakeholder groups and to further mainstream the sector by bringing in increased private sector capital, particularly from institutional investors (Hehenberger, Mair and Metz, 2019). These anchors provide the theoretical basis for such research and in themselves generate a number of compelling research questions. These theoretical bases can also be used to develop and answer more context-specific research questions that can be approached from different theoretical bases such as. What are the definitional boundaries of impact investing? How much impact is 'enough'? What issues or sectors qualify as impactful? For example, when is a renewable energy investment an impact investment? They also provide opportunities to extend these bases into progressive research which goes beyond traditional or well-established theoretical boundaries and research methods while retaining links to credible schools of thought. To this end, we provide illustrative research questions based on the preceding discussion as well as those that extend into the less well-charted territory. Table 3.1 offers research opportunities in impact investing with detailed research questions that focus on the above mentioned three key themes related to identity.

An institutional logics perspective opens research opportunities to view impact investing from its inherent hybrid logics, its legitimacy challenges and the associated institutional work that is arguably required for it to become mainstream. Institutional logics shape, and at the same time are reflected through, organizational structure, governance and capabilities. Concepts within broader institutional theory, including legitimacy viewed from an identity perspective, also inform future research opportunities around institutional logics. Institutional hybridity in impact investing creates legitimacy issues, where actors use various legitimizing strategies to reconcile competing institutional logics and identities. The process can be viewed as institutional work that has the potential to transform institutions to support the further ascendance of impact investing. While significant research has been undertaken in this space in the social enterprise and entrepreneurship literature, far less has looked at impact investing. Further exploration is needed to understand how impact investors and impact investment managers reconcile the myriad expectations that emanate from their own sources of capital, those of their investees, regulatory and legislative environments, and how their practices are shifting

Table 3.1   Impact investing research opportunities that focus on three key theoretical themes

Theoretical Themes and Focus	Potential Dimensions	Representative Research Questions
Institutional logics	• Hybridity • Legitimacy • Institutional work	1. What role does institutional logics play in the impact investing decision-making process? 2. How do institutional logics influence organizational structure, capabilities and governance in impact investing? 3. What forms of institutional resistance do impact investors face, and from what sources? 4. What legitimizing strategies do impact investors and/or investees deploy? 5. How does identity shape the legitimizing strategies of impact investors and/or investees? 6. To what extent are impact investors intentionally engaged in institutional work versus exploiting new opportunities?
Stakeholder management theory	• Locus of analysis • Stakeholder salience attributes • Objectives of and impacts for stakeholder groups • Social movements	1. How do we understand impact investing from different loci of stakeholders? Which locus is the most appropriate? 2. What roles do stakeholders play in shaping impact investing opportunities? 3. How can stakeholder salience explain stakeholder management in impact investing? 4. How do stakeholder proximity and connectivity contribute to the stakeholder salience in impact investing? 5. How is power (and whose power) shaping the emergent institutional form of impact investing? How is this varying in different geographic and political contexts? 6. How do organization- or industry-focused social movements (e.g. global climate strike) and activism address the interests of impact investing stakeholders? 7. How can insider or outsider activists be considered as stakeholders? What are their salience level (primary or secondary stakeholders to the targeted organizations)?

Theoretical Themes and Focus	Potential Dimensions	Representative Research Questions
Sensemaking from a behavioural perspective	• Ethical sensemaking • Prosocial behaviours • Altruism	1. How do investors reconcile the multiple objectives of impact investing? 2. What role do behavioural factors play in impact investing? 3. How (ir)rational is impact investing? What behavioural factors explain the (ir)rational behaviours of actors in the impact investing field? 4. How can a prosocial behaviour perspective illuminate the rationality of impact investing? 5. How could impact investors be considered as altruists or egoists with prosocial behaviours? Under what circumstances? 6. How does the sensemaking process of impact investors function to explain their prosocial behaviours? 7. How does identity shape the behaviours of actors in impact investing?

institutional norms in terms of the consideration of social and environmental impact in the investment industry. The research questions associated with institutional logics offer new ways of thinking to understand impact investing on an institutional level and have the potential to expand institutional theories.

With regard to stakeholder management theory, our future research questions are organized around loci of analysis, stakeholder salience attributes development, objectives of and impacts for stakeholder groups, and social movements. Key actors that could be the locus of stakeholder analysis in the impact investing field include investors, investees, community, the government and the natural environment. In impact investing research, investors are often at the centre of the analysis in the impact investing context. By changing the loci of analysis to other actors such as investees, the community, policy makers and the natural environment, it opens possibilities for a deeper understanding of stakeholder dynamics and development. Stakeholder salience attributes, including power, legitimacy, urgency and proximity, are useful tools with which to understand stakeholder relationships and dynamics. Developing these attributes further offers promising research opportunities. Stakeholder objectives and impacts are the sources of contestation, and at the same time can be used as legitimizing strategies. A more detailed discussion of these three themes can be found in the previous stakeholder management theory section.

Social movements are also a fertile context for stakeholder management theory development and relate to the above-mentioned three themes. Social movements are volatile and sometimes politicized, ranging from global social movements to community programmes, where activists can be considered as the stakeholder locus of community. There is also a close connection between organization theories and social movement theory, where many movements aim to change organization processes and adopt strategies from organizations (McAdam and Scott, 2005). Such novel combinations of theories and fields create especially compelling research opportunities. For example, climate justice has emerged as a global social movement, as highlighted by the youth-led climate protests of 2019, with the movement itself influencing and affecting climate change knowledge making (Jamison, 2010). Therefore, a consideration of the rise in demand for sustainable and impactful investment products alongside the increased climate activism compels us to consider impact investment as a form of activism itself, and as a response to general trends or specific issues.

Sensemaking from a behavioural perspective acknowledges the behavioural factors in impact investing, which challenges the utilitarian analysis with its focus on rationality. Individual and organizational sensemaking can be used to explore and explain those behaviours that cannot be understood by utilitarian concepts. Concepts of prosocial behaviours and associated concepts such as altruism can be employed in such research through the development of understandings of the ethical sensemaking processes of impact investors. Prosocial behaviours that benefit others are not only reflections of altruism but are also sometimes motivated by indirect reciprocity for reputational incentives, where egoists and altruists coexist in the heterogeneous social preferences models (Simpson and Willer, 2008). Impact investing is such an example of prosocial behaviour that could be underpinned by both altruism and egoism under different situations. Impact investors and other stakeholders' behaviours are also shaped by their identities, which influences the sensemaking process. The research questions associated with sensemaking in Table 3.1 reflect the behavioural factors involved in impact investing, showing the contested truths of these non-linear decisions.

Concluding thoughts

To conclude, we have offered three theoretical lenses through which to investigate the impact investing field, where institutional logics, stakeholder management theory and sensemaking are all interconnected through the concept of identity. An institutional logics perspective opens up research avenues for the hybridity of blended institutional logics, legitimacy and institutional work by which people, groups, and organizations evaluate their everyday activities and organize those activities. Stakeholder management theory and the stakeholder salience framework help managers to identify and prioritize stakeholder groups. Researchers are encouraged to shift their gaze away from the 'manager'-centred stakeholder analysis and attend more closely to various loci of stakeholder analyses. Further to this point, we offer a behavioural perspective to examine how investors navigate and shape their formal and informal institutional contexts and what motivates them to do so through ethical sensemaking. Sensemaking from a behavioural perspective in impact investing therefore brings to the fore notions of prosocial behaviour and altruism that cannot be fully explained by conventional rationality perspectives, even in a field (finance and economics) where that paradigm is dominant. Ethical sensemaking opens up research avenues in order to understand the underlying motivations of impact investing and the actual sensemaking processes during actors' decision making.

This chapter builds on previous literature reviews (Agrawal and Hockerts, 2019; Daggers and Nicholls, 2016; Höchstädter and Scheck, 2015) and contributes to the environment-focused impact investing literature by offering a brief picture of the development of the field and a focus on some of the key theoretical anchors upon which a research agenda can build. Impact investing is an emergent research field and environmentally focused expressions of it risk being subsumed by renewable energy or green finance research paradigms. This would be harmful to the scholarly and practical development of the field, as these forms of investment, while critical and already occurring at scale, lack the problem-solving focus of impact investment. We, therefore, encourage researchers to contribute to environmentally focused impact investing research to both build nuance into the impact investing literature and to shine a light on the limitations of more mainstream sustainable investment literature and practice.

References

Agrawal, A. and Hockerts, K. (2019). Impact investing: review and research agenda. *Journal of Small Business & Entrepreneurship*, 1–29, https://doi.org/10.1080/08276331.2018.1551457.
Alagappan, L., Orans, R. and Woo, C.K. (2011). What drives renewable energy development? *Energy Policy*, 39(9), 5099–104.

Albert, S. and Whetten, D.A. (1985). Organizational identity. *Research in Organizational Behavior*, 7, 263–95.

Azhgaliyeva, D. and Liddle, B. (2020). Introduction to the special issue: scaling up green finance in Asia. *Journal of Sustainable Finance & Investment*, 10(2), 83–91.

Barber, B.M., Morse, A. and Yasuda, A. (2019). Impact investing. *NBER Working Paper Series, w26582*.

Brandstetter, L. and Lehner, O.M. (2015). Opening the market for impact investments: the need for adapted portfolio tools. *Entrepreneurship Research Journal*, 5(2), 87–107.

Brickson, S.L. (2005). Organizational identity orientation: forging a link between organizational identity and organizations' relations with stakeholders. *Administrative Science Quarterly*, 40(4), 576–609.

Brickson, S.L. (2007). Organizational identity orientation: the genesis of the role of the firm and distinct forms of social value. *Academy of Management Review*, 32(3), 864–88.

Bridge, G., Bouzarovski, S., Bradshaw, M. and Eyre, N. (2013). Geographies of energy transition: space, place and the low-carbon economy. *Energy Policy*, 53, 331–40.

Bugg-Levine, A. and Emerson, J. (2011). Impact investing: transforming how we make money while making a difference. *Innovations: Technology, Governance, Globalization*, 6(3), 9–18.

Campbell-Lendrum, D. and Corvalán, C. (2007). Climate change and developing-country cities: implications for environmental health and equity. *Journal of Urban Health*, 84(S1), 109–17.

Chowdhry, B., Davies, S.W. and Waters, B. (2015). Incentivizing impact investing. Working paper, https://doi.org/10.2139/ssrn.2437238.

Daggers, J. and Nicholls, A. (2016). *The Landscape of Social Impact Investment Research: Trends and Opportunities*. Global Impact Investing Network (GIIN).

Dery, K., Kolb, D. and MacCormick, J. (2014). Working with connective flow: how smartphone use is evolving in practice. *European Journal of Information Systems*, 23(5), 558–70.

Dimaggio, P.J. (1988). Interest and agency in institutional theory. In L.G. Zucker (ed.), *Research on Institutional Patterns: Environment and Culture Cambridge* (pp. 3–21). Cambridge, MA: Ballinger Publishing Co.

Donaldson, T. and Preston, L.E. (1995). The stakeholder theory of the corporation: concepts, evidence, and implications. *Academy of Management Review*, 20(1), 65–91.

Driscoll, C. and Starik, M. (2004). The primordial stakeholder: advancing the conceptual consideration of stakeholder status for the natural environment. *Journal of Business Ethics*, 49(1), 55–73.

Dunham, L., Freeman, R.E. and Liedtka, J. (2006). Enhancing stakeholder practice: a particularized exploration of community. *Business Ethics Quarterly*, 16(1), 23–42.

Dutton, J.E. and Dukerich, J.M. (1991). Keeping an eye on the mirror: image and identity in organizational adaptation. *Academy of Management Journal*, 34(3), 517–54.

Edmiston, D. and Nicholls, A. (2018). Social impact bonds: the role of private capital in outcome-based commissioning. *Journal of Social Policy*, 47(1), 57–76.

Ehlers, T. and Packer, F. (2017, 17 September). Green bond finance and certification. *BIS Quarterly Review*.

Fassin, Y. (2012). Stakeholder management, reciprocity and stakeholder responsibility. *Journal of Business Ethics*, 109(1), 83–96.

Fehr, E. and Fischbacher, U. (2002). Why social preferences matter: the impact of non-selfish motives on competition, cooperation and incentives. *The Economic Journal*, 112(478), C1–C33.

Freeman, R.E. (1984). *Strategic Management: A Stakeholder Approach*. Cambridge, UK: Cambridge University Press.

Freeman, R.E. (1999). Divergent stakeholder theory. *Academy of Management Review*, 24(2), 233–36.

Friedland, R. and Alford, R.R. (1991). Bringing society back in: symbols, practices, and institutional contradictions. In W.W. Powell and P.J. DiMaggio (eds), *The New Institutionalism in Organizational Analysis* (pp. 232–63). Chicago, IL: University of Chicago Press.

Gioia, D.A., Schultz, M. and Corley, K.G. (2000). Organizational identity, image, and adaptive instability. *The Academy of Management Review*, 25(1), 63–81.

Glänzel, G. and Scheuerle, T. (2016). Social impact investing in Germany: current impediments from investors' and social entrepreneurs' perspectives. *VOLUNTAS: International Journal of Voluntary and Nonprofit Organizations*, 27(4), 1638–68.

Gordon, G.J. (2018). Environmental personhood. *Columbia Journal of Environmental Law*, 42(1), 49–92.

Granados, M.L. and Rosli, A. (2019). 'Fitting in' vs. 'standing out': how social enterprises engage with stakeholders to legitimize their hybrid position. *Journal of Social Entrepreneurship*, 11(2), 155–76.

Grimes, M. (2010). Strategic sensemaking within funding relationships: the effects of performance measurement on organizational identity in the social sector. *Entrepreneurship Theory and Practice*, 34(4), 763–83.

Hehenberger, L., Mair, J. and Metz, A. (2019). The assembly of a field ideology: an idea-centric perspective on systemic power in impact investing. *Academy of Management Journal*, 62(6), 1672–704.

Höchstädter, A.K. and Scheck, B. (2015). What's in a name: an analysis of impact investing understandings by academics and practitioners. *Journal of Business Ethics*, 132(2), 449–75.

Hoogendoorn, B., van der Zwan, P. and Thurik, R. (2019). Sustainable entrepreneurship: the role of perceived barriers and risk. *Journal of Business Ethics*, 157(4), 1133–54.

Houtbeckers, E. (2016). The everyday experiences of a sustainable entrepreneur: brokering for social innovation at the intersection of networks of practice. In K. Nicolopoulou, M. Karataş-Özkan, F. Janssen and J.M. Jermier (eds), *Sustainable Entrepreneurship and Social Innovation* (pp. 320–37). Abingdon: Routledge.

Hultman, N.E., Pulver, S. and Guimarães, L. et al. (2010). Carbon market risks and rewards: firm perceptions of CDM investment decisions in Brazil and India. *Energy Policy*, 40, 90–102.

Jackson, E.T. (2013). Evaluating social impact bonds: questions, challenges, innovations, and possibilities in measuring outcomes in impact investing. *Community Development*, 44(5), 608–16.

Jamison, A. (2010). Climate change knowledge and social movement theory. *Wiley Interdisciplinary Reviews: Climate Change*, 1(6), 811–23.

Jones, T.M. (1995). Instrumental stakeholder theory: a synthesis of ethics and economics. *Academy of Management Review*, 20(2), 404–37.

Kahneman, D. (2003). Maps of bounded rationality: psychology for behavioral economics. *American Economic Review*, 93(5), 1449–75.

Lawrence, T., Suddaby, R. and Leca, B. (2011). Institutional work: refocusing institutional studies of organization. *Journal of Management Inquiry*, 20(1), 52–58.

Lazzarini, S.G., Cabral, S. and De, L.C. et al. (2014). The best of both worlds? Impact investors and their role in the financial versus social performance debate. *University of St. Gallen Law & Economics Working Paper No. 2015-06.*

Lee, M., Adbi, A. and Singh, J. (2020). Categorical cognition and outcome efficiency in impact investing decisions. *Strategic Management Journal*, 41(1), 86–107.

Lehner, O.M., Harrer, T. and Quast, M. (2019). Building institutional legitimacy in impact investing. *Journal of Applied Accounting Research*, 20(4), 416–38.

Linnenluecke, M.K., Smith, T. and McKnight, B. (2016). Environmental finance: a research agenda for interdisciplinary finance research. *Economic Modelling*, 59, 124–30.

Mair, J., Mayer, J. and Lutz, E. (2015). Navigating institutional plurality: organizational governance in hybrid organizations. *Organization Studies*, 36(6), 713–39.

Masini, A. and Menichetti, E. (2012). The impact of behavioural factors in the renewable energy investment decision making process: conceptual framework and empirical findings. *Energy Policy*, 40, 28–38.

McAdam, D. and Scott, W.R. (2005). Organizations and movements. In G.F. Davis, D. McAdam, W.R. Scott and M.N. Zald (eds), *Social Movements and Organization Theory* (pp. 4–40). Cambridge, UK: Cambridge University Press.

Mendell, M. and Barbosa, E. (2013). Impact investing: a preliminary analysis of emergent primary and secondary exchange platforms. *Journal of Sustainable Finance & Investment*, 3(2), 111–23.

Mitchell, R.K., Agle, B.R. and Wood, D.J. (1997). Toward a theory of stakeholder identification and salience: defining the principle of who and what really counts. *The Academy of Management Review*, 22(4), 853–86.

Moore, M.-L., Westley, F.R. and Nicholls, A. (2012). The social finance and social innovation nexus. *Journal of Social Entrepreneurship*, 3(2), 115–32.

Moss, T.W., Short, J.C., Payne, G.T. and Lumpkin, G.T. (2011). Dual identities in social ventures: an exploratory study. *Entrepreneurship Theory and Practice*, 35(4), 805–30.

Mudaliar, A., Bass, R., Dithrich, H. and Nova, N. (2019). *Annual Impact Investor Survey*. Global Impact Investing Network (GIIN).

Ness, A.M. and Connelly, S. (2017). Situational influences on ethical sensemaking: performance pressure, interpersonal conflict, and the recipient of consequences. *Human Performance*, 30(2–3), 57–78.

Neville, B.A. and Menguc, B. (2006). Stakeholder multiplicity: toward an understanding of the interactions between stakeholders. *Journal of Business Ethics*, 66(4), 377–91.

Nicholls, A. (2010). The institutionalization of social investment: the interplay of investment logics and investor rationalities. *Journal of Social Entrepreneurship*, 1(1), 70–100.

Nunna, K.H.S.V.S. and Doolla, S. (2014). Responsive end-user-based demand side management in multimicrogrid environment. *IEEE Transactions on Industrial Informatics*, 10, 1262–72.

Ormiston, J., Charlton, K., Donald, M.S. and Seymour, R.G. (2015). Overcoming the challenges of impact investing: insights from leading investors. *Journal of Social Entrepreneurship*, 6(3), 352–78.

Ornetzeder, M. and Rohracher, H. (2006). User-led innovations and participation processes: lessons from sustainable energy technologies. *Energy Policy*, 34(2), 138–50.

Pache, A.-C. and Santos, F. (2013). Inside the hybrid organization: selective coupling as a response to competing institutional logics. *Academy of Management Journal*, 56(4), 972–1001.

Pham, L. (2016). Is it risky to go green? A volatility analysis of the green bond market. *Journal of Sustainable Finance & Investment*, 6(4), 263–91.

Ransome, W. and Sampford, C. (2010). *Ethics and Socially Responsible Investment: A Philosophical Approach*. Aldershot, UK: Ashgate.

Reboredo, J.C. (2018). Green bond and financial markets: co-movement, diversification and price spillover effects. *Energy Economics*, 74, 38–50.

Safarzynska, K. and Van den Bergh, J.C.J.M. (2011). Industry evolution, rational agents and the transition to sustainable electricity production. *Energy Policy*, 39(10), 6440–52.

Sanders, K. (2017). 'Beyond human ownership'? Property, power and legal personality for nature in Aotearoa New Zealand. *Journal of Environmental Law*, 30(2), 207–34.

Sangroya, D. and Nayak, J.K. (2017). Factors influencing buying behaviour of green energy consumer. *Journal of Cleaner Production*, 151, 393–405.

Schaltegger, S. and Wagner, M. (2011). Sustainable entrepreneurship and sustainability innovation: categories and interactions. *Business Strategy and the Environment*, 20(4), 222–37.

Shepherd, D.A. and Patzelt, H. (2011). The new field of sustainable entrepreneurship: studying entrepreneurial action linking 'what is to be sustained' with 'what is to be developed'. *Entrepreneurship: Theory and Practice*, 35(1), 137–63.

Silver, J.J., Gray, N.J. and Campbell, L.M. (2015). Blue economy and competing discourses in international oceans governance. *The Journal of Environment & Development*, 24(2), 135–60.

Simon, H.A. (1986). Rationality in psychology and economics. *The Journal of Business*, 59(4), 209–24.

Simpson, B. and Willer, R. (2008). Altruism and indirect reciprocity: the interaction of person and situation in prosocial behavior. *Social Psychology Quarterly*, 71(1), 37–52.

Smith, B.R. and Bergman, B.J. (2020). The other side of the coin: investor identity and its role in resource provision. *Journal of Business Venturing Insights*, 14, Article e00175.

Smith, I.H. and Woodworth, W.P. (2012). Developing social entrepreneurs and social innovators: a social identity and self-efficacy approach. *Academy of Management Learning & Education*, 11(3), 390–407.

Sparkes, R. and Cowton, C.J. (2004). The maturing of socially responsible investment: a review of the developing link with corporate social responsibility. *Journal of Business Ethics*, 52(1), 45–57.

Starik, M. (1995). Should trees have managerial standing? Toward stakeholder status for non-human nature. *Journal of Business Ethics*, 14(3), 207–17.

Stets, J.E. and Burke, P.J. (2000). Identity theory and social identity theory. *Social Psychology Quarterly*, 63(3), 224–37.

Stryker, S. and Burke, P.J. (2000). The past, present, and future of an identity theory. *Social Psychology Quarterly*, 63(4), 284–97.

Suchman, M.C. (1995). Managing legitimacy: strategic and institutional approaches. *Academy of Management Review*, 20(3), 571–610.

Suddaby, R., Bitektine, A. and Haack, P. (2017). Legitimacy. *Academy of Management Annals*, 11(1), 451–78.

Talan, G. and Sharma, G. (2019). Doing well by doing good: a systematic review and research agenda for sustainable investment. *Sustainability*, 11(2), 353.

Thiel, C.E., Bagdasarov, Z. and Harkrider, L. et al. (2012). Leader ethical decision-making in organizations: strategies for sensemaking. *Journal of Business Ethics*, 107(1), 49–64.

Thornton, P.H., Lounsbury, M. and Ocasio, W. (2012). *The Institutional Logics Perspective: A New Approach to Culture, Structure and Process.* Oxford: Oxford University Press.

Thornton, P.H. and Ocasio, W. (1999). Institutional logics and the historical contingency of power in organizations: executive succession in the higher education publishing industry, 1958–1990. *American Journal of Sociology*, 105(3), 801–43.

Thornton, P.H., Ocasio, W. and Lounsbury, M. (2015). The institutional logics perspective. In R.A. Scott, S.M. Kosslyn and M. Buchmann (eds), *Emerging Trends in the Social and Behavioral Sciences* (pp. 1–22). Hoboken, NJ: John Wiley & Sons.

Tracey, P. (2012). Religion and organization: a critical review of current trends and future directions. *The Academy of Management Annals*, 6(1), 87–134.

Tracey, P., Phillips, N. and Jarvis, O. (2011). Bridging institutional entrepreneurship and the creation of new organizational forms: a multilevel model. *Organization Science*, 22(1), 60–80.

Wabnitz, C.C.C. and Blasiak, R. (2019). The rapidly changing world of ocean finance. *Marine Policy*, 107, Article 103526.

Weber, M. and Henderson, A.M. (1947). *The Theory of Social and Economic Organization.* Edited by T. Parsons. New York: Oxford University Press.

Weick, K.E. (1995). *Sensemaking in Organizations.* Thousand Oaks, CA: SAGE.

Weick, K.E., Sutcliffe, K.M. and Obstfeld, D. (2005). Organizing and the process of sensemaking. *Organization Science*, 16(4), 409–21.

West, J., Bailey, I. and Winter, M. (2010). Renewable energy policy and public perceptions of renewable energy: a cultural theory approach. *Energy Policy*, 38(10), 5739–48.

Whetten, D.A. (2006). Albert and Whetten revisited: strengthening the concept of organizational identity. *Journal of Management Inquiry*, 15(3), 219–34.

Wry, T. and York, J.G. (2017). An identity-based approach to social enterprise. *Academy of Management Review*, 42(3), 437–60.

Zerbib, O.D. (2019). The effect of pro-environmental preferences on bond prices: evidence from green bonds. *Journal of Banking & Finance*, 98, 39–60.

Zink, T. and Geyer, R. (2017). Circular economy rebound. *Journal of Industrial Ecology*, 21(3), 593–602.

4. Market infrastructure for social ventures

Vanina A. Farber and Patrick Reichert

Introduction to resource acquisition for social ventures

The acquisition of resources – investors, employees or customers – is a key challenge for new organizations that lack experience and proven competencies (Zott and Huy, 2007). This process is arguably exacerbated for social ventures, hybrid organizations that use commercial operations to address social and environmental issues (Santos, Pache and Birkholz, 2015). Social ventures must not only navigate the hazards and uncertainties of the entrepreneurial process (Stinchcombe, 1965), but also reduce informational asymmetries related to both financial and social value creation, the so-called 'double bottom line' (Dees, 1998). On the other hand, the social mission of hybrid organizations enables access to a wide range of financial resources, ranging from private donation and public subsidy to earned-income strategies or fully commercial private investment (Di Domenico, Haugh and Tracey, 2010; Smith, Cronley and Barr, 2012).

Mirroring this innovation from the supply side, the emerging phenomenon of social finance calls upon the finance industry to promote ethics in finance by taking an active role to benefit and restore the trust of society in the wake of the recent financial crisis. At its core, social finance refers to the allocation of financial resources to primarily achieve social or environmental objectives, often at 'sustainable' but below-market financial returns on a risk-adjusted basis (Benedikter, 2011; Moore, Westley and Nicholls, 2012). The ensuing mantra of 'doing well by doing good' has sparked enthusiasm across a wide range of actors, including investors, policy makers, entrepreneurs and citizens (Falck and Heblich, 2007; Lehner, 2016).

The intersection of social entrepreneurial business models and social finance is quickly garnering attention, with scholarly research emerging on a vast array of topics such as environmental, social and governance (ESG) investing (Khan, Serafeim and Yoon, 2016), socially responsible investment (Renneboog, Ter Horst and Zhang, 2008), social banking (Cornée, Kalmi and Szafarz, 2016), impact investing (Höchstädter and Scheck, 2015), venture philanthropy (Di Lorenzo and Scarlata, 2019; Frumkin, 2003) crowdfunding (Lehner and Nicholls, 2014; Mollick, 2014), social impact bonds (Edmiston and Nicholls, 2017) and financial inclusion (Armendáriz and Labie, 2011). Despite general agreement that the financial instruments in these domains span the spectrum between pure grants and market-rate returns and seek to advance social objectives, a unified conceptualization of market infrastructure for social ventures has been slow to materialize.

In this chapter we provide a conceptualization of the market infrastructure for social ventures. We first examine the two-sided nature of social ventures (matching financial/social goals of investors and the pricing of their products/ services to balance break-even and profit expectations). Then we use a lifecycle view of social ventures to examine potential lines of research inquiry during the evolution from start-up to maturity.

A conceptualization of market structure for social ventures

Operating between the traditional nonprofit and business sectors, we view resource acquisition for social ventures as a two-sided market connecting altruistic funders to end customers (or beneficiaries). Classically defined, two-sided (or, more generally, multi-sided) markets are 'markets in which one or several platforms enable interactions between end-users and try to get the two (or multiple) sides "on board" by appropriately charging each side' (Rochet and Tirole, 2006, p. 645). In this sense, social ventures serve as a 'platform' or intermediary that brokers pricing between financiers (or donative funders if they are willing to accept lower than market returns) and customers (or beneficiaries if the price they pay is zero). Figure 4.1 illustrates this conceptualization of market structure for social ventures.

From Figure 4.1, two cases emerge at the extremes: business as usual and traditional third sector. At one end of the spectrum, we consider the 'business-as-usual' case where buyers (customers) pay full market price, the intermediary maximizes profits (full value capture) and ultimately transfers

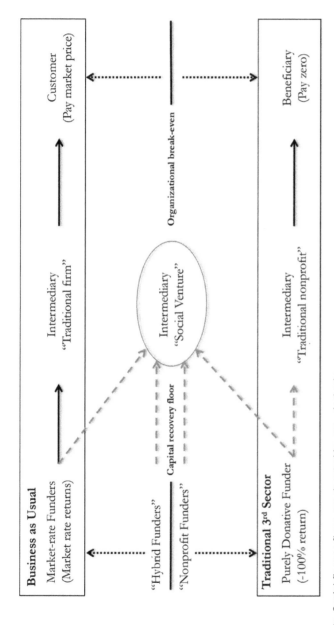

Note: Social finance flows are denoted by grey dashed arrows.
Source: Own illustration. Taxonomy of funders based on Cornée, Jegers and Szafarz (2018).

Figure 4.1   Market infrastructure for social ventures

the financial component of value to sellers (commercial investors) who receive full market returns. In a sense, the types of projects and businesses that market-rate funders find attractive define where social organizations are able to operate. That is, the market mechanism leads to activities being undertaken only as long as the benefits of further activity equal the incremental cost. The need for subsidized funding is a signal that the activity fails the market test, and thus may distort markets and individual incentives.

However, many circumstances bring about market failures, or a breakdown in the market mechanism. In the face of these market imperfections, subsidies help to achieve socially desirable outcomes, and thus market failures have long been used to justify public policy intervention (Bator, 1958; Wolf, 1979). However, the public policy remedies of service provision, subsidies or taxes, and regulation have been equally criticized as either inefficient (Le Grand, 1991) or repressive towards the demands of political minorities (Salamon, 1987). These dual problems of market failure on the one hand and government failure on the other led to the emergence of a private, voluntary sector to promote the public interest characterized by nonprofits and philanthropic foundations (Weisbrod, 1978). This sector is often referred to as the third sector and is characterized at the opposite end of the spectrum in Figure 4.1. In the third sector, buyers (or in this case, beneficiaries) do not pay for the services/products of the intermediary. Absent any revenue from customers, the intermediary relies upon full gifts from sellers (in this case fully donative social funders) in what we may consider as donative nonprofits or traditional charity.

In between these two extremes is where the 'zoo' of social entrepreneurial models has been argued to operate (Young and Lecy, 2014). Rather than maintain a clear distinction between private markets, welfare states and civil society, these hybrid markets emphasize competition and collaboration between for-profit, nonprofit and governmental actors in the provision of public and charitable goods (Evers, 2005; Marwell and McInerney, 2005). It is between this hybridization of sectors that forms the perimeters of this chapter. In the next section, we draw some generic features of how social ventures navigate these funding relationships and how they might leverage different funders and instruments as they advance in the business lifecycle.

Capital acquisition from start-up to growth to maturity

Access to capital is one of the most important elements for a social venture to fulfill its mission. Broadly, social ventures can access capital internally or externally. Internal financing is provided by cash flows generated through the provision of services or products. The products/services of the social venture can be paid either by the target group themselves (e.g., microfinance) or by third-party beneficiaries (parents, employers, cross-subsidies such as 'buy one-give one'). In many cases, however, the target group lacks any ability to pay (e.g., homeless shelters). In these cases, internal financing may occur via third-party contracting arrangements – for instance, through public sector grants that compensate the social venture for the provision of a good or service to a vulnerable population. Typically, contracting is done between public and nonprofit actors and is not usually accessible to for-profit ventures, although there is some experimentation on this subject through innovations such as social impact bonds.

External financing available to social ventures is typically used to cover tempo-rary negative operating cash flows or to finance investment in long-term assets such as buildings, equipment or other infrastructure-related expenses. In contrast to traditional for-profit start-ups, social ventures can also tap public subsidies and private donations to finance their activities. More recently, social ventures have also started to use more complex financial instruments such as equity, quasi-equity, debt and mezzanine capital. Since the social mission often places upside limits on the financial return of the venture, funders of social ventures often adapt their financing instruments through two mechanisms. First, funders can satisfice on the expected rate of financial return. Second, social funders can adapt financing instruments to better meet the needs of social ventures. Typical modifications may include the use of a deferred payment schedule or grace period for debt instruments or the use of convertible loans that turn into grants in case of unexpected low performance (Spiess-Knafl and Achleitner, 2012).

The financial return/social impact preferences of funders also carry implica-tions for the funding strategies of social ventures. From our funder typology in Figure 4.1, purely donative funders such as individual donors and charita-ble foundations might be willing to finance the income shortfalls of a social venture with grants. Nonprofit funders, such as a venture philanthropist, will prioritize social impact investment opportunities even where expected finan-cial return is negative but social impact is promising. Hybrid funders prefer opportunities that blend positive financial and social returns while market-rate funders will prefer investments that maximize financial return.

The existence of funders with diverse objectives is unique to the field of social ventures. The divergent preferences of funders often force social ven-tures to balance their financial objectives and social impact. For instance,

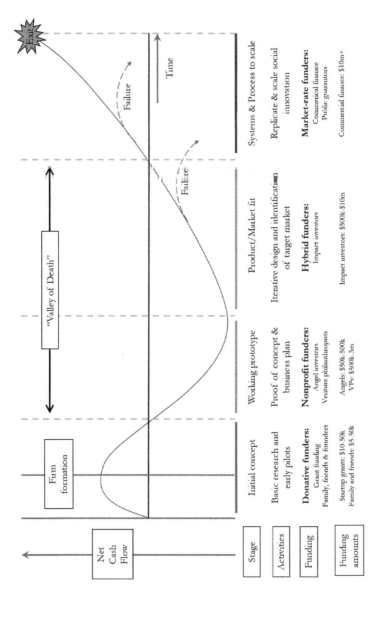

Source: Own illustration based on Agapitova and Linn (2015) and BFA Global (2020).

Figure 4.2   Business lifecycle of a social venture

a key debate in the field of microfinance concerns the trade-off between profitability and reaching poorer clients who are often located in expensive, difficult-to-reach rural villages. Additionally, social ventures may prioritize different financial-social blended finance instruments as they develop and scale up their businesses (Figure 4.2). That is, the promise of social entrepreneurship typically stresses the ability to achieve financial sustainability and operate independent of government and other philanthropic support (Di Domenico et al., 2010). However, commercial finance is often unable to provide the quantity, or perhaps more importantly, the *appropriate mix* of resources to meet the demand of this growing sector (Nicholls and Emerson, 2015). This paradigm leads to an apparently inconsistent business lifecycle: Social start-ups must rely on public and private donors, but mature social enterprises often strive for independence from donors.

In the following subsections, we explore the lifecycle stages and the associated funding sources and instruments. Each subsection is complemented with potential lines of research inquiry.

Donative funders

The primary tool at the disposal of donative funders is grant capital. Grants may come in either monetary or non-monetary forms. In the framework of consumer choice, the best a gift-giver can do is to give cash because he or she is unable to duplicate the choice the recipient would have made (unless the recipient is not perfectly informed about their utility function), which results in deadweight loss. In turn, this deadweight loss can be attributed as 'giver satisfaction' (Waldfogel, 1993). From a philanthropic perspective, this concept manifests in two ways: non-monetary gifts (i.e., tangible in-kind donations or voluntary labor) or the restriction of cash grants to fund specific activities and/or conditioning the release of grant funding upon fulfillment of specific conditions.

Donations are attractive to social ventures since they are not repayable (i.e., negative 100 percent rate of return for the funder) and do not give any enforceable control or voting rights to donors. Additionally, donations enable the pursuit of social opportunities that lack income-generating potential. However, grant funding also has a range of shortcomings. In many cases, grants come with strings attached that specify what the funds can be used for – for example, grants are reserved for project-related costs and donors are unwilling to fully cover the administrative costs of a social venture. Additionally, grant funding tends to be short-term oriented and carries substantial fundraising costs for the social venture (Spiess-Knafl and Achleitner, 2012).

Grant funding can also impose lasting effects on the financing strategy of the social venture. On one hand, we suggest that targeted grants can build organizational capacity and professionalism, which have positive long-term signaling effects on the organization (such as cash grants to establish project viability, new product development, etc.). On the other hand, continued untargeted cash support can signal that an organization will require ongoing subsidy in perpetuity. That is, market-rate funders would consider that continued cash grants signal that the social venture will never earn 'market' revenues or reach financial break-even.

Potential research streams

From our perspective, there remain a number of important research questions concerning the relationship between donative funders and social ventures. From the demand side, we believe there is substantial room to explore social finance mechanisms through the prism of pecking-order theory since social ventures must account for informational asymmetries related to both social and financial value creation. Social ventures could extend the pecking-order dichotomy between debt and equity to include grant funding. Surprisingly, this feature remains unexplored in the literature, with the exception of some work in nonprofit finance (Bowman, 2002; Calabrese, 2011). This is an especially important topic considering that the investment logics by donative funders, as well as nonprofit and hybrid investors, are widespread and range from impact-first funders who may deliberately accept no or below-market financial returns to finance-first investors who prioritize financial returns with a social impact floor (Höchstädter and Scheck, 2015).

Subsidy measurement and classification is another field ripe for academic inquiry. Since most economic data take a relatively narrow view of subsidies (i.e., a focus on cash grants), comparing subsidies across subfields in social entrepreneurship is a difficult task. Even straightforward questions such as the monetary valuation of voluntary labor have been of enduring interest to stakeholders like social funders, nonprofits, policy makers and economists (Orlowski and Wicker, 2015). Although there is general agreement in the literature that voluntary work is of substantial economic value, scholars have noted the difficulty of pinning down a precise definition of a volunteer as there are no standard practices in volunteering (Gaskin, 1999). And even if a precise definition of volunteering can be identified, a second complication in measuring volunteer work arises in deciding what the focus of the measurement should be. In standard economic analysis, two broad options are available. The first involves determining the economic value of volunteering by measuring its inputs – that is, labor time – and providing an assessment of the value of volunteer time. The second option for measuring the economic value of volunteering is to use an output-based approach (Salamon, Sokolowski and Haddock, 2011).

On the aggregate level, the problem is that non-market goods like voluntary labor are not included in the gross domestic product (GDP). One reason for this exclusion is that it is difficult to estimate the monetary value of voluntary work on the individual level. On the input side, traditional valuation methods cannot be applied since there is no market price (like a wage rate) for voluntary work. On the output side, problems arise due to the difficulty of sorting out the share of the output produced by the volunteer and due to the non-market nature of outputs often supplied by volunteers such as mentoring, advocating for a cause or providing goods or services to those unable to pay for them (Salamon et al., 2011). The development of an accounting framework that is able to consider the nuances of social venture business models could help stakeholders to debate the allocation of resources to achieve social goals and allow social ventures to better predict their potential for financial break-even.

Nonprofit funders

The shortcomings of donative capital have led social ventures to use other financing instruments. Equity capital is used to finance working capital, long-term investments or to cover temporary negative operating cash flows. Because nonprofit organizations cannot generally issue equity shares, equity financing is only available to for-profit recipients. Social ventures often take a for-profit legal form in efforts to attract equity from social funders. Strategic, philanthropic funders are increasingly among the first to finance these early stages of social venture development.

Early philanthropic capital investment aims to create impact by supporting social ventures on the path to building viable organizations and unlocking sustainable social innovations. Efforts to help new ventures navigate from a stage of proven start-up to early growth involve serious (i.e., multi-year) professional and personal commitments of key individuals and substantial resources (in the hundreds rather than the tens of thousands of US$ often provided by traditional philanthropic gifts). As a result, these commitments carry a high-risk profile.

Despite promises of both financial success and social impact over the long term, a systematic expectation of positive financial return is simply not realistic at this stage: organizational viability is unpredictable, scale is too limited, and risk of failure is too high (Wuffli and Farber, 2020). From a purely market-rate perspective, the small ticket size of an investment relative to the high costs of sourcing, due diligence and ongoing technical support during the investment lifecycle cannibalize the net returns of the few candidates that evolve into profitable growth companies. Often referred to as the 'death valley curve' in the venture capital industry, this dangerous phase in start-up development requires the funding of negative cash flows from operations (ibid.).

We believe that venture philanthropy is ideally suited to help social ventures overcome the challenges of the 'death valley' phase. Importantly, venture philanthropy is distinct from charity since it provides resources with the goal of generating a cash-on-cash return, therefore 'investment'. However, as it does not systematically lead to positive financial net returns within a reasonable time frame, this form of impact investment can be considered 'philanthropic'.

Potential research streams

To reduce information asymmetries during the funding process, entrepreneurs often communicate the latent quality of their venture to investors through signals (Connelly et al., 2011). Signals refer to costly and observable information about underlying quality (e.g., education, patent ownership, management team characteristics, board characteristics, referral source) (Ahlers et al., 2015; Scheaf et al., 2018). A substantial body of evidence has accrued over time on the effectiveness of signaling to reduce information asymmetries for profit-maximizing firms and the ability of young start-ups to attract angel and venture investment (Busenitz, Fiet and Moesel, 2005; Connelly et al., 2011; Janney and Folta, 2006; Schwienbacher, 2007). There is, however, little research on the signaling environment of hybrid firms such as social ventures.

We believe that venture philanthropy is the most empirically relevant setting in which to study entrepreneurial signaling to social funders. Venture philanthropy stands in contrast to purely donative charity, where information asymmetries surrounding a start-up's ability to generate future cash flows are less relevant. On the other hand, the non-distribution constraint of venture philanthropic foundations differentiates them from for-profit impact investors, who may attempt to maximize (and distribute) financial returns while simply using social impact as window dressing to acquire funds in a fast-growing market segment.

The venture philanthropist investment model integrates the socially oriented approach of grant making with the investment practices developed by traditional venture capitalists. Venture philanthropists offer tailored financing and value-added services to social ventures (Letts, Ryan and Grossman, 1997; Scarlata, Walske and Zacharakis, 2017). Financial instruments in venture philanthropy include grants, debt and equity/quasi-equity (Mair and Hehenberger, 2014). Value-added services resemble those found in traditional venture capital, including strategic involvement (e.g., board seat) or fulfilling a networking and support role to facilitate connections between investees and other potential investors or helping to professionalize the investee through financial and accounting management, human resource services, or marketing and communications (Di Lorenzo and Scarlata, 2019; Gorman and Sahlman, 1989). The combination of value-added activities with tailored financing suggests that venture philanthropists aid social enterprises on a path towards commercialization, a process that refers to the adoption of market-based principles and integration into the mainstream business sector (Armendáriz and Morduch, 2010). However, empirical tests of these assumptions remain elusive and primarily based on small sample case studies. More rigorous, systematic studies could increase our collective understanding of the strategic role nonprofit funders play in helping social ventures develop their business activities and attract more commercial capital in later growth stages. Distinguishing when philanthropic donors and public agencies can offset credit market imperfections to entice market-rate funders from situations where socially oriented funders will accept below-market financial returns in exchange for social impact should provide valuable insights into social finance.

Hybrid funders

The impact investment market has observed significant growth since the term was first used at a Rockefeller Foundation event in 2007. According to estimates from a recent (April 2019) report from the Global Impact Investing Network (GIIN), a leading data aggregator for the sector, assets under management (AuM) of more than 1340 organizations worldwide reached US$502 billion by 2018 (Dithrich and Mudaliar, 2019).

According to the GIIN's Impact Investor Survey (Bass, Cohen and Schiff, 2018), the vast majority of impact investors target risk-adjusted, market-rate returns (64 percent of respondents). The remaining funders accept below-market-rate returns, among which a minority of investors pursue impact-first strategies with financial returns close to capital preservation (16 percent of respondents).

When investors adopt an impact-first strategy, they accept finance ventures that have a less attractive risk-return profile and may yield lower returns or provide more patient capital (i.e., investments with a longer time horizon). In return, impact-first investors seed investments that promise ex-ante greater impact, potentially on a much larger scale or sustained over longer time horizons. Impact-first investors operate in what Etzel (2015) calls the 'sweet spot', bridging the gap between grant-making philanthropists and traditional market-rate investors.

Potential research streams

Whereas the non-distribution constraint of philanthropic foundations characterizes nonprofit funders, most hybrid funders such as impact investors operate through the use of limited liability partnerships (LLPs), whereby investors become limited partners (LPs) and venture capital managers are the general partners (GPs) of the fund. Typical debates in this nascent field seek to understand the trade-offs between financial return and social impact, how impact investors monitor the impact of their investments and the types of instruments that impact investors use to seed investment in social ventures. Additional lines of inquiry might choose to focus on impact funds themselves – for instance, by looking at the incentive structures in place for the GPs and the relationship between the GPs and LPs.

Some preliminary work from Brown (2006) analyzes the features that are central to the design of subsidizable ownership rights, which we summarize in Table 4.1. Information and public rights are usually determined by regulatory bodies, and therefore these ownership rights are non-subsidizable. Of the five remaining ownership rights, Brown (2006) makes a distinction between financial rights (liquidation, income and appreciation rights) and controlling rights (voting and transfer rights). Since equity returns are unknown ex ante to investment, quantifying equity subsidies is often difficult in practice. However, attaching restrictions to these ownership rights can create transparent ex ante subsidies – for example, a cap on the rate of return to investors. Future research could explore the application of these ownership rights across various empirical applications of social ventures to understand how they are adapted in practice.

New legal forms are also attempting to create limits on ownership rights and the financial upside of equity investments, such as common interest companies (CICs) in the United Kingdom and low-profit limited liability companies (L3Cs) in the United States. In the UK, CICs were introduced by the Companies Act 2004 with the aim of recognizing and promoting entrepreneurship in the

Table 4.1   Ownership rights and social ventures

Ownership rights	Description
Subsidizable ownership rights	
Liquidation rights	Rights to the residual assets of the enterprise after all other creditors have been paid
Income rights	Rights to receive a dividend or interest payment
Appreciation rights	Rights to any capital gain (or loss) in the value of the investment
Voting rights	Rights to control the affairs of the enterprise using agreed voting principles
Transfer rights	Rights to trade investment with another party, or to withdraw investment from the enterprise
Non-subsidizable ownership rights	
Information rights	Rights to information about the policies, practices and performance of the enterprise
Public rights	Rights of governments on behalf of their citizens to tax and regulate enterprises

Note: Based on Brown (2006).

social economy (Nicholls, 2010). Although CICs have a commercial legal form and can engage in any trade activities, their profits and assets have to be used in the general interest. CICs are subject to a dividend and interest cap as well as an asset lock – that is, assets may not be transferred or distributed to any organization apart from a CIC, a charity or a similar body established outside the UK) (Brown, 2006; Nicholls, 2010).

Low-profit limited liability companies were recognized as a distinct legal entity with the passage of the L3C law in Vermont in April 2008. L3Cs are a special-ized form of the traditional LLC, offering the protection of a corporation and flexibility of a partnership, but are explicitly formed to further a social mission and to qualify as a program-related investment (PRI) for private foundations. Statutorily, L3Cs have three main pillars: (1) they must be organized to accom-plish a charitable purpose; (2) they must not be created primarily to accumu-late property or earn a profit; and (3) they must not be created to further any political or legislative objective (Artz, Gramlich and Porter, 2012).

The creation of new legal forms offers social funders additional opportunities to further diversify their philanthropic donations. Additionally, equity invest-ment allows social ventures to compete on the bundle of financial return and social impact available to funders. The result is an investment universe that opens up new opportunities for blended value (Emerson, 2003) and allows funders to construct an optimal basket of financial return and social impact. We encourage more academic perspectives on this front.

Market-rate funders and exit opportunities

As it stands today, there are limited exit options for equity capital investors in social ventures. The current impact investing market caters to wealthy individuals, foundations and family offices. Non-accredited investors and/or retail investors as well as pensions funds are not yet able to participate in social finance markets. A fully functioning social stock exchange (SSE) could there fore serve as an attractive exit option for social funders as well as provide an additional funding source for mature social enterprises with a proven business model. Although there are currently a number of initiatives to set up a fully functioning social stock exchange, a fully functioning public marketplace for social ventures has yet to emerge.

Although very different in their status and characteristics, the four SSEs profiled in a 2014 *Forbes* article have all failed to emerge as functioning social venture marketplaces.[1] Two of the initiatives, the Social Stock Exchange (SSX) in the United Kingdom and Mission Markets of the United States, have failed altogether. The other two promising candidates, the Social Venture Connexion (SVX) of Canada and the Impact Exchange (IX) of Singapore, pivoted towards a curated stream of financing opportunities that connect social funders to social ventures in private transactions.

Some key issues that pose challenges to the creation of an SSE are the valuation of the social venture, the protection of the social mission and the social report-ing. Valuation methods for social ventures remain elusive and many question whether social funders are paying a premium or a discount on a relative valuation (Spiess-Knafl and Achleitner, 2012). Mission lock can potentially be achieved through various measures, such as the equity restrictions mentioned previously. Other examples offered include the control of a minority stake (e.g., above 25 percent) by a foundation to protect the social mission or the establishment of articles of associations with reference to the social mission or poison pills to avoid unsolicited takeover bids (ibid.). Social reporting is another hurdle challenging the development of a robust secondary market for social venture shares, although initiatives such as the Impact Reporting & Investment Standards (IRIS) in the United States are unifying impact reporting for social ventures. In recent years, sustainability reporting has also been formalized through the creation of new organizations in mainstream markets such as the Sustainability Accounting Standards Board (SASB), the Global Reporting Initiative (GRI) guidelines and the International Integrated Reporting Council (IIRC).

Potential research streams

While it's easy to see how below-market investors can provide capital benefits to an enterprise, as a socially neutral investor seeking market-rate returns would not provide any capital on favorable terms, it is less clear how and when funders expecting market returns create subsidy. For example, if a funder is not willing to make a financial sacrifice, what can he or she contribute that the market wouldn't do anyway? Brest and Born (2013) make the case for a wider view of subsidy (or social impact in their terms) through the concept of additionality – for example, 'donor' participation in an investment that would not otherwise occur. Because subsidies in social finance often accrue in imperfect markets, non-concessionary funders may have the ability to circumvent market failures that a socially neutral investor may not observe. Future research could aim to first tackle this issue of 'additionality' in social finance – for instance, by identifying potential hidden concessions in the form of risk or extra and costly due diligence that ordinary investors would not undertake.

These concessions, however, are hard to identify externally. Some advancement has been made in the creation of new legal forms that aim to explicitly address the concessions made by donors/investors. In the absence of the non-distribution constraint that limits the upside financial return in nonprofits, new legal forms such as the CIC and L3C attempt to replicate profitability constraints on public benefit companies by imposing dividend caps or creating an asset lock to restrict share transferability. Although these are initial steps to curtail the use of impact investment or venture philanthropy as simple market dressing, further research could attempt to move this discussion on legal form and financial returns into the broader financial literature since to date, research on legal form has tended to be siloed within legal studies and specialized journals in social entrepreneurship. Understanding the motivations of social funders could also benefit from more applied methods, such as a survey on the risk preferences of social investors.

Though still in their nascent stages of development, SSEs are useful to study for three main reasons. First, SSEs can help social ventures to commercialize their financing, scale operational activities and break their dependency on grant funding. Second, SSEs ostensibly do the actual work of differentiating social from traditional finance by creating a separate marketplace for social ventures. This is achieved through the development of specific listing criteria for social ventures wishing to transact on the SSE platform, establishing the requirements for listed firms to comply with in order to stay listed (e.g., the production of financial and social reports), implementing investor screens to ensure the 'right' types of social funders can access the SSE platform, as well as creating the mechanisms for the enforcement of these rules such as de-listing conditions and grievance mechanisms (Dadush, 2015). Third, emerging SSEs are self-regulated to the extent that the rules they create and implement among their members – listed businesses and investors – are not being forced upon them by an official government regulator. This is particularly true regarding the rules pertaining to the issuance of social impact securities, since regulations already exist for traditional securities. A reasonable expectation is that SSE accountability will largely come from the social finance market itself, and thus the study of SSEs allow us to document and analyze the creation of the types of rules for administering a new market and the types of strain put on it from market participants.

Conclusion

The 2008 financial crisis has called into question how financial markets operate and how they benefit society (Shiller, 2013; Zingales, 2015). Financial economists have historically nuanced this view through theory crafting, suggesting that finance benefits society implicitly by helping to manage risk (Froot, Scharfstein and Stein, 1993) and provide price signals (Hayek, 1945), or through the design of securities to alleviate informational asymmetries (Myers and Majluf, 1984) and minimize monitoring costs (Diamond, 1984). There is also substantial empirical evidence suggesting that finance is positively associated with economic growth (Demirgüç-Kunt and Levine, 1996; Levine, 2005), entrepreneurship (Guiso, Sapienza and Zingales, 2004) and less inequality (Beck, Demirgüç-Kunt and Levine, 2007). Nevertheless, these positive views on the role of finance do not seem to be shared by society at large.

The contribution made by financial markets and financial institutions to the prosperity of society has been questioned, and the need to develop new investment opportunities able to create blended returns and shared value has emerged (Lehner, 2016; Porter and Kramer, 2011). Around the globe, new investment models able to reflect responsible behavior have been claimed in order to keep financial markets in tune with the development of society.

This chapter explores the financing levers that social funders and social ventures use to build sustainable industries that deliver social or environmental impact. In sectors where both philanthropic and market-rate funders compete over altruistic investments, the utility functions of funders need to also consider social returns. These considerations are further compounded when the clients of a social enterprise are simultaneously the intended beneficiaries. Our exploration of this market suggests that social ventures face trade-offs between their social and financial objectives, which in turn makes the evaluation of profitability in social ventures more difficult. Since social funders can both crowd in and crowd out market-rate investors, understanding the dynamics of 'blended-value' investing becomes of paramount importance. We believe that thorough investigation of the intersection of these new models of business and investment is warranted in order to help the social venture market develop as it transitions towards the future.

Note

1. *Forbes* (2014, 27 March), 'Stock exchanges for social enterprises? Here's where you can find them', accessed 6 May 2020 at https://www.forbes.com/sites/ashoka/2014/03/27/stock-exchanges-for-social-enterprises-heres-where-you-can-find-them/#196e49d64e5a.

References

Agapitova, N. and Linn, J.F. (2016). Scaling up social enterprise innovations: approaches and lessons. *Global Economy & Development at Brookings Working Paper, No. 95.*

Ahlers, G.K., Cumming, D., Günther, C. and Schweizer, D. (2015). Signaling in equity crowdfunding. *Entrepreneurship Theory & Practice*, 39(4), 955–80.

Armendáriz, B. and Labie, M. (2011). *The Handbook of Microfinance*. Singapore: World Scientific.

Armendáriz, B. and Morduch, J. (2010). *The Economics of Microfinance* (2nd ed.). Cambridge, MA: MIT Press.

Artz, N., Gramlich, J. and Porter, T. (2012). Low-profit limited liability companies (L3Cs). *Journal of Public Affairs*, 12(3), 230–38.

Bass, R. Cohen, A. and Schiff, H. (2018). *Annual Impact Investor Survey 2018* (8th ed.). New York: Global Impact Investing Network (GIIN).

Bator, F.M. (1958). The anatomy of market failure. *Quarterly Journal of Economics*, 72(3), 351–79.

Beck, T., Demirgüç-Kunt, A. and Levine, R. (2007). Finance, inequality and the poor. *Journal of Economic Growth*, 12(1), 27–49.

Benedikter, R. (2011). *Social Banking and Social Finance*. New York: Springer.

BFA Global (2020). Startup acceleration. Accessed 10 May 2020 at https://bfaglobal
.com/catalyst-fund/inclusive-fintech.
Bowman, W. (2002). The uniqueness of nonprofit finance and the decision to borrow.
Nonprofit Management and Leadership, 12(3), 293–311.
Brest, P. and Born, K. (2013). When can impact investing create real impact. *Stanford
Social Innovation Review*, 11(4), 22–31.
Brown, J. (2006). Equity finance for social enterprises. *Social Enterprise Journal*, 2(1),
73–81.
Busenitz, L.W., Fiet, J.O. and Moesel, D.D. (2005). Signaling in venture capitalist–new
venture team funding decisions: does it indicate long-term venture outcomes?
Entrepreneurship Theory & Practice, 29(1), 1–12.
Calabrese, T.D. (2011). Testing competing capital structure theories of nonprofit
organizations. *Public Budgeting & Finance*, 31(3), 119–43.
Connelly, B.L., Certo, S.T., Ireland, R.D. and Reutzel, C.R. (2011). Signaling theory:
a review and assessment. *Journal of Management*, 37(1), 39–67.
Cornée, S., Jegers, M. and Szafarz, A. (2018). Theory of social finance. *Working Papers
CEB 18-010*. Université Libre de Bruxelles.
Cornée, S., Kalmi, P. and Szafarz, A. (2016). Selectivity and transparency in social
banking: evidence from Europe. *Journal of Economic Issues*, 50(2), 494–502.
Dadush, S. (2015). Regulating social finance: can social stock exchanges meet the
challenge? *University of Pennsylvania Journal of International Law*, 37(1), 139–230.
Dees, J.G. (1998). Enterprising nonprofits. *Harvard Business Review*, 76, 54–69.
Demirgüç-Kunt, A. and Levine, R. (1996). Stock markets, corporate finance, and eco-
nomic growth: an overview. *The World Bank Economic Review*, 10(2), 223–39.
Diamond, D.W. (1984). Financial intermediation and delegated monitoring. *The
Review of Economic Studies*, 51(3), 393–414.
Di Domenico, M., Haugh, H. and Tracey, P. (2010). Social bricolage: theorizing social
value creation in social enterprises. *Entrepreneurship Theory & Practice*, 34(4),
681–703.
Di Lorenzo, F. and Scarlata, M. (2019). Social enterprises, venture philanthropy and the
alleviation of income inequality. *Journal of Business Ethics*, 159(2), 307–23.
Dithrich, H. and Mudaliar, A. (2019). *Sizing the Impact Investing Market*. New York:
Global Impact Investing Network (GIIN).
Edmiston, D. and Nicholls, A. (2017). Social impact bonds: the role of private capital in
outcome-based commissioning. *Journal of Social Policy*, 47(1), 57–76.
Emerson, J. (2003). The blended value proposition: integrating social and financial
returns. *California Management Review*, 45(4), 35–51.
Etzel, M. (2015, 9 November). Philanthropy's new frontier – impact investing. *Stanford
Social Innovation Review*. Accessed 31 March 2020 at https://ssir.org/articles/entry/
philanthropys_new_frontierimpact_investing.
Evers, A. (2005). Mixed welfare systems and hybrid organizations: changes in the
governance and provision of social services. *International Journal of Public
Administration*, 28(9–10), 737–48.
Falck, O. and Heblich, S. (2007). Corporate social responsibility: doing well by doing
good. *Business Horizons*, 50(3), 247–54.
Froot, K.A., Scharfstein, D.S. and Stein, J.C. (1993). Risk management: coordinating
corporate investment and financing policies. *Journal of Finance*, 48(5), 1629–58.
Frumkin, P. (2003). Inside venture philanthropy. *Society*, 40(4), 7–15.
Gaskin, K. (1999). Valuing volunteers in Europe: a comparative study of the volunteer
investment and value audit. *Voluntary Action*, 2(1), 33–49.

Gorman, M. and Sahlman, W.A. (1989). What do venture capitalists do? *Journal of Business Venturing*, 4(4), 231–48.

Guiso, L., Sapienza, P. and Zingales, L. (2004). Does local financial development matter? *Quarterly Journal of Economics*, 119(3), 929–69.

Hayek, F.A. (1945). The use of knowledge in society. *American Economic Review*, 35(4), 519–30.

Höchstädter, A.K. and Scheck, B. (2015). What's in a name: an analysis of impact investing understandings by academics and practitioners. *Journal of Business Ethics*, 132(2), 449–75.

Janney, J.J. and Folta, T.B. (2006). Moderating effects of investor experience on the signaling value of private equity placements. *Journal of Business Venturing*, 21(1), 27–44.

Khan, M., Serafeim, G. and Yoon, A. (2016). Corporate sustainability: first evidence on materiality. *The Accounting Review*, 91(6), 1697–724.

Le Grand, J. (1991). The theory of government failure. *British Journal of Political Science*, 21(4), 423–42.

Lehner, O.M. (ed.) (2016). *Routledge Handbook of Social and Sustainable Finance*. Abingdon: Routledge.

Lehner, O.M. and Nicholls, A. (2014). Social finance and crowdfunding for social enterprises: a public–private case study providing legitimacy and leverage. *Venture Capital*, 16(3), 271–86.

Letts, C.W., Ryan, W. and Grossman, A. (1997). Virtuous capital: what foundations can learn from venture capitalists. *Harvard Business Review*, 75, 36–50.

Levine, R. (2005). Finance and growth: theory and evidence. In P. Aghion and S.N. Durlauf (eds), *Handbook of Economic Growth* (pp. 865–934). Amsterdam: Elsevier (North-Holland Publishing).

Mair, J. and Hehenberger, L. (2014). Front-stage and backstage convening: the transition from opposition to mutualistic coexistence in organizational philanthropy. *Academy of Management Journal*, 57(4), 1174–200.

Marwell, N.P. and McInerney, P.B. (2005). The nonprofit/for-profit continuum: theorizing the dynamics of mixed-form markets. *Nonprofit and Voluntary Sector Quarterly*, 34(1), 7–28.

Mollick, E. (2014). The dynamics of crowdfunding: an exploratory study. *Journal of Business Venturing*, 29(1), 1–16.

Moore, M.L., Westley, F.R. and Nicholls, A. (2012). The social finance and social innovation nexus. *Journal of Social Entrepreneurship*, 3(2), 115–32.

Myers, S.C. and Majluf, N.S. (1984). Corporate financing and investment decisions when firms have information that investors do not have. *Journal of Financial Economics*, 13(2), 187–221.

Nicholls, A. (2010). Institutionalizing social entrepreneurship in regulatory space: reporting and disclosure by community interest companies. *Accounting, Organizations and Society*, 35(4), 394–415.

Nicholls, A. and Emerson, J. (eds) (2015). *Social Finance*. Oxford: Oxford University Press.

Orlowski, J. and Wicker, P. (2015). The monetary value of voluntary work: conceptual and empirical comparisons. *VOLUNTAS: International Journal of Voluntary and Nonprofit Organizations*, 26(6), 2671–93.

Porter, M.E. and Kramer, M.R. (2011). Creating shared value. *Harvard Business Review*, 89(1/2), 62–77.

Renneboog, L., Ter Horst, J. and Zhang, C. (2008). Socially responsible investments: institutional aspects, performance, and investor behavior. *Journal of Banking & Finance*, 32(9), 1723–42.

Rochet, J.C. and Tirole, J. (2006). Two-sided markets: a progress report. *RAND Journal of Economics*, 37(3), 645–67.

Salamon, L.M. (1987). Of market failure, voluntary failure, and third-party government: toward a theory of government–nonprofit relations in the modern welfare state. *Nonprofit and Voluntary Sector Quarterly*, 16(1–2), 29–49.

Salamon, L.M., Sokolowski, S.W. and Haddock, M.A. (2011). Measuring the economic value of volunteer work globally: concepts, estimates, and a roadmap to the future. *Annals of Public and Cooperative Economics*, 82(3), 217–52.

Santos, F., Pache, A.-C. and Birkholz, C. (2015). Making hybrids work. *California Management Review*, 57(3), 36–58.

Scarlata, M., Walske, J. and Zacharakis, A. (2017). Ingredients matter: how the human capital of philanthropic and traditional venture capital differs. *Journal of Business Ethics*, 145(3), 623–35.

Scheaf, D.J., Davis, B.C. and Webb, J.W. et al. (2018). Signals flexibility and interaction with visual cues: insights from crowdfunding. *Journal of Business Venturing*, 33(6), 720–41.

Schwienbacher, A. (2007). A theoretical analysis of optimal financing strategies for different types of capital-constrained entrepreneurs. *Journal of Business Venturing*, 22(6), 753–81.

Shiller, R.J. (2013). *Finance and the Good Society*. Princeton, NJ: Princeton University Press.

Smith, B.R., Cronley, M.L. and Barr, T.F. (2012). Funding implications of social enterprise: the role of mission consistency, entrepreneurial competence, and attitude toward social enterprise on donor behavior. *Journal of Public Policy & Marketing*, 31(1), 142–57.

Spiess-Knafl, W. and Achleitner, A.K. (2012). Financing of social entrepreneurship. In C. Volkmann, K.O. Tokarski and K. Ernst (eds), *Social Entrepreneurship and Social Business* (pp. 157–73). Wiesbaden: Springer Gabler.

Stinchcombe A.L. (1965). Organizations and social structure. In J.G. March (ed.), *Handbook of Organizations* (pp. 142–93). Chicago, IL: Rand McNally.

Waldfogel, J. (1993). The deadweight loss of Christmas. *American Economic Review*, 83(5), 1328–36.

Weisbrod, B. (1978). Problems of enhancing the public interest: toward a model of government failures. In B.A. Weisbrod, J.F. Handler and N.K. Komesar (eds), *Public Interest Law*. Berkeley, CA: University of California Press, pp. 30–41.

Wolf, C. (1979). A theory of nonmarket failure: framework for implementation analysis. *The Journal of Law & Economics*, 22(1), 107–39.

Wuffli, P. and Farber, V. (2020). *The elea Way*. Abingdon: Routledge.

Young, D.R. and Lecy, J.D. (2014). Defining the universe of social enterprise: competing metaphors. *VOLUNTAS: International Journal of Voluntary and Nonprofit Organizations*, 25(5), 1307–32.

Zingales, L. (2015). Presidential address: does finance benefit society? *Journal of Finance*, 70(4), 1327–63.

Zott, C. and Huy, Q.N. (2007). How entrepreneurs use symbolic management to acquire resources. *Administrative Science Quarterly*, 52, 70–105.

5. The best of both worlds? Impact investors and their role in the financial versus social performance debate[1]

Sergio G. Lazzarini, Sandro Cabral,
Leandro S. Pongeluppe, Luciana C. de M. Ferreira and
Angelica Rotondaro

Introduction

A central question in the study of impact-oriented strategies is how organizations can craft profitable business models while at the same addressing social and environmental goals (Barnett and Salomon, 2006; Luo et al., 2015; Margolis and Walsh, 2003) – leading to what some scholars refer to as *blended* creation of economic and social value (Nicholls, 2009; Zahra and Wright, 2015). Some emphasize that the sheer pursuit of profitability can encourage firms to grow by developing sustainable stakeholder relations or by catering to growing, low-income segments (Aguilera et al., 2007; London and Hart, 2004; Prahalad and Hammond, 2002; Tantalo and Priem, 2016). Yet, research has also underscored the myriad tensions that firms face to sustain blended value. Thus, in efforts to appropriate economic rents, firms may excessively focus on short-term profits (Slawinski and Bansal, 2015), neglect disadvantaged groups (Karnani, 2011; Roodman, 2012), and steer away from social objectives (Battilana and Dorado, 2010; Ebrahim, Battilana and Mair, 2014; Ioannou and Serafeim, 2015; Karnani, 2007a, 2007b, 2011; Katz, 2007).

Given these diverging views on how firms manage concurrent social and economic objectives, a natural question arises: when and under what conditions will firms promote synergistic (instead of tensioned) strategies supporting the creation of blended value? We contend that blended strategies require the support of coherent, complementary organizational choices and that tensions will fundamentally derive from a blatant *misalignment* between those choices. For instance, a social enterprise facing pressure from short-term investors suffers from a more fundamental problem: the presence of investors who are not particularly aligned with the social mission of the firm. Alternatively, the entrepreneur can attract a blend of investors with mixed (financial and social) motivations (Roundy, Holzauer and Dai, 2017), and use contractual mechanisms that compensate for the social impact that they generate (Bugg-Levine, Kogut and Kulatilaka, 2012).

In other words, changes in assumptions about the underlying motivation of agents as well as about the various complementary mechanisms that they use can help realign activities and objectives that at first glance would appear counter synergistic (Makadok and Coff, 2009). Accordingly, we draw from the literature on organizational complementarities (Makadok and Coff, 2009; Milgrom and Roberts, 1995; Soda and Furlotti, 2017; Zott and Amit, 2010) to propose that the creation of blended value results from bundles of mutually consistent, self-reinforcing organizational attributes attenuating potential tensions between social and financial goals. We use grounded theory to identify these attributes and propose alternative models leading to various forms of blended value creation. Our theorizing benefits from the recent emergence of so-called *impact investors* and especially the diverse strategies that they use to support enterprises with blended indicators of profitability and social impact (Brest and Born, 2013; Flammer, 2015; Flammer and Bansal, 2017; Harji and Jackson, 2012; Roundy et al., 2017).

Our proposed models of blended value are based on the results of 65 in-depth interviews and five roundtables, totaling 93 informants. Our qualitative efforts allow us to identify organizational attributes supporting blended models combining financial and social goals, as well as distinct *types* of blended value creation. By highlighting the importance of aligned and complementary organizational choices supporting blended value creation, our study advances existing discussions on the challenges faced by firms combining economic and social dimensions of performance. In addition, given our focus on the field of impact investing, we unveil the mechanisms in which financial markets help support, instead of derail, the social orientation of the firm. In our discussion, investors are neither profit-maximizing actors neglecting social benefits nor passive actors simply avoiding firms with negative impact; they are instead active players whose varying motivations and choices buttress heterogeneous organizational models with mixed social and economic objectives. Thus, we also contribute to the literature on social entrepreneurship and impact-oriented strategies by shedding light on the 'investor side' of social businesses and especially on the mechanisms that investors – and their supported entrepreneurs – employ to create and sustain blended value. We conclude by providing a host of suggestions for future research, both empirical and theoretical.

Theoretical background and context

Tensions in the pursuit of blended value

Over recent decades we have witnessed a vibrant debate on whether firms can capture economic value while at the same time addressing social and environmental needs (Barnett, 2007; Barnett and Salomon, 2006; Flammer, 2015; Flammer and Bansal, 2017; Luo et al., 2015; Margolis, Elfenbein and Walsh, 2007; Margolis and Walsh, 2003). As organizational goals are influenced by a complex web of stakeholders (Donaldson and Preston, 1995; Freeman, 1984), firms can develop stakeholder-centered strategies to build their reputation and develop sustainable operations that, in turn, lead to long-term financial performance (Aguilera et al., 2007; Porter and Kramer, 2006; Tantalo and Priem, 2016).

In a different direction, another research stream has underscored the conflicts that emerge from the pursuit of multiple social and economic objectives. Some scholars point out the risk that firms targeting vulnerable groups will simply try to expand and leverage their commercial activities without worrying about their social development in the long run (Hall et al., 2012; Karnani, 2011). More recently, an extensive literature has emerged to explain the dilemmas involved in socially oriented enterprises that at the same time need to generate economic return to fund their operations (Battilana and Dorado, 2010; Ebrahim et al., 2014; Ioannou and Serafeim, 2015; Pache and Santos, 2010). Indeed, research has shown that social enterprises often prioritize one dominant objective and only a few proactively manage to combine financial and social goals (Mair, Mayer and Lutz, 2015).

Yet, while some organizations pursue disproportionate emphasis on a single dimension, either financial or social, other firms try to actively juxtapose multiple demands (Hahn et al., 2015). Thus, Emerson (2003) introduced the term *blended value* to characterize a situation where firms develop sustainable operations and generate tangible social benefits (social value), such that these very practices support profitable business models (economic value). Over time, the concept of performance has changed to incorporate a more encompassing combination of financial, social and environmental indicators

(Hubbard, 2009; Nicholls, 2009). In this view, organizational strategies create channels through which these multiple goals become potentially interdependent. However, the nature of these channels remains understudied. Zahra and Wright (2015), for instance, ask: 'What are the dimensions of different forms of hybrid organizations with for profit and social goals and how does this influence the measurement of blended value?' (p. 625). Below we draw from the literature of organizational complementarities to help identify these dimensions and their interactions.

Organizational complementarities: from conflict to synergy

A critical step in the analysis of alternative mechanisms to reconcile economic and social value is to recognize that tensions or conflicts do not necessarily arise from the existence of multiple goals, but from *misaligned* choices preventing blended value creation. For instance, in his critical assessment of the microcredit industry, Roodman (2012, p. 108) writes:

> Some argue that in going fully commercial, leaders of for-profit microfinance institutions are selling more than parts of their companies to investors, they are also selling their souls. The charge is that to hit quarterly earnings targets, these institutions will profit at the expense of their customers rather than in service to them.

If investors expect these microcredit firms to act as regular commercial banks, then conflicts will indeed escalate, as they will require high profitability from loans to financially constrained clients. Would it be possible to realign organizational choices to avoid this inherent tension?

A way to examine this process of alignment is to consider that organizations comprise bundles of attributes that can potentially reinforce one another. Indeed, strategy research has conceptualized firms as systems of complementary attributes whereby each particular choice increases the benefits of adopting other elements in the system (Milgrom and Roberts, 1995; Porter, 1996; Soda and Furlotti, 2017). This view is also consistent with the idea of building coherent 'business models' comprising self-reinforcing attributes – an idea that is not only widespread among practitioners (Osterwalder and Pigneur, 2010) but also increasingly adopted by scholarly work (Baden-Fuller and Morgan, 2010).

In this view, complementarities are particularly crucial in the case of organizations combining multiple and potentially conflicting objectives. Specifically, tensions will arise whenever managers adopt misaligned, incongruent choices. Along these lines, Makadok and Coff (2009) proposed a model to study complementary choices in organizations requiring multi-task managerial effort following distinct objectives. Multi-tasking in hybrid organizations is usually seen as counter-synergistic because devoting more effort to one activity can undermine effort to other important activities. However, Makadok and Coff (2009) show that activities that are apparently counter-synergistic can become synergistic or complementary if we relax some underlying assumptions on the behavior of organizational players, including their underlying motivation to engage in particular tasks or activities.

In our specific context – namely, impact investment – tasks leading to economic value creation can be synergistic or counter-synergistic to tasks conducive to social value creation. Scholars assessing potential conflicts in the pursuit of multiple social and economic objectives implicitly assume that these tasks are counter-synergistic. However, changes in key organizational choices, including the attraction of agents with distinct motivations, can lead to configurations where complementary choices mitigate tension and even promote multi-tasking synergy. In the previous microfinance example, the attraction of investors motivated to support socially oriented businesses changes the type of the pressure that they can exert on the managers of the microcredit firm. These investors may actually confront managers if they *fail* to target disadvantaged groups. Also, investors and managers can incorporate social performance dimensions into formal reporting mechanisms and even craft incentive contracts whereby part of their compensation is tied to indicators of *both* economic and social value creation.

As is usual in the study of systems of complementary choices, multiple solutions based on varied combinations of attributes are expected to emerge (Brynjolfsson and Milgrom, 2013). Accordingly, as we explain below, we examine the emerging movement of impact investing to assess how investors and entrepreneurs adopt new and varied models to combine social and economic objectives.

Impact investors and their influence on blended value

Financial investors are usually seen as a major source of tension for firms pursuing blended value. Some argue that financial markets and financially motivated investors encourage companies to emphasize short-term profitability and neglect potential positive or negative externalities that those companies may generate (see, e.g., Davis, 2009; Kemper and Martin, 2010). In this view, linking with our previous discussion, investors are counter-synergistic to the overall objective to generate blended value. Yet, investors are far from being a uniform, monolithic group. An early research stream has examined the phenomenon of socially responsible investing (SRI), which infuses dimensions of corporate ethics and social responsibility in the context of portfolio management and investment decisions (Barnett and Salomon, 2006; Renneboog, Ter Horst and Zhang, 2008). The *impact investing* movement, in contrast, involves investors who *actively* pursue and influence the strategy of for-profit entrepreneurial ventures with a clear mandate to achieve and even measure positive social performance (Brest and Born, 2013; Harji and Jackson, 2012). In other words, impact investors actively seek businesses with evidence of blended value creation, although with distinct and varied emphasis on each dimension (Freireich and Fulton, 2009; J.P. Morgan, 2010).

These mixed motivations towards financial or social objectives are not only a critical attribute of the impact investing movement (Roundy et al., 2017) but also a central element in our theorising. Going back to our previous discussion, organizational tasks can be synergistic or counter-synergistic depending on the underlying motivational assumptions of agents and the organizational mechanisms that they use. For instance, Bridges Ventures, an impact investing fund in the United Kingdom, has managed impact-oriented funds with distinct expectations of financial return and social impact. While some funds have high financial targets much in line with the traditional venture capital industry, some other funds seek to attract investors willing to accept a 'financial trade-off', given that some of the invested firms cross-subsidize internal operations to guarantee delivery to vulnerable population targets (Rangan and Appleby, 2013). Impact investors have also created mechanisms to monetize the social value that they generate – such as in the case of the social or development impact bonds, where governments or nonprofits compensate investors according to pre-specified impact targets (Bugg-Levine et al., 2012; Social Finance, 2013). In this context, our subsequent empirical analysis essentially unveils alternative self-reinforcing models through which investors and their target entrepreneurs achieve distinct forms of blended value creation.

Methodology

Using the nascent field of impact investing as our empirical setting, we use grounded theory (Corbin and Strauss, 2008) to expand our understanding of how investors support models to cope with the inherent tensions between financial and social goals. Our choice of grounded theory is justified because programmatic research on the determinants of blended value is at an early stage in general (Zahra and Wright, 2015) and even more so in our context involving the emergence of impact-oriented investors. The qualitative, context-rich orientation of grounded theory allows us not only to unveil alternative models in this field but also the complex interactions between their underlying attributes.

Instead of departing from a *tabula rasa* (Kelle, 2007), we benefited from discussions and findings from the existing literature to help structure our interviews and guide our data collection process (Suddaby, 2006; Turner, 1983). With our specific research question in mind – what organizational attributes and complementarities between these attributes can promote blended value – we started with a set of 'conceptual blocks' to collect and categorize the data (Turner, 1983). These blocks, which emerged from our extensive review of the literature, focus on key conceptual/topical elements serving as an initial guide for our empirical investigation (Locke, 2001). The open-ended questions used in our interviews were anchored on seven complementary blocks: (1) types of targeted markets and beneficiaries; (2) types of targeted entrepreneurs; (3) challenges to creating blended value; (4) investment mechanisms; (5) assessment of blended value (social and financial performance indicators); (6) investor preferences; and (7) future of the industry.

Sample of interviewees

Starting from these seven blocks, we then collected our qualitative data based on interviews and interactions with different players involved in impact investing. We started our initial data analysis by selecting an initial sample of professionals involved in the field of impact investment. To obtain new valuable informants, we applied the snowball or chain sampling procedure (Patton, 2005), in which new respondents are recommended by the existing informants so as to increase the richness of our sample. This process was repeated four times until we reached 'theoretical saturation' – that is, when no fundamentally new information was obtained from the interviews nor from our successive interactions between theory and data (Strauss and Corbin, 1990).

Our interviews focus on a single country where the field of impact investing is in rapid development: Brazil. A study found that impact investing in Latin America had a total capital allocation of around $2 billion dollars, with Brazil as the largest single market with around $300 million (Leme, Martins and Hornberger, 2014). The Brazilian Social Finance Task Force, an informal network of investors, entrepreneurs and nonprofit organizations, estimated that the total amount of socially oriented investments in Brazil could be as high as $15 billion dollars by 2020 (Força Tarefa de Finanças Sociais, 2015). The focus on the Brazilian context creates an opportunity to examine alternative organizational models for blended value in a setting where the impact investing movement is active and growing, while at the same time minimizing the effect of potential extraneous variables that might appear if our study covered distinct and disparate institutional contexts.

In total, we conducted 65 in-depth interviews and five roundtables (discussion groups), totaling 93 participants with approximately 55 hours and 25 minutes of interaction.[2] We benefited from a diverse set of interviewees that allowed us to gain a more complete view of the phenomenon, incorporating multiple relevant stakeholders and providing different perspectives of the same issues (Dubois and Araujo, 2007). We interviewed a group of impact investors involved in conventional financial firms such as venture capital and private equity funds; wealth and savings management firms such as family offices and pension funds; nonprofit firms and government agencies dealing with or interested in impact investing. We also interviewed socially oriented entrepreneurs at various stages in their business cycles (either mature or early stage) as well as other stakeholders in the field (consultants focused on project design or impact measurement, regulatory agencies, universities, and so forth).

Data collection and data analysis: operational procedures

Our interviews were semi-structured, following a guide with specific questions anchored on the seven conceptual blocks discussed earlier, while at the same time guaranteeing some flexibility for the interviewer to exploit new emerging issues (Kvale and Brinkmann, 2009; Opdenakker, 2006). Our roundtables, in turn, normally involved a group of entrepreneurs, consultants, investors and academics discussing a particular theme. Finally, we complemented our interviews and interactions with secondary data based on our own research as well as documents or articles suggested by the interviewees.

All the interviews were recorded and analyzed using the ATLAS.ti* software. Our research team performed a constant comparison between conceptual blocks, based on emerging statements from the interviews and ancillary documents (Glaser and Strauss, 1967; Walker and Myrick, 2007). Inspired by Petriglieri (2015), and based on our analysis of interviews and documents, we then defined *axial codes* representing key constructs or issues that were frequently mentioned. Based on emerging statements from the interviews, we performed a simple content analysis by counting the number of times interviewees mentioned each key concept.[3] We then established connections between our initial conceptual blocks and the axial codes emanating from the interviews (Bergh et al., 2014; Krippendorff, 2004). We then proceeded to aggregate the concepts that emerged from the analysis of axial codes and triangulated information (Dubois and Gadde, 2002), thus arriving at *aggregate attributes* that then served as key elements to categorize organizational models supporting blended value.

Findings: key aggregate attributes of organizational models

Figure 5.1 summarizes the associations between our initial conceptual blocks, the axial codes emerging from the data, and our final proposed aggregate attributes. The figure also shows the frequency of occurrence of the codes identified by our procedure and how they led to aggregate organizational attributes whose interactions can potentially explain synergistic effects in the creation of blended value. The final aggregate attributes are explained below.[4]

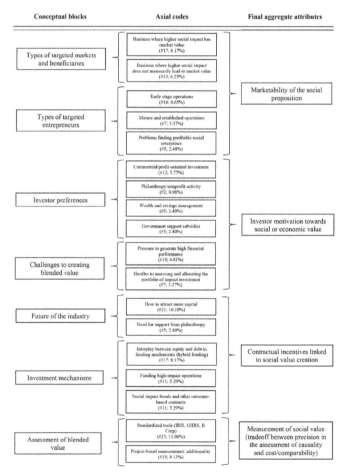

Figure 5.1   Codes, frequency of appearances (#) and aggregation

Marketability of the social proposition

Our data suggest that there are at least two ways in which firms can translate their social proposition into market-based sources of value, which is crucial for the creation of blended value. First, firms can address existing market failures by delivering products or services that are valued by low-income consumer segments more efficiently. Second, firms can also design products or services for which their social impact is valuable to consumers, and therefore can yield a price premium. If the model involves activities that meet one of those conditions, we say that the social proposition is *marketable*. By marketability we imply that social impact can be monetized via consumer segments directly or indirectly by the firm. Consider the following quote from a manager of a cosmetics firm selling products at a premium based on specialized inputs coming from low-income communities located in conservation areas in the Amazon rainforest:

> When we deal with low-income suppliers, we explain how the project works... After the deal is closed our marketing guys go there and talk to the community. Then, the marketing department develops a new concept of why to use the product... You grasp the meaning that [the community] assigns to the forest input and translate it into a marketing concept attracting more customers. (Interview #2: Social enterprise in maturity stage, pers. comm., 2012)

Related to our previous theoretical discussion, marketability essentially implies that actions leading to social value creation (e.g., targeting low-income customers) are naturally aligned with actions that create economic value (e.g., these low-income customers represent profitable growth opportunities). Our interviews revealed, however, three main obstacles that limit marketability, and consequently create counter-synergistic effects in the pursuit of blended value. First, consumers may have budgetary constraints to pay for high impact (Santos, Pache and Birkholz, 2015) and in some more extreme cases firms may even be unable to charge for their products or services. Second, considering the inherent purchasing constraints of these target populations, early-stage entrepreneurs need to learn and experiment with alternatives to generate sufficient revenues. Third, entrepreneurs (and investors) may face incentives to cut costs at the expense of actions that would otherwise generate social benefits, especially when internal targets incentivize profitability (Cabral, Lazzarini and Azevedo, 2013; Hart, Schleifer and Vishny, 1997).

Investor motivation

Our data also reveal that the type of *investor motivation* is a critical variable influencing models designed to create blended value. In our context, investors are motivated to support impact-oriented business for a variety of reasons, depending on their underlying preferences for economic gain and fairness (Bolton and Ockenfels, 2000). On the one hand, investors may follow the usual assumption of *self-interest*: they may invest in businesses for personal economic gain. On the other hand, investors may have an intrinsic interest in achieving results other than pure profitability; sometimes there is even an altruistic desire to create tangible benefits for vulnerable populations and avoid societal harm. In this case, investors display *other-regarding* preferences (Bolton and Ockenfels, 2000; Charness and Rabin, 2002) and are, thus 'willing to sacrifice own consumption to reward kindness' (Sobel, 2009, p. 12).

We verified in our fieldwork that impact investors often mix these two motives, although to varying degrees. Some investors, even if valuing signals of positive impact, are more interested in the financial return of their investees (Døskeland and Pedersen, 2015). These conventional investors are more aligned with the more traditional SRI trend, defining socio-environmental criteria to include or exclude certain firms in a portfolio mimicking market-based returns. Other investors, while still requiring positive returns, are more willing to accommodate profitability constraints that emerge in some businesses.

For instance, as discussed before, early-stage social enterprises benefit from more 'patient' investors that are less concerned with short-term results and more interested in the potential value that the social enterprise can generate in the long run (Slawinski and Bansal, 2015). Family offices are an example of patient investors with increased social orientation (Alto, 2012). Consistent with research findings that family businesses have motivations beyond short-term profitability (Berrone et al., 2010; Miller and Le Breton-Miller, 2006), we observed several offices managing the inherited wealth of families involved in the funding of socially oriented ventures. These investors exhibit mixed self- and other-regarding preferences, and in some cases, their other-regarding preferences are closely connected with their self-interest. For instance, pension funds, as institutional investors, must follow regulations requiring an assessment of social and environmental risks.

However, as we have gleaned in our empirical work, the field has also benefited from the actions of investors willing to sacrifice economic returns to support the creation of social value. Some nonprofits, for instance, support impact-oriented businesses either as investors or, even more commonly, as partners providing additional sources of revenue (e.g., scholarships to low-income students in private schools), helping with potential impact-oriented interventions, or funding the measurement of impact:

> Impact investment is not the silver bullet that will solve all the social problems of our society. There are some areas where philanthropy and donations will be necessary. (Interview #15: Private/venture capital, pers. comm., 2013)

Contractual incentives

Our analysis reveals that investors have also used various *contractual incentives* in models designed to cope with various potential counter-synergistic effects involved in the creation of blended value. These contracts are mainly between impact investing funds and their investors, social enterprises and impact investing funds, and investors/entrepreneurs and external payers. The first type of contract, between funds and their investors, usually involves arrangements where the performance fee of fund managers depends not only on financial targets (as is usual in the venture capital industry) but also on socio-environmental indicators. For instance, one interviewed impact investing fund has a payment structure where half their performance fee is conditional on impact targets. The second type of contract, between social enterprises and funds, usually involves adherence to social mission and feasibility of the socially oriented business proposition. These factors guide decisions to allocate financial resources and even – if targets are not met – exit their investees:

> Within the [fund name] program in December 2011... we got an angel investment. That investment consisted in a loan, which we had to repay in a year if we have not achieved their social and financial requirements. But in three months after the initial investment, they [the fund] have already agreed to evolve our partnership into a bigger investment. Finally, in December 2012, we received a higher amount of capital, where they became minority partners, holding a seat on the board. (Interview #19: Early stage social entrepreneur, pers. comm., 2013)

The third type of contract involves arrangements between investors/entrepreneurs and external payers providing outcome-based payments or bonuses conditional on social value creation. For instance, we observed in our context a public–private partnership (PPP) in which a state government tried to attract private capital to support the preservation of a natural area through tourism and forest conservation management practices. The contract was structured in such a way that the government would compensate entrepreneurs (and their investors) based on a host of socio-environmental indicators.

Measurement of social value

A final critical aspect that emerged from our field interactions is the role of *measurement mechanisms* to assess the creation of blended value. Given that financial tools to measure economic value are already well known, we focus on the more recent discussion on how to measure social value, which is still in flux (see, e.g., Rawhouser, Cummings and Newbert, 2017). Our analysis revealed that alternative ways to measure social value deal with a fundamental trade-off between cost, comparability and the precision of causal assessment. Some of our interviewees reported the use of standardized tools, such as Impact Reporting and Investment Standards (IRIS), Global Impact Investing Report System (GIIRS), and the B Corp certification. Because the use of these tools is widespread and mostly based on self-reporting, investors do not consider them expensive. Also, given their standardized nature, they enable measurements that are, by design, comparable. However, some of our interviewees viewed those standardized tools more critically:

> Although GIIRS is the most common methodological framework, it looks like a checklist of sustainability. So, internally, we seek other forms of impact assessment that are really related to our social goal. (Interview #21: Private/venture capital, pers. comm., 2013)

Some investors and entrepreneurs have therefore adopted project-specific metrics and have even used their own measurements to assess the causal impact of their interventions (in education, for instance, scores from student learning tests are often used). In the assessment of causality, the field has adopted varied techniques to compute the *additionality* of the project, that is, a comparison of actual outcomes to what would have happened to the target population without the intervention. Social value creation, in this perspective, is usually measured by comparing the outcomes of the target population to a control group of comparable individuals (e.g., Brest and Born, 2013; Kroeger and Weber, 2014). Although these additionality based methods have received increasing attention because of their more precise assessment of impact (Duflo, Glennerster and Kremer, 2007), they are seen as substantially more expensive and, in some cases, even unfeasible. For instance, entrepreneurs usually self-select their beneficiaries and are sometimes reluctant to exclude potential beneficiaries serving as control groups.

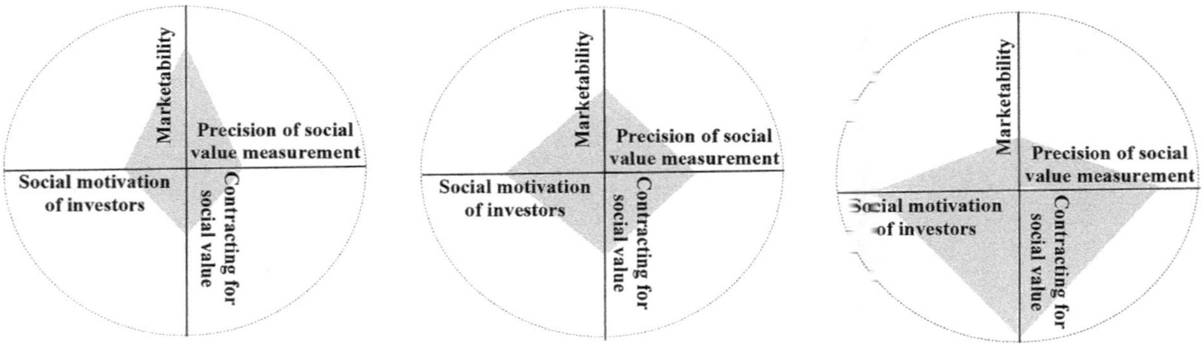

Type of blended value: economic value is central, reinforced by signals of social value creation.

Key synergistic mechanism: firms address opportunities for market growth in lower-income populations and/or signal differentiated product attributes, increasing profitability and attracting more conventional investors.

Type of blended value: moderate emphasis on economic value, with social value creation as a precondition.

Key synergistic mechanism: attraction of "tamed" market investors (with mixed self- and other-regarding preferences) helps address limitations to marketability and guarantee minimal targets for social value creation.

Type of blended value: social value is central and contractually monetized to enhance economic value.

Key synergistic mechanism: socially oriented investors (with other-regarding preferences) and outcome-based payments linked with more precise measurement of social value help address critical constraints to marketability.

Figure 5.2   Models for blended value creation and their key synergistic mechanisms

Self-reinforcing models for blended value creation

Based on our revealed attributes, discussed before, we now describe three general types of blended value creation, as well as their underlying self-reinforcing attributes. We describe these attributes (summarized in Table 5.1) and show how they complement one another, via synergistic relations (depicted in Figure 5.2 and detailed below).

Model 1: Economic value is central, reinforced by signals of social value creation

Investors pursuing this model typically select more mature enterprises operating with goods and services that can deliver profits in the short run and are also expected to generate positive social outcomes. An example in our data, discussed before, is a cosmetics firm operating with products whose inputs come in part from low-income supplier communities located in remote rural areas. By explicitly advertising its environment-friendly activities and supplier development efforts (e.g., through above-market pricing of the inputs or infrastructure support), the firm can charge a price premium for its final products.

With this type of positioning, the social enterprise manages to attract competitive investors who seek returns aligned with the conventional market but want to incorporate signals of impact in their portfolio of assets. They include private equity firms, investment bankers and institutional funds with a tradition of investing in mature, established firms. In addition, because they target more mature businesses where financial performance partially derives from socially enhancing activities, they tend to channel funds through conventional vehicles (such as institutional funds or stock markets) with no need to adopt impact-based contractual incentives. With respect to measurement, increased funding from traditional investors will typically be associated with relatively simple, standardized metrics. Because these investors place higher emphasis on financial performance, they will be relatively less interested in a more precise measure of social performance. Instead, they may simply want to invest in 'signals' that their portfolio includes firms concerned with the socio-environmental impact of their activities – including advertising and reporting tools describing the social action of their investees or standardized tools.

In sum, high marketability attenuates counter-synergistic tensions on the investor side by luring investors mainly motivated by economic self-interest. Scant adoption contracts to incentivize social value and the use of simple mechanisms to measure impact are also complementary to this type of investor and the higher marketability of the social project.

Table 5.1   Types of self-reinforcing models for blended value creation

Attribute of the Model for Blended Value Creation	Alternative Self-reinforcing Models		
	#1 Economic value is central, reinforced by signals of social value creation	#2 Moderate emphasis on economic value, with social value creation as a precondition	#3 Social value is central and contractually monetized to enhance economic value
Marketability of the social proposition	Investors select mature, established businesses where social and market-based activities complement each other and lead to a natural and concurrent alignment between social and economic value creation (e.g., growing low-income markets and/ or higher-end segments willing to pay a premium for products with positive signals of impact)	Investors select businesses where social and market-based activities are partially aligned. Constraints to marketability include: Early-stage operations with uncertainty on whether the social proposition will generate future demand Moderate hazard that vulnerable groups will be neglected or de-emphasized	Investors select businesses where social and market-based activities are poorly aligned. Critical limits to marketability arise due to: Severe budgetary or structural constraints of the targeted market segments Acute hazard that enterprises will economize on activities that would otherwise generate social value
Investor motivation	Mostly based on self-interest: opportunity to invest in profitable social businesses or pursue differentiation via signals of impact in the portfolio	Mixed self- and other-regarding preferences: investors target profitable business but with a longer-term financial orientation and increased attention to evidence of social value creation guiding capital allocations	Increased participation of investors with other-regarding preferences (emphasizing social value creation) and stimulating the adoption of contractual mechanisms to compensate for impact (which can also help attract investors with mixed or economic-centered preferences)

Contractual incentives	Scant use of formal contractual mechanisms linked with social targets	Use of contractual mechanisms to allocate investments according to indicators of economic and social performance. Moderate use of compensation linked with social value creation	High emphasis on contractual mechanisms to compensate investors and entrepreneurs according to concrete evidence of social value creation
Measurement of social value	Simple signals of impact: advertising and reporting of socially oriented investments; in some cases, with standardized tools (e.g., IRIS, GIIRS, B Corp certification)	Use of standardized measurement tools, although with increased adoption of project-specific metrics and more precise evidence of social value in more mature projects	Project-specific metrics with higher emphasis on more precise, robust evidence of social value creation (in some cases, with verification of additionality)

Example in the data

Cosmetics firm charging a price premium for its environmentally friendly products and compensating its supplier communities with above-market supplier prices	Start-up with a new web search mechanism helping individuals to locate drugs distributed through a government program. Most of the revenue of the start-up comes from partnerships with health service providers	Public–private partnership attracting private capital to support the preservation of a natural area, whereby the local government compensates investors according to socio-environmental indicators

Model 2: Moderate emphasis on economic value, with social value creation as a precondition

The second model involves situations in which an excessive emphasis on financial performance may jeopardize the pursuit of promising social initiatives, such as in the case of nascent social entrepreneurs and emerging technologies to address social or environment challenges, for which there is an uncertain future demand. In some cases, there is also a moderate risk that investors will force entrepreneurs to prioritize profitability even at the expense of activities necessary to support high social performance. An example in our database is a start-up that created a new web-based mechanism to search for locations where individuals can get medicine for free sponsored by the government. Most of the revenue of the start-up comes from partnerships with health service providers, including health insurance companies. There was an internal tension arising not only from the need of the start-up to grow and achieve a stable cash flow, but also from the possibility of entering a partnership with health service providers targeting higher-income populations to simply reduce their spending on medication for their clients. However, this tension reduced with the presence of an impact-investing fund with clear dual mandates to achieve profitability and generate benefits for vulnerable target populations. In this case, the fund managers clearly expressed their disapproval of actions that would broaden its market scope to include higher-income clients.

Therefore, this second model is associated with projects whose nature requires a longer-term orientation and some moderate risk that profitability will be prioritized at the expense of social value creation. These projects will attract 'tamed' investors whose motivation balances economic self-interest and other-regarding preferences. Unlike the first model, these investors tend to adopt more specialized contractual arrangements to allocate their capital according to the indicators of social and economic performance of their investees, as well as impact-based incentives for fund managers conditional on these indicators. In this model, while profitability remains important to attract capital, achieving social impact is a precondition; departure from an initial social mission can even trigger exit and divestment. As for the measurement of social value, in this model investors typically adopt standardized tools in the impact investment field, although increasingly using project-specific measures tailored to the business of the social enterprise.

Thus, the presence of investors with mixed motivation helps support businesses with moderate limits to marketability and reduce counter-synergistic tensions that would otherwise arise with more economically motivated investors. The mixed motivation of those investors is reinforced by the presence of contractual arrangements defining investment allocations and managerial compensation based on blended social and economic indicators. For this reason, unlike the first model, investors have moved beyond simple signals of impact and have progressively adopted project-based measures, albeit with less emphasis on (costly) verification of additionality.

Model 3: Social value is central and contractually monetized to enhance economic value

The third model essentially involves cases where positive externalities cannot be fully 'internalized' in the form of economic value accruing to the social entrepreneur. There are severe limits to marketability, as a function of budget or structural constraints of beneficiaries, as well as expenses to support positive social interventions. In this case, counter-synergistic effects abound; severe constraints to marketability require the attraction of investors and sponsors whose preferences are more other-regarding. Impact investing funds with more balanced social and economic orientation, although usually more aligned with the second model, also create specialized investment vehicles with lower return targets to attract investors willing to accept lower profitability as long as their capital supports enterprises with higher expected impact.

In this model, we also observe higher participation of nonprofits (mission-oriented foundations and institutes) and state agencies (such as multilateral development institutions) – which, as mentioned before, participate as either investors or external payers, compensating other investors (and their entrepreneurs) for the social value that they generate. This model also involves higher reliance on contractual mechanisms with explicit clauses linking payments to indicators of social value creation – such as PPPs where government payments depend on socio-environmental indicators, as well as more sophisticated outcome-based contracts where those service providers are funded by investors whose returns are also linked with social metrics (social and development impact bonds). Because these external payers will not want to pay for social outcomes that would otherwise be achieved without the presence of impact investors and their extra capital, in this model we observe a more frequent use of more precise project-specific measurements, in some cases even with verification of additionality.

Thus, this model essentially involves synergistic mechanisms to 'internalize externalities', attenuating constraints to marketability and increasing the attraction of investors with varied motivations. While other-regarding investors will typically act as sponsors of complementary tasks (e.g., feasibility or impact measurement studies), the use of more precise measurements and especially monetary payments according to evidence of social value creation helps attract more profit-oriented investors providing extra capital.

Discussion and suggestions for future research

Our work informs the ongoing debate on whether organizations can achieve superior economic performance while at the same time address social and environmental needs (Barnett, 2007; Barnett and Salomon, 2006; Flammer, 2015; Flammer and Bansal, 2017; Luo et al., 2015; Margolis et al., 2007; Margolis and Walsh, 2003). Crucially, we argue that entrepreneurs and investors, and the mechanisms they choose to support their projects, are largely heterogeneous. Some projects may be more conducive to blended value creation, whereas other projects may exhibit inherent tensions that undermine the reconciliation of profitability and socio-environmental performance. In this chapter, we offer a general, encompassing theoretical framework that accommodates these two perspectives and identifies the precise synergistic mechanisms through which social enterprises (and their investors) can create blended value. Consistent with research emphasizing conflicts when firms combine multiple goals, we describe the source and nature of internal tensions but also change underlying motivational assumptions and consider a broader range of complementary choices that can attenuate initial counter-synergistic effects preventing blended value creation (in line with Makadok and Coff, 2009).

Our framework also highlights the role of investors as actors who can help address inherent conflicts when entrepreneurs jointly pursue blended value. This shift of attention towards investors, and especially investors trying to *attenuate* the tensions arising from the reconciliation of financial and social performance, represents an important departure from most of the existing literature. Our study describes a group of investors who actively create new mechanisms to support and help create blended value. Hence, by focusing on the nascent field of impact investing – which has received scant attention in the literature – we contribute to this debate through a more refined portrayal of investors as actors with varied motivations and mechanisms to support enterprises with combined financial and social goals. All in all, our work highlights several opportunities for future research, described below:

1. Unpacking the role and motivations of investors. Given the relevant importance of investor motivation as a driving force enhancing or attenuating potential counter-synergistic effects involved in the pursuit of blended value, future research could more directly describe and measure the preferences of investors towards financial and social goals. In our second and third models, some investors express other-regarding preferences – that is, they value actions that truly generate social benefits – while our first model involves investors who are more economically self-interested – that

is, they require higher financial compensation in their impact-oriented investments. Much more work is needed to identify these types of investors and the extent to which some of them are willing to sacrifice or not their appropriation of economic value in return for more robust evidence of social value creation.[5]

2. Distinct blended models as configurations. The analysis of complementarities is consistent with a long tradition in management research proposing configurations that could conceptually represent heterogeneous organizations and heterogeneous organizing principles (e.g., Miller, 1986). Our three proposed models emerge from grounded theorizing based on qualitative data. New techniques, such as configurational methods (Fiss, 2007), have allowed researchers to compare a larger number of cases and identify complex interactions between multiple attributes. Future research could therefore apply these methods to measure these attributes and potentially unveil other types of configurations beyond what we proposed in the analysis of our qualitative data.

3. The role of the local context. Because our theorizing is based on universal, conceptually informed attributes, we believe that our proposed self-reinforcing models express fundamental forces and synergistic effects present in multiple and varied contexts. Yet, our analysis is focused on an emerging market where the field of impact investing is in development and influenced by a host of local conditions (such as local policies, legal systems, and so forth). Future research could, for instance, check how our proposed models may need to be adapted in other contexts where the field is more mature and with distinct institutional traits (e.g. more developed capital markets). For instance, our third model, where social value is central and contractually monetized, is facilitated by previous local experiences in outcome-oriented contracting and effective public–private collaborations in myriad sectors.

4. The interplay between alternative arrangements to incentivize blended value. Future research should also examine how other organizational choices, such as the presence of contracts rewarding for superior impact, interact with the motivation of agents. For instance, some claim that external incentives may 'crowd out' other-regarding preferences (Deci and Ryan, 1985); alternatively, others propose that these incentives may help reduce the temptation to deviate from contractual targets, which in turn fosters trust and cooperation (Poppo and Zenger, 2002). A more detailed analysis of investor motivation can greatly inform the design and evolution of contractual and measurement tools to support blended value.

5. Measuring impact in distinct blended value models. The study of measurement innovations, which has started receiving scholarly interest (e.g.,

Kroeger and Weber, 2014), should also be a fertile source for future research as the field progressively experiments with new contracts and metrics. A key issue in this debate is how to reconcile cost, comparability and precision; more precise project-specific techniques required in the second and especially the third model are more expensive and their measurements are less comparable than cheaper standardized tools. The study of alternative measurement techniques, in turn, could also improve our understanding of various forms of contractual arrangements to reward for superior social value. What are the trade-offs involved in these measurement tools and how do they influence the design and stability of those contracts? Tracking the evolution of such a measurement and contracting ecosystem should itself be a rewarding research agenda in the field of impact investing and more generally in the study of strategies for blended value.

Notes

1. We are grateful for the financial support of the Latin America Economy Impact Innovations Fund (The Rockefeller Foundation, Avina and Omidyar, in a proposal coordinated by ICE), Insper and the University of St. Gallen. We also benefited from comments by Michael Barnett, Paola Criscuolo, Lien de Cuyper, Ilze Kivleniece, Jean-Louis Laville, Gideon Markman, Anita McGahan as well as seminar participants at Imperial College Business School and the 2014 Academy of Management Conference. We also thank Luc Wüst for his invaluable research assistance.
2. A more detailed description of our interviewees is available upon request.
3. We are aware that the mere counting the number of times a code appears does not necessarily imply the importance of a topic. Nevertheless, it provides a rough indication of the importance of each topic, therefore informing our subsequent theorizing.
4. A more detailed description of our aggregate attributes as well as a list of illustrative quotes from the interviews are available upon request.
5. Investor motivation is leading decision-making processes in major venture capital and private equity funds. One example is BlackRock, whose CEO announced in 2019 they will more thoroughly access the climate risk of their investments and are pushing the Task Force on Climate-related Financial Disclosures (TCFD).

References

Aguilera, R.V., Rupp, D.E., Williams, C.A. and Ganapathi, J. (2007). Putting the S back in corporate social responsibility: a multilevel theory of social change in organizations. *Academy of Management Review*, 32(3), 836–63.

Alto, P. (2012). Impact investing: will hype stall its emergence as an asset class? *Social Space*, November, 40–47.

Baden-Fuller, C. and Morgan, M.S. (2010). Business models as models. *Long Range Planning*, 43(2), 156–71.

Barnett, M.L. (2007). Stakeholder influence capacity and the variability of financial returns to corporate social responsibility. *Academy of Management Review*, 32(3), 794–816.

Barnett, M.L. and Salomon, R.M. (2006). Beyond dichotomy: the curvilinear relationship between social responsibility and financial performance. *Strategic Management Journal*, 27(11), 1101–22.

Battilana, J. and Dorado, S. (2010). Building sustainable hybrid organizations: the case of commercial microfinance organization. *The Academy of Management Journal*, 53(6), 1419–40.

Bergh, D.D., Connelly, B.L. Ketchen, D.J. and Shannon, L.M. (2014). Signalling theory and equilibrium in strategic management research: an assessment and a research agenda. *Journal of Management Studies*, 51(8), 1334–60.

Berrone, P., Cruz, C., Gomez-Mejia, L.R. and Larraza-Kintana, M. (2010). Socioemotional wealth and corporate responses to institutional pressures: do family-controlled firms pollute less? *Administrative Science Quarterly*, 55(1), 82–113.

Bolton, G.E. and Ockenfels, A. (2000). ERC: a theory of equity, reciprocity, and competition. *American Economic Review*, 90(1) 166–93.

Brest, B.P. and Born, K. (2013). When can impact investing create real impact? *Stanford Social Innovation Review*, 22–31. Accessed 19 January 2021 at https://community-wealth.org/sites/clone.community-wealth.org/files/downloads/article-brest-born.pdf.

Brynjolfsson, E. and Milgrom, P. (2013). Complementarity in organizations. In R. Gibbons and J. Roberts (eds), *The Handbook of Organizational Economics* (pp. 11–55). Princeton, NJ: Princeton University Press.

Bugg-Levine, A., Kogut, B. and Kulatilaka, N. (2012). A new approach to funding social enterprises. *Harvard Business Review*, 90(1–2), 1–7.

Cabral, S., Lazzarini, S.G. and Azevedo, P.F. (2013). Private entrepreneurs in public services: a longitudinal examination of outsourcing and statization of prisons. *Strategic Entrepreneurship Journal*, 7(1), 6–25.

Charness, G. and Rabin, M. (2002). Understanding social preferences with simple tests. *The Quarterly Journal of Economics*, 117(3), 817–69.

Corbin, J. and Strauss, A. (2008). *Basics of Qualitative Research: Techniques and Procedures for Developing Grounded Theory*. London: SAGE.

Davis, G.F. (2009). The rise and fall of finance and the end of the society of organizations. *The Academy of Management Perspectives*, 23(3), 27–44.

Deci, E.L. and Ryan, R.M. (1985). The general causality orientations scale: self-determination in personality. *Journal of Research in Personality*, 19(2), 109–34.

Donaldson, T. and Preston, L.E. (1995). The stakeholder theory of the corporation: concepts, evidence, and implications. *Academy of Management Review*, 20(1), 65–91.

Døskeland, T. and Pedersen, L.J.T. (2015). Investing with brain or heart? A field experiment on responsible investment. *Management Science*, 62(6), 1632–44.

Dubois, A. and Araujo, L. (2007). Case research in purchasing and supply management: opportunities and challenges. *Journal of Purchasing and Supply Management*, 13, 170–81.

Dubois, A. and Gadde, L. (2002). Systematic combining: an abductive approach to case research. *Journal of Business Research*, 55(7), 553–60.

Duflo, E., Glennerster, R. and Kremer, M. (2007). Using randomization in development economics research: a toolkit. In P.T. Schultz and J.A. Strauss (eds), *Handbook of Development Economics*, Vol. 4 (pp. 3895–962). Amsterdam: North-Holland Publishing.

Ebrahim, A., Battilana, J. and Mair, J. (2014). The governance of social enterprises: mission drift and accountability challenges in hybrid organizations. *Research in Organizational Behavior*, 34, 81–100.

Emerson, J. (2003). The blended value proposition: integrating social and financial returns. *California Management Review*, 45(4), 35–51.

Fiss, P.C. (2007). A set-theoretic approach to organizational configurations. *Academy of Management Review*, 32(4), 1180–98.

Flammer, C. (2015). Does corporate social responsibility lead to superior financial performance? A regression discontinuity approach. *Management Science*, 61(11), 2549–68.

Flammer, C. and Bansal, P. (2017). Does a long-term orientation create value? Evidence from a regression discontinuity. *Strategic Management Journal*, 38, 1827–47.

Força Tarefa de Finanças Sociais (2015). *Finanças Sociais: Soluções Para Desafios Sociais e Ambientais*. Accessed 19 January 2021 at http://forcatarefafinancassociais.org.br/wp-content/uploads/2015/10/Finan%C3%A7as-Sociais_Solu%C3%A7%C3%B5es.pdf.

Freeman, R.E. (1984). *Strategic Management: A Stakeholder Approach*. London: Pitman.

Freireich, J. and Fulton, K. (2009). *Investing for Social & Environmental Impact: A Design for Catalyzing an Emerging Industry*. Monitor Institute. Accessed 19 January 2021 at https://www2.deloitte.com/content/dam/Deloitte/global/Documents/Financial-Services/gx-fsi-monitor-Investing-for-Social-and-Environmental-Impact-2009.pdf.

Glaser, B. and Strauss, A. (1967). *The Discovery of Grounded Theory*. Chicago, IL: Aldine.

Hahn, T., Pinkse, J., Preuss, L. and Figge, F. (2015). Tensions in corporate sustainability: towards an integrative framework. *Journal of Business Ethics*, 127(2), 297–316.

Hall, J., Matos, S., Sheehan, L. and Silvestre, B. (2012). Entrepreneurship and innovation at the base of the pyramid: a recipe for inclusive growth or social exclusion? *Journal of Management Studies*, 49(4), 785–812.

Harji, K. and Jackson, E.T. (2012). *Accelerating Impact Achievements, Challenges and What's Next in Building the Impact Investing Industry*. New York: The Rockefeller Foundation.

Hart, O.D., Shleifer, A. and Vishny, R.W. (1997). The proper scope of government: theory and an application to prisons. *Quarterly Journal of Economics*, 112(4), 1127–61.

Hubbard, G. (2009). Measuring organizational performance: beyond the triple bottom line. *Business Strategy and the Environment*, 18(3), 177–91.

Ioannou, I. and Serafeim, G. (2015). The impact of corporate social responsibility on investment recommendations: analysts' perceptions and shifting institutional logics. *Strategic Management Journal*, 36(7), 1053–81.

J.P. Morgan (2010). *Impact Investments: An Emerging Asset Class*. The Rockefeller Foundation. Accessed 19 January 2021 at https://www.rockefellerfoundation.org/wp-content/uploads/Impact-Investments-An-Emerging-Asset-Class.pdf.

Karnani, A. (2007a). Employment, not microcredit, is the solution. *Ross School of Business Working Paper Series, No. 1065*.

Karnani, A. (2007b). Doing well by doing good – case study: 'Fair & Lovely' whitening cream. *Strategic Management Journal*, 28(13), 1351–7.

Karnani, A. (2011). 'Doing well by doing good': the grand illusion. *California Management Review*, 53(2), 69–86.

Katz, B.R. (2007, 16 February). The BOP debate: Aneel Karnani responds. *Next Billion. net*.

Kelle, U. (2007). 'Emergence' vs. 'forcing' of empirical data? A crucial problem of 'grounded theory' reconsidered. *Historical Social Research*, 19, 133–56.

Kemper, A. and Martin, R.L. (2010). After the fall: the global financial crisis as a test of corporate social responsibility theories. *European Management Review*, 7, 229–39.

Krippendorff, K. (2004). Reliability in content analysis: some common misconceptions and recommendations. *Human Communication Research*, 30(3), 411–33.

Kroeger, A. and Weber, C. (2014). Developing a conceptual framework for comparing social value creation. *Academy of Management Review*, 39(4), 513–40.

Kvale, S. and Brinkmann, S. (2009). *Interviews: Learning the Craft of Qualitative Research Interviewing*. Thousand Oaks, CA: SAGE.

Leme, A., Martins, F. and Hornberger, K. (2014). *The State of Impact Investing in Latin America*. Boston, MA: Bain & Company.

Locke, K. (2001). *Grounded Theory in Management Research*. Thousand Oaks, CA: SAGE.

London, T. and Hart, S.L. (2004). Reinventing strategies for emerging markets: beyond the transnational model. *Journal of International Business Studies*, 35(5), 350–70.

Luo, X., Wang, H., Raithel, S. and Zheng, Q. (2015). Corporate social performance, analyst stock recommendations, and firm future returns. *Strategic Management Journal*, 36(1), 123–36.

Mair, J., Mayer, J. and Lutz, E. (2015). Navigating institutional plurality: organizational governance in hybrid organizations. *Organization Studies*, 36(6), 713–39.

Makadok, R. and Coff, R. (2009). Both market and hierarchy: an incentive-system theory of hybrid governance forms. *Academy of Management Review*, 34(2), 297–319.

Margolis, J.D., Elfenbein, H.A. and Walsh, J.P. (2007). Does it pay to be good? A meta-analysis and redirection of research on the relationship between corporate social and financial performance. Working paper. Accessed 19 January 2021 at https://ssrn.com/abstract=1866371.

Margolis, J.D. and Walsh, J.P. (2003). Misery loves rethinking companies: social initiatives by business. *Administrative Science Quarterly*, 48(2), 268–305.

Milgrom, P. and Roberts, J. (1995). Complementarities and fit strategy, structure, and organizational change in manufacturing. *Journal of Accounting and Economics*, 19(2), 179–208.

Miller, D. (1986). Configurations of strategy and structure: towards a synthesis. *Strategic Management Journal*, 7(3), 233–49.

Miller, D. and Le Breton-Miller, I. (2006). Family governance and firm performance: agency, stewardship, and capabilities. *Family Business Review*, 19(1), 73–87.

Nicholls, A. (2009). 'We do good things, don't we?': 'blended value accounting' in social entrepreneurship. *Accounting, Organizations and Society*, 34(6), 755–69.

Opdenakker, R. (2006). Advantages and disadvantages of four interview techniques in qualitative research. *Forum Qualitative Sozialforschung/Forum: Qualitative Social Research*, 7(4), Article 11.

Osterwalder, A. and Pigneur, Y. (2010). *Business Model Generation: A Handbook for Visionaries, Game Changers, and Challengers*. Hoboken, NJ: John Wiley & Sons.

Pache, A.-C. and Santos, F.M. (2010). When worlds collide: the internal dynamics of organizational responses to conflicting institutional demands. *Academy of Management Review*, 35(3), 455–76.

Patton, M.Q. (2005). Qualitative research. In B.S. Everitt and D.C. Howell (eds), *Encyclopedia of Statistics in Behavioral Science* (pp. 1633–6). Chichester: John Wiley & Sons.

Petriglieri, J.L. (2015). Co-creating relationship repair: pathways to reconstructing destabilized organizational identification. *Administrative Science Quarterly*, 60(3), 518–57.

Poppo, L. and Zenger, T. (2002). Do formal contracts and relational governance function as substitutes or complements? *Strategic Management Journal*, 23(8), 707–25.

Porter, M.E. (1996). What is strategy? *Harvard Business Review*, 74(6), 61–78.

Porter, M.E. and Kramer, M.R. (2006). Strategy and society: the link between competitive advantage and corporate social responsibility. *Harvard Business Review*, 84(12), 78–92.

Prahalad, C.K. and Hammond, A. (2002). Serving the world's poor, profitably. *Harvard Business Review*, 80(9), 48–59.

Rangan, V.K. and Appleby, S. (2013). Bridges Ventures. *Harvard Business School Case* 514-001, October.

Rawhouser, H., Cummings, M. and Newbert, S.L. (2017). Social impact measurement: current approaches and future directions for social entrepreneurship research. *Entrepreneurship Theory and Practice*, 43(1), 82–115.

Renneboog, L., Ter Horst, J. and Zhang, C. (2008). Socially responsible investments: institutional aspects, performance, and investor behavior. *Journal of Banking & Finance*, 32(9), 1723–42.

Roodman, D. (2012). *Due Diligence: An Impertinent Inquiry Into Microfinance*: Washington, DC: Center for Global Development and Brookings Institution Press.

Roundy, P., Holzhauer, H. and Dai, Y. (2017). Finance or philanthropy? Exploring the motivations and criteria of impact investors. *Social Responsibility Journal*, 13(3), 491–512.

Santos, F., Pache, A.-C. and Birkholz, C. (2015). Making hybrids work. *California Management Review*, 57(3), 36–59.

Slawinski, N. and Bansal, P. (2015). Short on time: intertemporal tensions in business sustainability. *Organization Science*, 26(2), 531–49.

Sobel, J. (2009). Generous actors, selfish actions: markets with other-regarding preferences. *International Review of Economics*, 56(1), 3–16.

Social Finance (2013). *A Technical Guide to Developing Social Impact Bonds*. London: Social Finance Ltd.

Soda, G. and Furlotti, M. (2017). Bringing tasks back in: an organizational theory of resource complementarity and partner selection. *Journal of Management*, 43(2), 348–75.

Strauss, A.L. and Corbin, J.M. (1990). *Basics of Qualitative Research: Techniques and Procedures for Developing Grounded Theory* (15th ed.). Newbury Park, CA: SAGE.

Suddaby, R. (2006). What grounded theory is not. *Academy of Management Journal*, 49(4), 633–42.

Tantalo, C. and Priem, R.L. (2016). Value creation through stakeholder synergy. *Strategic Management Journal*, 37(2), 314–29.

Turner, B.A. (1983). The use of grounded theory for the qualitative analysis of organizational behavior. *Journal of Management Studies*, 20(3), 333–48.

Walker, D. and Myrick, F. (2007). Grounded theory. *Qualitative Research*, 16(4), 547–59.

Zahra, S.A. and Wright, M. (2015). Understanding the social role of entrepreneurship. *Journal of Management Studies*, 53(4), 610–29.

Zott, C. and Amit, R. (2010). Business model design: an activity system perspective. *Long Range Planning*, 43(2–3), 216–26.

6. Challenges for social impact measurement in the non-profit sector

Ericka Costa

Introduction

In the last 20 years, the debate around measuring, accounting, reporting and evaluating non-financial performance has begun to gain momentum at the global level. A variety of actors need to understand the potential positive impact of investment beyond financial returns, including individual and institutional investors, venture firms and non-profit and governmental organizations (O'Donohue et al., 2010, Santos, 2012). As a result, individuals and institutions have actively deployed capital into low-income domestic markets to gain both financial and social returns, such as job creation, community facilities, social housing and other broad societal benefits (Thornley and Dailey, 2010). Within these emergent needs, financial accounting and measurement systems have shown themselves to be overly focused on economic and financial returns on investment, providing no understanding of the social impacts gained through the funding (Reheul, Caneghem and Verbruggen, 2014). Currently, national regulators still tend to require accountability based strictly on financial measurements (European Commission, 2014; Williams and Taylor, 2013).

This debate has particular relevance for non-profit organizations (NPOs) such as social enterprises and hybrid organizations. NPOs have become key players in providing public services both at the European (Defourny and Nyssens, 2010; Manetti, 2014; Santos, 2012) and worldwide levels (Costa, Parker and Andreaus, 2014). Indeed, all types of organizations – both for-profit and non-profit – produce social impact; however, social impact typically refers to the value that non-governmental organizations (NGOs), social enterprises, social ventures and social programmes create (Arena, Azzone and Bengo,

2015; Bagnoli and Megali, 2011). Financiers and investors certainly agree on the need to measure NPOs' social impact because their decisions in favour of a given impact investment rely at least partially on this (Ebrahim, 2009, 2010). On one hand, financial indicators help investors to assess potentially profitable opportunities, inform investment decisions and allow for monitoring of these investments; on the other hand, investors interested in generating non-financial returns adopt and request non-financial indicators to inform their investment decisions. These indicators often assist in analysing and monitoring the social and/or environmental outcomes or impacts of a project, venture or organization (Best and Harji, 2013).

The 2009 financial crisis resulted in the restriction of public funding for societal needs while simultaneously increasing requests for assistance and economic support by NPOs and other organizations, a situation increasing competition in fund-raising (Groupe d'Experts de la Commission sur l'Entrepreuriat Social [GECES], 2014). The worldwide financial crisis indeed dampened the world economy, generating financial sustainability issues for different organizations. Therefore, today's funders and investors must have confidence that their investments will foster societal change and alleviate the targeted social inequalities (Best and Harji, 2013; Grieco, Michelini and Iasevoli, 2015; Nicholls, 2018; Nicholls, Nicholls and Paton, 2015).

In response to this situation, many scholars and practitioners have investigated various 'non-financial accountability' practices in non-profit organizations. The notion of 'social impact' (Ebrahim and Rangan, 2014) has emerged from the idea of 'blended value accounting' (BVA) (Nicholls, 2009) to the 'social accounting project for NPOs' (Costa et al., 2014). To date, notions of social impact and social impact measurement continue to present many limitations and potentialities (Ebrahim and Rangan, 2010). These limitations have yet to be completely resolved, thus opening up further avenues of research. In order to illuminate the potential challenges in the current social impact measurement debate, this chapter aims to introduce the most recent and relevant debates around social impact and social impact measurement while encouraging future avenues of research. The chapter will therefore discuss the following: (1) the relevance of a 'one-size-fits-all' approach to social impact measurement and the possibility of adopting standardized and replicable metrics for all NPOs across Europe (Clark et al., 2004; Maas and Liket, 2011b); (2) the emergent need to adopt a multi-stakeholder perspective in social impact measurement (Bengo et al., 2016; Costa and Pesci, 2016); and (3) the current debate around the Sustainable Development Goals (SDGs) and the role of NPOs' social impact measurements within this context (Bebbington and

Unerman, 2018; Organisation for Economic Co-operation and Development [OECD], 2019).

The next section of this chapter discusses the rationale that moved the NPO accountability debate towards new blended accountability systems encompassing both economic and social value. The third section focuses on the multiple definitions of social impact while adopting the impact value chain as a basis for the discussion. The fourth section reflects on the theory of change as the backbone of the impact value chain, while the fifth presents various approaches to social impact measurement, classifying them according to Bengo et al.'s (2016) proposal. The sixth section proceeds to highlight possible challenges in measuring, accounting and reporting impacts via three main themes: comparability and standardization, the multi-stakeholder approach and the SDGs. The chapter concludes with final thoughts.

Why has social impact measurement emerged in the NPO context?

In the NPO context, regulators typically restrict accountability to financial measurements (Andreaus and Costa, 2014; Rehuel et al., 2014; Torres and Pina, 2003). Accounting information may be an important and regular mechanism for discharging major aspects of accountability. Financial accountability enables primary external users to assess the NPO's financial position and its acquisition and spending of funds (Rehuel et al., 2014). When NPOs deal with financial accountability and present the conventional financial statement and balance sheet, they usually adopt formats designed for for-profit organizations. The conventional financial accountability process seeks to (1) provide information on how resources are obtained and used during the period; (2) present the resources available for future use at the end of the period; and (3) report on the continuance of services in the future (Torres and Pina, 2003). However, research has shown that this approach faces limitations when applied to NPOs (Williams and Taylor, 2013). Meanwhile, accounting theories encounter shortcomings when dealing with these organizations for two primary reasons. First, the bottom line for NPOs is not based on the maximization of economic value for shareholders; rather, the goal is to create 'social value' for the broader community. Second, NPOs have a multi-stakeholder nature, and therefore their activities benefit a wide range of stakeholders (not only the owners). Indeed, as highlighted by Maddocks (2011), financial accountability captures only a partial picture of such organizations, because it does not help in understanding many factors in non-profit settings, such as success, performance and impact (Torres and Pina, 2003).

When applied to NPOs, traditional financial accountability, which deals with economic and financial metrics, becomes a meaningless bureaucratic constraint: it needs to be respected due to regulations, yet it fails to capture the effectiveness and mission-oriented activities of NPOs. In NPO financial reporting, the bottom line is not an indicator of success; therefore, the information provided by conventional reporting needs to be complemented with information about effectiveness and social performance (ibid.). Indeed, because of their multi-stakeholder nature and their roles within society in promoting and fostering the well-being of the people they serve, NPOs prefer to adopt different narratives in order to communicate their performance and achievements to stakeholders (Ebrahim, 2009; Moore, 2000).

Various studies have pointed out the limitations of financial accountability (Reheul et al., 2014; Torres and Pina, 2003; Vermeer, Raghunandan and Forgione, 2009) by highlighting the function and effects of accounting and reporting in such organizations. Because they are social-value oriented, they cannot simply be measured by traditional financial indicators or by market share. Many have proposed a more nuanced and blended form of accountability (Nicholls, 2009), engaging both economic and social dimensions. To reflect the dual nature of NPOs – with both financial and social value – these organizations have begun to experiment with certain accounting practices measuring not only economic performance but also social results (Bagnoli and Megali, 2011; Manetti, 2014; Nicholls, 2009). Difficulties aligning these measurement systems arise because these two types of value creation are intrinsically connected rather than opposing one another in a zero-sum equation (Emerson, 2003). As Epstein and McFarlan (2011) have highlighted, financial and non-financial measures are indeed closely related in the NPO context because financial resources are meaningless if not employed to achieve the mission. Meanwhile, it is not possible to achieve a social purpose without efficiently employing financial resources.

In short, researchers have turned their attention to broader forms of NPO accountability in the last 20 years, largely because NPOs' performance cannot be measured and reported by conventional accounting systems. Calls have emerged to include a social dimension in NPO accountability, encompassing social impact for a variety of stakeholders (Ebrahim, 2009, 2010). Within this broad debate on NPO accountability, I believe that it is possible to identify some prominent keywords: 'social accounting', 'blended value accounting', and more recently, 'social impact'.

The 'social accounting project' (Gray, 2002) aims to find an alternative and new form of accounting 'which goes beyond the economic' (p. 687). Social accounting provides an alternative to the conventional accounting framework in order to improve shareholders' financial decisions while reinventing capitalism. The social accounting project has embraced the multi-stakeholder approach for NPOs (Gray, Bebbington and Collison, 2006; Unerman and O'Dwyer, 2006) in order to help organizations 'justify their pursuit of social and environmental goals in economic terms' (Gray, Dillard and Spence, 2011, p. 13).

'Blended value accounting' recognizes that all organizations create both financial and social value, and these two types of values are intrinsically connected rather than being in opposition in a zero-sum equation (i.e., to generate more social value, an organization must sacrifice its financial performance) (Emerson, 2003; Nicholls, 2009). In other words, generating increased social wealth does not necessarily imply a sacrifice in terms of economic-financial results. In a holistic approach, both elements contribute to creating value (Manetti, 2014).

The notion of 'social impact' has recently emerged as a new mantra expressing civil society's demand for 'accountability' (Ebrahim and Rangan, 2010). Borrowing from established literature in performance measurement (Arena et al., 2015), social impact can be defined as 'a logic chain of results in which organizational inputs and activities lead to a series of outputs, outcomes and ultimately to a set of societal impacts' (Ebrahim and Rangan, 2010, p. 3). The notion of accountability prominently focuses on both the responsibility to take certain actions and the responsibility to provide an account (not only financial) for those actions (Gray, Adams and Owen, 1996). By comparison, the idea of social impact is fundamentally connected to a given action's effects and consequences. Consistent with a long-term orientation, social impact refers to all societal and environmental changes – both positive and negative, intended and unintended – created by activities and investments. Societal impacts include issues such as equalities, livelihoods, health, nutrition, poverty, security and justice (Defourny and Nyssens, 2010).

These differences highlight the need to create a more complex, multi-directional and multi-stakeholder accountability system (Christensen and Ebrahim, 2006; Ebrahim, 2005; Najam, 1996; Williams and Taylor, 2013), one that does not simply focus on the economic bottom line but offers different measurements for a greater number of stakeholders (Costa and Pesci, 2016).

What is social impact?

Social impact is a concept that still involves many complexities and controversies (Bengo et al., 2016; Ebrahim and Rangan, 2014). The literature contains no shared definition of social impact, but it can be broadly understood as the long-term changes and effects that an activity incurs. However, a uniform definition proves difficult given the proliferation of terminology and diversity of contexts (Maas and Liket, 2011b; Rawhouser, Cummings and Newbert, 2019). Many researchers support the idea that social impact is an ambiguous 'social construction', with many differences in terms of 'vocabulary' and methodology (Ebrahim and Rangan, 2014). In terms of vocabulary, many different words collocate with social measures, such as 'impact', 'output', 'effect', 'outcome' and 'social return'. For instance, the literature has conceptualized social impact using terms like social value (Santos, 2012), social performance (Nicholls, 2009), social value creation (Emerson, 2003), social return (Clark et al., 2004) and social return on investment (SROI) (Arvidson et al., 2013). Although similar, these terms represent distinct constructs. While these different terms have been used synonymously in the literature, in this chapter I will adopt the so-called impact value chain approach (Figure 6.1), which differentiates outputs from outcomes and impacts. Therefore, this chapter employs the term 'social impact' to maintain consistency.

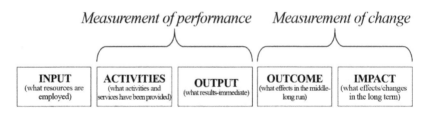

Source: Adapted from Clark et al. (2004) and Ebrahim and Rangan (2010).

Figure 6.1   Impact value chain

The impact value chain (Clark et al., 2004) has been driven by the 'theory-driven evaluation' method, according to which organizations observe how different programmes and initiatives cause intended or observed outcomes and impacts (Ebrahim and Rangan, 2010, 2014; Epstein and McFarlan, 2011). This method defines the impact value chain (Clark et al., 2004) as a 'logic chain of results' in which organizational *inputs* (the resources provided into the initiative, e.g., money, staff time, capital assets) are used to support *activities* and services (e.g., health services, schooling, job training, etc.). These activities ultimately result in the delivery of *outputs* to a target beneficiary population (i.e., results that a social enterprise or NPO can measure or assess directly). The identified output can lead to different effects and changes in beneficiaries' attitudes, behaviours, knowledge, skills and/or status (i.e., the *outcome* of the social enterprise's activity). Short-term benefits and changes then can foster a societal *impact* on the broader society in the long term (Clark et al., 2004; Costa and Pesci, 2016; Ebrahim and Rangan, 2010, 2014; Epstein and McFarlan, 2011).

Figure 6.1 also highlights how the adoption of the impact value chain can help differentiate between the *input–activities–output* by measuring NPO performance and the *outcome–impact*, which refers to measuring the NPO's change. In other words, the impact value chain encourages an understanding that output differs from outcome–impact. Indeed, it borrows from evaluation theory by conceptualizing impacts as different from outputs. Kolodinsky, Stewart and Bullard (2006) highlight that output could be countable from the NPO's perspective, while impact refers to the user's perspective. Extending this idea, I personally think that NPOs could internally measure input–activities–output, but measuring outcome–impact requires the adoption of a multi-stakeholder perspective in order to engage external perspectives and perceptions about the impact (Costa and Pesci, 2016).

The notion of impact requires a degree of nuance as well. Some definitions, such as the one proposed by Clark et al. (2004), refer to impact as 'the portion of the total outcome that happened as a result of the activity of the venture, above and beyond what would have happened anyway' (p. 7). This approach adopts the so-called counterfactuality (which is also adopted in cost–benefit analysis) and argues in favour of considering what might have happened if the organization had not undertaken the activities. Other scholars favour this approach to impact because it attempts to 'isolate' the portion of impact that occurred because of the NPO's specific intervention (Grieco et al., 2015).

Other approaches employ the impact value chain, considering outcome and impact in a broader sense, without focusing on the contractual analysis. This approach explores the significant benefits that NPOs could foster (Ebrahim and Rangan, 2010) – namely, the changes produced by an intervention or activity on the community of interest in the medium term. In this case, qualitative outcomes are also included in terms of the well-being generated, such as better living or health conditions. Within this approach, qualitative outcomes include long-term effects on the root causes pursued by the organization. These causes may be positive or negative, primary or secondary, and produced directly or indirectly by the intervention. Example impacts would include the reduction of poverty or the achievement of certain rights (Costa and Pesci, 2016; Ebrahim and Rangan, 2010, 2014).

What distinguishes these two perspectives (the first more focused on the counterfactual analyses and the second more narrow) is the interpretation and adoption of the theory of change (Davies, 2018; Taplin and Clark, 2012), as further discussed in the next section.

Social impact and theory of change

The varying definitions of social impact provided in the previous section share a commonality: each of them refers to social impact as a *changing status* for people and communities; these changes occur as a result of the NPO's initiatives and activities. In this sense, change involves people modifying their lives in terms of their norms, values, aspirations and beliefs; it may also include the community in terms of its political systems, environment, health or well-being.

This notion of social impact takes the theory of change (ToC) as a point of departure. Although the idea of adopting the ToC in order to evaluate programmes is not new (Weiss, 1995), its use has increased in recent years, particularly amongst international development aid organizations (Davies, 2018). As a construct, it appears often in the social impact debate (Clark et al., 2004; Ebrahim and Rangan, 2010; GECES, 2014). Weiss (1995) described the ToC as 'a theory of how and why an initiative works', one that can be tested empirically by measuring indicators for every step expected on the hypothesized causal pathway to impact. In other words, 'Theory of change is a rigorous yet participatory process whereby groups and stakeholders in a planning process articulate their long-term goals and identify the conditions they believe have to unfold for those goals to be met' (Taplin and Clark, 2012, p. 2).

ToC defines long-term goals and then maps backward to identify changes that need to happen earlier (preconditions). ToC therefore refers to both *process* and *product* (Taplin et al., 2013). In terms of process, the ToC is developed in collaboration with stakeholders and modified throughout the intervention development as well as the evaluation process; it involves an ongoing process of reflection to explore change and how it happens (James, 2011). In terms of product, the ToC adopts some form of diagrammatic representation, usually supported by a text commentary (Davies, 2018). Following a ToC approach, the identified changes are mapped graphically in causal pathways of outcomes, showing each outcome in logical relationship to all other potential results

(Taplin et al., 2013). The adopted diagrams are capable of succinctly representing multiple and intersecting pathways and are often enriched with a narrative component (Davies, 2018).

In presenting their contingency framework, Ebrahim and Rangan (2010) recognize the adoption of ToC in relation to the idea of social impact while considering two different approaches to ToC. Indeed, the relationship between the input–activities–output and the effect, namely outcome–impact, can be *focused* or *complex*: 'For a focused theory of change, the relationship between cause and effect is linear and clearly understood. A complex theory of change refers to cause–effect relationships that are only weakly understood, and where there may be multiple causal factors at play' (Ebrahim and Rangan, 2010, p. 22).

Focus and complex ToC co-exist in the delivery of NPOs' activities because they both depend on the single intervention they operate. For instance, offering jobs to disadvantaged people or providing clean water in particular areas could be very complex in terms of the activity's organization, but it could potentially be fairly straightforward in terms of 'isolating' the part of the change that could be allocated to a single intervention. By comparison, vaccination campaigns or advocacy activities are typically more complex and shaped by many factors that may be poorly understood and non-linear. This kind of activity and intervention may also involve a multitude of different actors, making it difficult to attribute a policy change to a single NPO's action.

As previous studies have highlighted (James, 2011), the application of ToC to the non-profit sector has increased in recent years among international NGOs, foundations and evaluators in North America, Europe and Australia. These organizations have received increased pressure from individual and institutional investors, ventures and governments to understand the potential long-term impact of their investments beyond financial returns (O'Donohue et al., 2010). Therefore, NPOs have started to reflect more on change, rather than just activity, seeking to define new ways of representing change as a reflection of more complex and systemic understandings of development. To help NPOs become more aware of their impacts, many different social impact measurements have emerged. Both academics and practitioners have provided various methodologies and metrics to guide NPOs' social impact measurements (for a review, see Costa and Pesci, 2016).

One size fits all (or not?): different approaches to social impact measurement

In the past 20 years, performance and social impact measurement in NPOs has gained increasing attention among researchers and professionals. Indeed, the development of various measurement methods responds to the changing needs of management information resulting from increased interest in impact measurement (Maas and Liket, 2011a, 2011b). From an academic perspective, I think that we are in a so-called 'creative chaos' phase according to which many different social impact measurements offer varying perspectives, purposes and approaches. Unfortunately, these divergent approaches present a poor systematic analysis; it is difficult for NPOs to decide on the most relevant method for use (Arena et al., 2015, Costa and Pesci, 2016, Maas and Liket, 2011b).

Several reasons account for the large number of methods. First, because of the lack of a single definition of social impact, confusion surrounds the methods that could be adopted. Indeed, NPOs vary in terms of size, sector, country and governance mechanisms; therefore, they select the indicators that appear most suitable for their organizations (Costa and Pesci, 2016). Second, because NPOs have multiple stakeholders by their very nature (Christensen and Ebrahim, 2006; Ebrahim, 2005; Najam, 1996), the NPOs may prefer a specific type of measurement over another (Williams and Taylor, 2013). Given the complexities related to such measurements, the number of methods and documents designed to address social impact measurement is remarkable (Costa and Pesci, 2016; Grieco et al., 2015; Maas and Liket, 2011b).

The debate on social impact measurement ranges from those who favour the so-called 'one-size-fits-all' metric to those who prefer a more tailored measurement. The one-size-fits-all approach involves the indiscriminate application of a sort of golden standard for social impact measurement to all NPO activities and interventions (Arvidson et al., 2013). These measurements and universal standards are to be applied to all sectors and all types of data in order to facilitate comparison with other similar NPOs (GECES, 2014). This approach is preferred by lenders and public investors who are mainly interested in justifying the allocations of public money as well as attracting other sources of public and private financing (European Commission, 2014).

The second approach involves defining tailored and idiosyncratic metrics in order to better highlight differences within a variety of NPO realities; this approach includes identifying specific metrics able to meet specific stakeholders' needs (Costa and Pesci, 2016; Nicholls, 2009). Both approaches can lead to a sort of 'accountability dilemma' (Ebrahim and Rangan, 2010), and both have been subject to criticism. On the one hand, a 'gold standard' cannot represent and measure the significant impacts of every single NPO and its variety of stakeholders; meanwhile, the meaningful social value of NPOs cannot be captured by a mere numerical indicator (Arena et al., 2015; Grieco et al., 2015). On the other hand, it can be time intensive to create overly detailed, tailored and scrupulous metrics that may be non-comparable and subjective (Bagnoli and Megali, 2011).

Recently, some academic studies have offered different classifications able to 'guide' NPOs in selecting the most appropriate social impact metric (Arena et al., 2015; Bengo et al., 2016, Costa and Pesci, 2016; Maas and Liket, 2011a; Thornley and Dailey, 2010). In order to make the analysis as comprehensive as possible, I have adopted Bengo et al.'s (2016) classifications while also including the various metrics proposed by other contributions. I find Bengo et al.'s (2016) classifications quite useful in helping NPOs discern among different metrics. This discussion will focus only on a few of them (one example per method). Please see Table 6.1 for a more detailed analysis of all possible metrics.

Bengo et al. (2016) proposed the following classifications of social impact measurement:

- *Synthetic measures*: these include approaches that lead to the calculation of a synthetic indicator or metrics that provide a measure of the NPO's social impact.
- *Process-based models*: these focus on narrowing down the impact value chain into the elements of inputs, outputs, outcomes and impacts.
- *Dashboards and scorecards*: these aim at identifying a set of KPIs to cover different performance dimensions that represent the NPO's activities and results.

The first group includes all approaches intended to provide a global and quantifiable performance indicator and that therefore focus on the final outcome of an NPO's project. This group includes the well-known SROI developed by the Roberts Enterprise Development Fund (REDF) for social enterprises and tested by the New Economics Foundation (NEF) in 2007 (Sadownik, 2013). SROI could be considered an adapted cost–benefit analysis because it assigns a monetary value to social, economic and environmental benefits and costs. It does so by discounting the cash flows associated with the benefits and costs derived from a given activity and for a certain period of time (Arvidson et al., 2013). The SROI transforms the social impact into a monetary value thanks

Table 6.1   Different methodologies and metrics of social impact
measurement

Methods	Description	Examples		
Synthetic measures	They suggest the calculation of a synthetic indicator/metrics to provide a measure of the global performance of an NPO	• Social return on investment (SROI) by the Roberts Enterprise Development Fund (Emerson, Wachowicz and Chun, 2000) • Local Multiplier 3 (LM3) by Sacks (2002) • Gamma model, by Grabenwarter and Liechtenstein (2011) • Total social impact (TSI) rating by Dillenburg, Greene and Erekson (2003)		
Process-based models	They focus on the process of 'production' of a social service/product, articulating indicators and metrics into inputs, outputs, outcomes and impacts	Without key performance indicators (KPIs)	• Contingency framework by Ebrahim and Rangan (2010) • Five-step model by Costa and Pesci (2016)	
		With KPIs	• Multidimensional control system by Bagnoli and Megali (2011) • Methodology for impact analysis and assessment by Hornsby (2012) • Social impact assessment by Global Social Venture Competition (2017) • Stepwise method by Arena et al. (2015)	

Methods	Description	Examples	
Dash-boards and scorecards	They include dashboards and scorecards aimed at identifying a set of indicators and metrics to cover different performance dimensions that are considered representative of the results of an NPO	Criteria to define performance dimensions and KPIs	• Adapted balanced scorecard by Kaplan and Norton (2001) • Layered balanced score-card by Somers (2005) • Multi-bottom-line bal-anced scorecard by Bull (2007) • Public value scorecard by Moore (2003)
		Stakeholder perspective	• Social added value eval-uation system by Bassi (2011) • Performance manage-ment system by Simmons (2003)
		Guidelines	• Fit for purpose model by the Development Trusts Association (2008) • Social impact for local economy (SIMPLE) by McLoughlin et al. (2009) • Performance assessment model for social enter-prise by Yang, Huang and Lee (2014)
		Synthetic measure	• Integration of the dash-board approach with a synthetic indicator by Meadows and Pike (2010)

Source: Adapted from Bengo et al. (2016).

to financial proxies that are attributed to intangible social value constructs. Arvidson et al. (2013) outline some of the challenges of SROI use, including its participatory approach, which allows stakeholder discretion in the design of each SROI exercise (Costa and Pesci, 2016).

The second group includes models that refer to the ToC and to the impact value chain in order to unpack the social impact measurement into the single elements of the chain, namely the input, output, outcome and, ultimately, impact. All the models proposed in this approach are articulated as guidelines for developing a set of indicators/metrics; however, some of them focus on identifying the social impact dimensions (Ebrahim and Rangan, 2010; Costa and Pesci, 2016), while others also offer a set of KPIs to guide NPOs in their social impact measurement (see, for instance, Bagnoli and Megali, 2011). Some have critiqued this approach as 'cherry picking' because organizations select the most suitable models/frameworks.

Finally, the third group includes a variety of methods – similar but distinct from one another – which define a set of indicators covering various areas of the performance dimensions. Within the dashboard and scorecard category, Bengo et al. (2016) identified four different metrics: (1) the *adapted* balanced scorecard (Kaplan and Norton, 2001), which includes the NPO's mission at the core of the model; (2) the *stakeholder perspective*, which falls into the definition of performance dimensions (Bassi, 2011; Simmons, 2003); (3) *guidelines*, which drive the selection process for the performance dimensions and the KPIs (McLoughlin et al., 2009); and (4) integration of the *dashboard approach with a synthetic indicator* (Meadows and Pike, 2010), which includes KPIs that reflect different strategies to different stakeholders' point of view, by also adopting a synthetic indicator.

Importantly, these classifications could be helpful not only for the academic audience, but also for policy makers and the NPOs themselves. To date, I believe that too much emphasis has been devoted to synthetic measures, which can be attractive for investors and funding bodies. However, the selection of a proper measurement system could play a crucial role in influencing political bargaining processes and power relationships among different actors within organizations and policy makers. Therefore, we need to consider multi-voiced approaches that include the possibility of adopting different metrics among varying actors/stakeholders.

Challenges in measuring, accounting and reporting impact

Having presented the dominant conversation around social impact and social impact measurement, its motivations and prominent methodologies, this section turns to potential challenges in measuring, accounting and reporting social impact. The purpose of this section is to open up possible avenues for future research while also adding my personal views based on field experience with Italian NPOs.

Comparability and standardization

I think the 'big question' today still rests with the idea of comparability and standardization. As Costa and Pesci (2016) highlighted, two opposite approaches have emerged: (1) definition of 'standardized universal' measurement units that facilitate comparisons between organizations and over time; and (2) the development of idiosyncratic measurement units that tailor social impact measurements to stakeholders' needs. Within these two extremes, there exists a 'continuum' of nuanced positions: (a) standardized universal metrics; (b) standardized metrics by sector; and (c) standardized processes.

Aligning with the first approach, some scholars and organizations (Best and Haji, 2013; Clark et al., 2004; Thornley and Dailey, 2010) favour a more standardized impact measurement following the investor perspective. Clark et al. (2004) criticize the absence of comparable standards for social impact accounting, such as for financial accounting. Indeed, the provision of standardized financial metrics is traditionally the central topic of accounting. In for-profit companies, generally accepted accounting principles (GAAP) have been established to help measure and report on financial returns. However, a similar set of accounting principles and legal structures have yet to come to fruition in the NPO sector, preventing comparable standards for measuring social impacts (Clark et al., 2004; Maas and Liket, 2011a). The impact of activities on society, as defined by the social value or social change created, is often not accompanied by a straightforward market value, making it complicated or maybe even impossible to meaningfully capture with conventional accounting methods (Gray, 2002; Maas and Liket, 2011a).

The need for standardized metrics comes from the current welfare economics paradigm, according to which the value of a social good may be priced at what a beneficiary or consumer would be willing to pay for it (Nicholls, 2009). However, this evaluation fails to consider situations where there are no comparable goods or services available to the market, such as those in which

NPO organizations operate. NPOs typically deal in so-called 'market failure' spaces (Nicholls, 2009), where the prices of goods and services are not market based. Moreover, NPOs also operate across a broad spectrum of heterogeneous activity, and therefore it is very difficult to demonstrate comparable performance reporting measures. As Nicholls (2009, p. 758) pointedly asks, 'How, for example, can a reduction in social exclusion via employment creation be quantitatively compared to the rehabilitation of a drug user?' These observations opened an avenue for a second position for those who favour a standardized approach by sector.

Indeed, some scholars (Bengo et al., 2016; Maas and Liket, 2011b; Rawhouser et al., 2019) argue for differences between the industries in which NPOs are situated. These authors support the idea that having a more sectorial standard sould help impact assessment and measurement to be more congruent with NPOs' activities, which are, by definition, multi-sectorial (Rawhouser et al., 2019). A survey conducted by the Global Impact Investing Network (GIIN) and J.P. Morgan confirms the relevance of this issue, with results showing that more than two-thirds of respondents agree that there is a need for standardized impact metrics to foster industry development (cited in Bengo et al., 2016).

Moreover, Rawhouser et al. (2019) highlight the absence of a validated multi-sectorial social impact database, which would be useful in guiding NPOs' activities and performance. Therefore, they promote an improvement in external validity for both multi-sector and single-sector social impact standards. In more detail, the opportunities for single-sector standards relate to (1) the alignment with NPO stakeholder interests; (2) the ability to analyse the processes that result in social impact; and (3) the possibility of better linking the specific activities with the particular types of outcomes associated with these activities.

The GECES sub-group proposed a third perspective in this debate in June 2014, underscoring the benefits of a standard for social impact measurement, ideally agreed-upon worldwide. However, GECES (2014) recognizes that no single set of indicators can be devised following a top-down approach to measuring social impact in European (or global) NPOs. Therefore, it advocates for a *standard process* of social impact measurement, while allowing NPOs to freely adopt different metrics within a sort of 'defined library'. The GECES proposal includes five stages: (1) identify objectives; (2) identify stakeholders; (3) set relevant measurements; (4) measure, validate and value; and (5) report, learn and improve. This proposal moves towards a more standardized, synthetic measurement process, but at the same time highlights the need for a flexible approach tailored to organizations' goals and needs (European

Commission, 2014). As the GECES sub-group clearly explains, this process allows 'freedom as to which indicator to use, in order that the measurement remains appropriate to the intervention and stakeholders' needs' (p. 24). The role of stakeholders and stakeholder engagement is relevant in the current debate around social impact measurement, as further discussed in the following section (Sadownik, 2013).

The multi-stakeholder perspective in social impact measurement

The role of stakeholders and stakeholder-engagement processes is well known in accountability circles, thus NPO accountability has been considered a relational concept (Unerman and O'Dwyer, 2006). In the relational approach to accountability, organizations are required to explain and take responsibility for their actions for stakeholders, thus addressing the 'to whom' questions of accountability (Christensen and Ebrahim, 2006; Ebrahim, 2005; Najam, 1996; Williams and Taylor, 2013).

Several studies have investigated the multiple stakeholders 'to whom' NPOs are accountable. These perspectives indicate that in developing this 'multi-demands' accountability system, NPOs should satisfy the competing claims of multiple stakeholders; as such, NPOs must prioritize their stakeholders within their own aims and expectations (Williams and Taylor, 2012).

The discussion around social impact has also turned to the relevance of stakeholders. For instance, the five standardized steps suggested by the GECES (2014) includes identifying stakeholders (step 2) and reporting activities to them (step 5). Therefore, any definition of social impact should include stakeholder consultation and/or engagement. To date, however, the prominent approach focuses on the NPO's perspective of stakeholders and highlights the importance of taking into account which stakeholders these metrics will serve (Bengo et al., 2016). The direction of the relationship therefore moves from the NPO to the stakeholders and then vice versa. However, as suggested by Costa and Pesci (2016), when social impact measurement deals with a stakeholder-based approach, it needs to be based on stakeholder engagement, which differs from simply acknowledging the existence of many stakeholder viewpoints. Such stakeholder engagement should be based on many different consultative forums with stakeholders, with the aim of extending beyond a multi-stakeholder consensus-seeking approach and producing indicators that appropriately respond to stakeholders' needs (Maas and Liket, 2011b; Sadownik, 2013).

Accordingly, what is needed in order to maintain a multi-stakeholder approach in social impact measurement? Drawing from Kolodinsky et al. (2006) and Costa and Pesci (2016), it is possible to highlight future areas of investigation for this particular topic in social impact measurement. First, as Kolodinsky et al. (2006) clearly argue, output could be countable from the NPO's perspective, but impact refers to the user's perspective. Extending on this idea, I believe that, while input–activity–output could be measured internally by the NPOs through consultation with diverse stakeholders, it is necessary to adopt an external multi-stakeholder perspective in order to measure the outcome–impact view while engaging external perspectives and perceptions about the impact received. As noted by Costa and Pesci (2016), stakeholder engagement should involve a process that encompasses all the steps/stages of social impact measurement and not only those related to stakeholder identification and stakeholder communication regarding the identified metrics. On the contrary, the stakeholder-based approach in social impact measurement should consider who is affected (directly or indirectly) by the NPO's impact and allow these stakeholders to define the measures themselves. The role of NPOs is therefore to consult stakeholders, ask them how they perceive the impacts, and understand these perceptions. Then, together with the affected stakeholders, it is possible to propose and set metrics.

Taking stakeholder views as the basis for social impact measurement affirms the position that measurement is a social activity, and thus, measurement criteria are socially constructed (e.g., Roberts and Scapens, 1985). If we acknowledge the socially constructed nature of social impact measurement it also becomes necessary to adopt a more tailored and customized view of social impact measurement where no universal and golden metrics are defined; on the contrary, these metrics and indicators emerge in the context of interactions among the specific NPO and the specific stakeholders affected by their activities and output. Together, they enact the specific value provided.

Social impact, NPOs and SDGs

In 2016, the United Nations (2016) endorsed the so-called 2030 Agenda for Sustainable Development as a worldwide framework for understanding and achieving environmental and human development ambitions up to the year 2030 (Bebbington and Unerman, 2018). The SDGs have rapidly gained traction and salience among a broad range of actors, such as public policy bodies, NPOs, public sector and private sector organizations, businesses and professional bodies, and of course, academic scholars and universities.

Indeed, the SDGs framework has the merit of integrating social, economic and environmental dimensions within each of the 17 proposed goals while bringing attention to the long-term effects of organizational actions. However, there remains opacity regarding how these goals might relate to each another, as well as the underlying drivers of the impacts that the SDGs seek to address (ibid.).

Two main perspectives have emerged in this discussion. Social accounting scholars have contributed by highlighting the role of accounting studies in this arena (Bebbington, Russell and Thomson, 2017; Bebbington and Unerman, 2018) while impact investing scholars have highlighted the need for new and innovative impact measurements.

From the accounting perspective, Bebbington et al. (2017) noted how accounting-like practices and accounting-like actors are situated in the intersection between academic disciplines, theories, professional practices and policies. These practices relate to the challenges, problems, structures, systems, obstacles and conflicts associated with sustainable development and its application. Therefore, it is urgent that we rethink the conventional accounting paradigm, which has focused on economic and financial revenues, thus helping impact founders to assess, interpret and monitor the overall performance of organizations.

From the finance side, the OECD (2019) highlights the changing paradigm brought into being by Agenda 2030 in terms of financial investor markets. The 2030 Agenda has indeed called for an ambitious financing strategy for sustainable development, with the dual challenge of (1) mobilizing and catalysing innovative resources, not only public, but also private, domestic and international; and (2) gaining a social impact in addition to financial returns. Within this context, the definition and measurement of social impact has become critical. The OECD (2019) report sets out four pillars for the 'impact imperative', which aims to better direct investment for sustainable development in the following ways:

1. 'Ensuring financing is going where it is needed most'. For too many years, financial resources have targeted the 'usual' businesses, leaving behind the less remunerative markets. The OECD (2019) is promoting the development of vibrant local financial markets by encouraging commercial finance with the help of blended finance models.
2. 'Applying innovative approaches to reaching the SDGs'. The public and private sectors should collaborate in order to innovate and facilitate the development of ecosystems to catalyse innovation and experimentation.

Additional funding is not sufficient to meet the SDGs' challenges; a more effective and efficient approach is needed.

3. 'Addressing data and measurement challenges'. The OECD promoted transparent and standardized data sharing in order to coordinate efforts in developing and implementing data standards while establishing linkages between existing data platforms. Building on the OECD mapping study, a specific subset of relevant transaction-based indicators has been developed in order to generate a global reporting framework that also includes financial and impact data.

4. 'Evaluating the social, environmental and economic results of public initiatives'. The so-called policy imperative requires the ex post assessment of policy initiatives' social and environmental outcomes in order to ensure that the 'impact' evaluation does not become an exercise in futility.

These four pillars are intended to ensure that financing for sustainable development achieves real impact as a result of collective effort.

In sum, I personally believe that the debate regarding NPO accountability and social impact over the last 20 years could provide insightful and inspiring contributions to the present debate, because of NPOs' dual nature (both financial and social; Bagnoli and Megali, 2011, Manetti, 2014; Nicholls, 2009). NPOs always have struggled with financial metrics (Rehuel et al., 2014; Torres and Pina, 2003) that were only able to partially represent their value to and impact on society. In this sense, I think that the overall rethinking of the conventional accounting framework and its related measurement systems extends beyond meeting the individual SDGs' expectations; indeed, the adoption of the SDG framework provides opportunities and drives the need for research into new measurement systems – systems able to encompass economic, financial and social dimensions. In so doing, they may refocus the overall accounting and finance system while becoming more impactful.

Concluding thoughts

This chapter has addressed the topic of measuring, accounting, reporting and evaluating impact, with a focus on the non-profit sector. This chapter started by discussing the limitations of conventional accounting frameworks when applied to NPOs (Andreaus and Costa, 2014; Rehuel et al., 2014; Torres and Pina, 2003) before exploring the increasing pressures NPOs face in terms of funding, particularly after the global financial crisis (Best and Harji, 2013; GECES, 2014). Within this context, I briefly presented the debate around social impact measurement with its different approaches and measurements. The chapter has also addressed the notion of impact, the ToC and impact measurement. In these concluding remarks, I would like to elucidate on my personal viewpoints regarding social impact measurement before recapping possible avenues for future research.

First, in terms of the notion of social impact, I believe that more emphasis should be placed on outcomes without obsessing over measuring impact when and where it is not possible. In this sense, I would like to echo Ebrahim and Rangan (2010) who argued that 'measuring impact makes sense under a severely limited set of circumstances' (Ebrahim and Rangan, 2010, p. 29). Outside this realm, it makes sense to measure outcomes and outputs – or, sometimes, inputs and activities. Ebrahim and Rangan (2010) indeed clearly refer to the 'control of variables' for measuring impact (please see their example on the American Red Cross), and they explain that organizations sometimes have no access to data and no access to the desired impact. Therefore, organizations can measure the *outcome*. I would place more emphasis on this position by reinforcing Ebrahim and Rangan's (2010) thinking and by supporting the idea of adopting outcome measurements more, when needed. Combined with financial performance measurements, outcome measurements allow organizations to take a more informed view of their performance while better understanding how NPOs affect the communities that they serve (Epstein and McFarlan, 2011).

Second, by presenting different methods and methodologies in social impact measurement, the chapter has adopted Bengo et al.'s (2016) classifications in order to discuss diverse possibilities and approaches to social impact measurement. Among the different possibilities, I would like to reinforce the idea of a multi-stakeholder approach that does not offer a 'one-size-fits-all' approach'. Indeed, as Kolodinsky et al. (2006) highlight, output can be countable from the NPO's perspective, while impact refers to the user's perspective. As already pointed out in the second section, I believe that, while input–activity–output could be measured internally by the NPOs, it is necessary to adopt an external multi-stakeholder perspective in order to measure the outcome–impact view. In other words, I support the idea that organizations cannot measure their own activities and the output; rather, measures must start from NPOs' various stakeholders, thus allowing participation and consultation at different levels. This measure would include many NPO actors and enable multiple and idiosyncratic impact measures.

Third, because accountability and social impact measurement involves ensuring that the various informative needs of stakeholders are met, the NPO's accountability framework should explicitly consider its mission as a category (Costa et al., 2014; Williams and Taylor, 2012). I am personally in favour of focusing on the mission and mission-based activities as the 'core' of the NPO's impact measurement in order to reinforce lateral and downward accountability (Najam, 1996). Mission-based activities should be internally oriented rather than focused on upward accountability and external scrutiny.

The chapter also opened three avenues of research that require further investigation. These areas of research relate to the standardization and comparability of social impact measurement and the possibility of adopting standardized and replicable metrics for all NPOs across Europe (Clark et al., 2004; Maas and Liket, 2011b). Another area of future research rests in the multi-stakeholder perspective in social impact measurement as well as the need to better develop complex and inclusive metrics that can respond to different needs (Bengo et al., 2016; Costa and Pesci, 2016). Finally, a new frontier of research emerging today is the contribution of social impact to NPOs and NGOs in the SDGs context (Bebbington and Unerman, 2018; OECD, 2019).

References

Andreaus, M. and Costa E. (2014). Toward an integrated accountability model for non-profit organizations'. In E. Costa, L. Parker and M. Andreaus (eds), *Accountability and Social Accounting for Social and Non-profit Organizations (Advances in Public interest Accounting)* (pp. 153–76). Bingley, UK: Emerald Group Publishing.

Arena, M., Azzone, G. and Bengo, I. (2015). Performance measurement for social enterprises. *VOLUNTAS: International Journal of Voluntary and Nonprofit Organizations,* 26(2), 649–72.

Arvidson, M., Lyon, F., McKay, S. and Moro, D. (2013). Valuing the social? The nature and controversies of measuring social return on investment (SROI). *Voluntary Sector Review,* 4(1), 3–18.

Bagnoli, L. and Megali, C. (2011). Measuring performance in social enterprises. *Nonprofit and Voluntary Sector Quarterly,* 40(1), 149–65.

Bassi, A. (2011). *Il valore aggiunto sociale del terzo settore: verso un sistema di indicatori per la misurazione della performance delle imprese sociali.* Milan: QuiEdit.

Bebbington J., Russell, S. and Thomson I. (2017). Accounting and sustainable development: reflections and propositions. *Critical Perspectives on Accounting,* 48(C), 21–34.

Bebbington, J. and Unerman, U. (2018). Achieving the United Nations Sustainable Development Goals: an enabling role for accounting research. *Accounting, Auditing & Accountability Journal,* 31(1), 2–24.

Bengo, I., Arena, M., Azzone, G. and Calderini, M. (2016). Indicators and metrics for social business: a review of current approaches. *Journal of Social Entrepreneurship,* 1(2), 1–24.

Best, H. and Harji, K. (2013). *Social Impact Measurement Use Among Canadian Impact Investors*. Human Resources and Skills Development Canada and Purpose Capital.

Bull, M. (2007). Balance: the development of a social enterprise business performance analysis tool. *Social Enterprise Journal*, 3(1), 49–66.

Christensen, R.A. and Ebrahim, A. (2006). How does accountability affect mission? *Nonprofit Management and Leadership*, 17(2), 195–209.

Clark, C., Rosenzweig, W., Long, D. and Olsen, S. (2004). Double bottom line project report: assessing social impact in double bottom line ventures. *Working Paper Series 13*. Center for Responsible Business, University of California Berkeley.

Costa, E., Parker, L. and Andreaus, M. (2014). The rise of social and non-profit organizations and their relevance for social accounting studies. In E. Costa, L. Parker and M. Andreaus (eds), *Accountability and Social Accounting for Social and Non-profit Organizations (Advances in Public Interest Accounting)* (pp. 3–21). Bingley, UK: Emerald Group Publishing,

Costa, E. and Pesci, C. (2016). Social impact measurement: why do stakeholders matter? *Sustainability Accounting, Management and Policy Journal*, 7(1), 99–124.

Davies, R. (2018). Representing theories of change: a technical challenge with evaluation consequences. *CEDIL Inception Paper, 15*. Centre of Excellence for Development Impact and Learning. Accessed May 2020 at https://cedilprogramme.org/wp-content/uploads/2018/11/Inception-Paper-No-15-Rick-Davies-Representing-theories-of-change.pdf.

Defourny, J. and Nyssens, M. (2010). Conceptions of social enterprise and social entrepreneurship in Europe and the United States: convergences and divergences. *Journal of Social Entrepreneurship*, 1(1), 32–53.

Development Trusts Association (DTA) (2008). *Fit for Purpose: The Development Trusts Association Healthcheck for Community Enterprise Organisations*. Accessed January 2021 at https://www.nefconsulting.com/wp-content/uploads/2017/05/dta-Fit-for-Purpose.pdf.

Dillenburg, S., Greene, T. and Erekson, H. (2003). Approaching socially responsible investment with a comprehensive ratings scheme: total social impact. *Journal of Business Ethics*, 43(3), 167–77.

Ebrahim, A. (2005). Accountability myopia: losing sight of organizational learning. *Nonprofit and Voluntary Sector Quarterly*, 34(1), 56–87.

Ebrahim, A. (2009). Placing the normative logics of accountability in 'thick' perspective. *American Behavioral Scientist*, 52(6), 885–904.

Ebrahim, A. (2010). The many faces of nonprofit accountability. *Harvard Business School Working Paper, 10–069*.

Ebrahim, A. and Rangan, V.K. (2010). The limits of nonprofit impact: a contingency framework for measuring social performance. *Harvard Business School Working Paper, 10–099*, pp. 1–53.

Ebrahim, A. and Rangan, V.K. (2014). What impact? A framework for measuring the scale and scope of social performance. *California Management Review*, 56(3), 118–41.

Emerson, J. (2003). The blended value proposition: integrating social and financial returns. *California Management Review*, 45(4), 35–51.

Emerson, J., Wachowicz, J. and Chun, S. (2000). *Social Return on Investment: Exploring Aspects of Value Creation in the Nonprofit Sector*. The Roberts Foundation.

Epstein, M.J. and McFarlan F.W. (2011). Measuring the efficiency and effectiveness of a nonprofit's performance. *Strategic Finance*, 93(4), 27–34.

European Commission (2014). *Social Innovation: A Decade of Changes*. Luxembourg: European Commission. Accessed May 2020 at https://espas.secure.europarl.europa.eu/orbis/document/social-innovation-decade-changes.

Global Social Venture Competition (2017). Social impact assessment guidelines. Accessed January 2021 at http://gsvc.crearevalore.com/wp-content/uploads/2013/10/GSVC2017SocialImpactAssessmentGuidelines_PT.pdf.

Grabenwarter, U. and Liechtenstein, H. (2011), In search of gamma – an unconventional perspective on impact investing. *IESE Business School Working Paper*. University of Navarra.

Gray, R. (2002). The social accounting project and *Accounting, Organizations and Society*: privileging engagement, imaginings, new accountings and pragmatism over critique? *Accounting, Organizations and Society*, 27(7), 687–708.

Gray, R., Adams, C. and Owen, D. (1996). *Accounting and Accountability: Changes and Challenges in Corporate Social and Environmental Reporting*. Upper Saddle River, NJ: Prentice Hall.

Gray, R., Bebbington, J. and Collison, D. (2006). NGOs, civil society and accountability. making the people accountable to capital. *Accounting, Auditing and Accountability Journal*, 19(3), 319–48.

Gray, R., Dillard, J. and Spence, C. (2011). A brief re-evaluation of 'the social accounting project'. In A. Ball and S.P. Osborne (eds), *Social Accounting and Public Management: Accountability for the Common Good* (pp. 12–22). New York: Routledge.

Grieco, C., Michelini, L. and Iasevoli, G. (2015). Measuring value creation in social enterprises: a cluster analysis of social impact assessment models. *Nonprofit and Voluntary Sector Quarterly*, 44(6), 1173–93.

Groupe d'Experts de la Commission sur l'Entrepreuriat Social [GECES] Sub-group on Impact Measurement (2014). *Proposed Approaches to Social Impact Measurement in European Commission Legislation and in Practice Relating to EuSEFs and the EaSI*. Accessed January 2021 at https://op.europa.eu/en/publication-detail/-/publication/0c0b5d38-4ac8-43d1-a7af-32f7b6fcf1cc.

Hornsby, A. (2012). *The Good Analyst, Impact Measurement & Analysis in the Social-Purpose Universe*. London: Investing for Good.

James, C. (2011). *Theory of Change Review. A Report Commissioned by Comic Relief*. Accessed May 2020 at https://www.dmeforpeace.org/wp-content/uploads/2017/06/James_ToC.pdf.

Kaplan, R.S. and Norton, D.P. (2001). Transforming the balanced scorecard from performance measurement to strategic management. Part II. *Accounting Horizons*, 15(2), 147–60.

Kolodinsky, J., Stewart, C. and Bullard, A. (2006). Measuring economic and social impacts of membership in a community development financial institution. *Journal of Family and Economic Issues*, 27(1), 27–47.

Maas, K. and Liket, K. (2011a). Talk the walk: measuring the impact of strategic philanthropy. *Journal of Business Ethics*, 100(3), 445–64.

Maas, K. and Liket, K. (2011b). Social impact measurement: classification of methods. In R.L. Burritt, S. Schaltegger and M. Bennett et al. (eds), *Environmental Management Accounting and Supply Chain Management* (pp 171–202). Dordrecht: Springer.

Maddocks, J. (2011). Debate: sustainability reporting: a missing piece of the charity-reporting jigsaw. *Public Money & Management*, 31(3), 157–8.

Manetti, G. (2014). The role of blended value accounting in the evaluation of socio-economic impact of social enterprises. *VOLUNTAS: International Journal of Voluntary and Nonprofit Organizations*, 25, 443–64.

McLoughlin, J., Kaminski, J. and Sodagar, B. et al. (2009). A strategic approach to social impact measurement of social enterprises: the SIMPLE methodology. *Social Enterprise Journal*, 5(2), 154–78.

Meadows, M. and Pike, M. (2010). Performance management for social enterprises. *Systemic Practice and Action Research*, 23(2), 127–41.

Moore, M.H. (2000). Managing for value: organizational strategy in for-profit, non-profit and governmental organizations. *Nonprofit and Voluntary Sector Quarterly*, 29, 183–208.

Moore, M.H. (2003). The public value scorecard: a rejoinder and an alternative to strategic performance measurement and management in non-profit organizations. *Hauser Center for Nonprofit Organizations Working Paper, 18*.

Najam, A. (1996). NGO accountability: a conceptual framework. *Development Policy Review*, 46, 339–53.

Nicholls, A. (2009). 'We do good things, don't we?': 'blended value accounting' in social entrepreneurship. *Accounting, Organizations and Society*, 34, 755–69.

Nicholls, A. (2018). A general theory of social impact accounting: materiality, uncertainty and empowerment. *Journal of Social Entrepreneurship*, 9(2), 132–53.

Nicholls, A., Nicholls, J. and Paton, R. (2015). Measuring social impact. In A. Nicholls, R. Paton and J. Emerson (eds), *Social Finance* (pp. 253–81). Oxford: Oxford University Press.

O'Donohue, N., Leijonhufvud, C. and Saltuk, Y. et al. (2010). *Impact Investments: An Emerging Asset Class*. New York: J.P. Morgan Global Research.

Organisation for Economic Co-operation and Development (OECD) (2019). *Social Impact Investment 2019: The Impact Imperative for Sustainable Development*. Paris: OECD Publishing.

Rawhouser, H., Cummings, M. and Newbert, S.L. (2019). Social impact measurement: current approaches and future directions for social entrepreneurship research. *Entrepreneurship Theory and Practice*, 43(1), 82–115.

Reheul, A.M., Caneghem, T. and Verbruggen, S. (2014). Financial reporting lags in the non-profit sector: an empirical analysis. *VOLUNTAS: International Journal of Voluntary and Nonprofit Organizations*, 25, 352–77.

Roberts, J. and Scapens, R. (1985). Accounting systems and systems of accountability – understanding accounting practices in their organizational context. *Accounting Organizations and Society*, 10(4), 443–56.

Sacks, J. (2002). *The Money Trail: Measuring Your Impact on the Local Economy Using LM3*. London: New Economics Foundation.

Sadownik, B. (2013). The demonstrating value initiative: social accounting for social enterprise. In L. Mook (ed.), *Accounting for Social Value* (pp. 139–66). Toronto: University of Toronto Press.

Santos, F.M. (2012). A positive theory of social entrepreneurship. *Journal of Business Ethics*, 111(3), 335–51.

Simmons, J. (2003). Balancing performance, accountability and equity in stakeholder relationships: towards more socially responsible HR practice. *Corporate Social Responsibility and Environmental Management*, 10(3), 129–40.

Somers, A.B. (2005). Shaping the balanced scorecard for use in UK social enterprises. *Social Enterprise Journal*, 1(1), 43–57.

Taplin, D.H. and Clark, H. (2012). Theory of change basics: a primer on theory of change. ActKnowledge Inc. Accessed May 2020 at https://www.theoryofchange.org/wp-content/uploads/toco_library/pdf/ToCBasics.pdf.

Taplin, D.H., Clark, H., Collins, E. and Colby, D.C. (2013). Theory of change, technical papers. ActKnowledge Inc. Accessed May 2020 at http://www.theoryofchange.org/wp-content/uploads/toco_library/pdf/ToC-Tech-Papers.pdf.

Thornley, B. and Dailey, C. (2010). Building scale in community impact investing through nonfinancial performance measurement. *Community Development Investment Review*. Federal Reserve Bank of San Francisco. Accessed May 2020 at https://www.pacificcommunityventures.org/wp-content/uploads/sites/6/2015/07/Thornley_Dailey.pdf.

Torres, L. and Pina, V. (2003). Accounting for accountability and management in NPOs: a comparative study of four countries: Canada, the United Kingdom, the USA and Spain. *Financial Accountability & Management*, 19(3), 265–85.

Unerman, J. and O'Dwyer, B. (2006). Theorising accountability for NGO advocacy. *Accounting, Auditing & Accountability Journal*, 19(3), 349–76.

United Nations (2016). *The Sustainable Development Goals Report 2016*. Accessed January 2021 at https://unstats.un.org/sdgs/report/2016/The%20Sustainable%20Development%20Goals%20Report%202016.pdf.

Vermeer, T., Raghunandan, K. and Forgione, D. (2009). Audit fees at US non-profit organizations. *Auditing: A Journal of Practice & Theory*, 28(2), 289–303.

Weiss, C.H. (1995). Nothing as practical as good theory: exploring theory-based evaluation for comprehensive community initiatives for children and families. In J.P. Connell, A.C. Kubisch, L.B. Schorr and C.H. Weiss (eds), *Approaches to Evaluating Community Initiatives: Concepts, Methods, and Contents* (pp. 65–92). Washington, DC: Aspen Institute.

Williams, A.P. and Taylor, J.A. (2013). Resolving accountability ambiguity in non-profit organizations. *VOLUNTAS: International Journal of Voluntary and Nonprofit Organizations*, 24, 559–80.

Yang, C.L., Huang, R.H. and Lee, Y.C. (2014). Building a performance assessment model for social enterprises – views on social value creation. *Science Journal of Business and Management*, 2(1), 1–9.

7. At the intersection of financial and non-financial accounting impact measurements

Caterina Pesci and Andrea Girardi

Accounting for recording financial impacts

Accounting normative approach

Accounting can be defined in different ways, but, despite the possible nuances of its potential definitions, it has been established that accounting is a science whose system of measurement could, ideally, be built in several ways (Alexander and Nobes, 1994; Frank, 1979; Schipper and Trombetta, 2010).

Examining accounting from a normative point of view, scholars have discussed several important issues – for example, how to define the building blocks of a proper measurement system for recording organizational facts by using different sets of evaluation metrics (Mattessich, 1995). In this vein, Mattessich (2002) distinguished between normative and conditional-normative accounting approaches, considering the latter as able to synthesize the opposing views of the more orthodox normative approach and the positive stance.

Despite the opposition between the normative and the positive stances (Ball and Brown, 1968; Kaplan and Ruland, 1991; Milne, 2002; Watts and Zimmerman, 1978, 1990), accounting has developed over time both as a normative and as a positive science, depending on the cognitive needs that scholars aim to address. In particular, the normative foundations of accounting determine its features as a measurement system and should not be considered an outdated topic, given its importance in influencing the results on which all theoretical discussions are based (Tinker, Merino and Neimark, 1982).

In this regard, referring to the normative foundation of accounting, Riahi-Belkaoui (2004, p. ix) stated: 'A single generally accepted accounting theory does not exist. Several attempts have been made to formulate such a theory...the various attempts have resulted in different frameworks for financial reporting standards'. This highlights how the normative approach is not a unified block; rather, it is a nuanced set of different approaches. The differentiation among possible accounting approaches comes from the fact that accounting develops 'in response to perceived needs adapting to meet changes in the demands made on it' (Alexander and Nobes, 1994, p. 4). In addition, accounting depends on the value theory adopted, so that 'while value theory has traditionally provided the logics for exchange relations, accounting has provided the system for measuring and reporting reciprocity and exchange' (Tinker et al., 1982, p. 174).

Accounting normative foundations: the role of GAAP

Currently, recognized normative foundations of accounting have been established through the so-called generally accepted accounting principles (GAAP), including, for example, the International Financial Accounting Standards (IFRS) issued by the International Accounting Standards Board (IASB), and the US GAAP, issued by the Financial Accounting Standards Board (FASB).

In the normative perspective of the standard setters, accounting faces two key issues: (1) what is the objective of the accounting measurements (Bryer, 1993); and (2) what are the key assumptions (axioms or postulates) needed to achieve the measurement's aim (Moonitz, 1961; Sprouse and Moonitz, 1962)?

The normative foundation of accounting can be based on GAAP: after having clearly defined the measurement's objective (i.e., providing information on big companies to help investors to take financial decisions versus providing information on small enterprises to protect external stakeholders), a measurement system must be set that is endowed with proper axioms/postulates. The objective of the accounting system is the key differentiator and guides the formulation of proper accounting postulates. Some key accounting issues that must be covered by these postulates include the definition of the accounting boundaries; the definition of accounting general principles guiding the records; the definition of records typologies; the definition of the unit of measurement; and the definition of evaluation criteria. The accounting postulates are true axioms on which the whole theorem that we tend to call 'accounting' stands. By changing the axioms, the system, as the result of a theorem, deeply changes (Haller, Ernstberger and Froschhammer, 2009; Tsalavoutas, André and Evans, 2012).

The conceptual framework as the main normative foundation of GAAP

One useful exercise for understanding how accounting develops, after having defined its objectives and postulated its basic definitions, can be to deepen the content of the conceptual framework issued by the IASB (Abela et al., 2014; Whittington, 2008). A conceptual accounting framework aims to provide the basic definitions (general aim and postulates) that define the normative foundation of accounting (Peasnell, 1982). In other words, the conceptual framework contains the backbone of the type of accounting defined by the IASB and defines what should fall under that normative approach. The IASB's conceptual framework, however, has been the object of a project to converge the US GAAP and the IASB's GAAP as part of the EU project of accounting harmonization that began in 2005 (Whittington, 2005); for these reasons, it has been chosen as a significant example of accounting's normative foundation (Jones and Wolnizer, 2003).

The content of the renewed IASB's framework covers the following topics, which are considered general principles (IASB, 2018):

1. Definition of the objective of general purpose financial reporting.
2. Definition of the qualitative characteristics of useful financial information.
3. A description of the reporting entity and its boundary.
4. Definitions of an asset, a liability, equity, income and expenses, and guidance supporting these definitions.
5. Criteria for including assets and liabilities in financial statements (recognition) and guidance on when to remove them (derecognition).
6. Measurement bases and guidance on when to use them.
7. Concepts and guidance on presentation and disclosure.
8. Concepts relating to capital and capital maintenance.

Point 1 defines the IASB's accounting objective, which is 'to provide financial information about the reporting entity which is useful to existing and potential investors, lenders and other creditors in making decisions related to providing resources to the entity' (IASB, 2018, p. 46). Through this definition, the IASB identifies the scope of its system of measurement, which is devoted to providing information for decision-making purposes to certain types of stakeholders who have a direct monetary interest in the entity's business.

Thus, the IASB's financial accounting model has at its core the exigency of satisfying the informational needs of investors and other lenders, and this specific objective should guide all the postulates on which IASB's accounting type is based because they must be coherent with this finalism. In considering the IASB's objective, however, it is important to understand that its specificity also determines its main limitation: this type of accounting is developed for stakeholders who have a monetary interest in the entity's existence, while all the other stakeholders should complement information with other sources.

Point 2 defines the general qualitative characteristics of useful financial information and specific related principles. These characteristics are explained in detail. The fundamental characteristics are relevance and faithful representation. In addition, the enhancing qualitative characteristics are comparability, verifiability, timeliness, understandability and cost constraints. Materiality is intended as an aspect of relevance, while prudence is considered as a support to neutrality.

These qualitative characteristics act as general pillars in support of the main issues of the financial statements and their core elements, which are the objects of points 3 and 4. Point 3 defines the main financial statements – that is, the statement of financial position and the statement of financial performances (the former a statement of comprehensive income) – in terms of objective and meaning. The connection between points 3 and 4 is immediate because it is explicated that the objective of financial statements is to provide information on the elements composing them: assets, liabilities, equity, income and expenses. Point 4 establishes what to record and what must be excluded by the IASB's GAAP records. The definitions of assets and liabilities are the true main pillars of point 4 because, from them, the other definitions (equity, income and expenses) follow. This specific choice is one of the most influential of the axioms provided by the IASB's framework and determines the type of entity theory on which all the IASB's accounting is founded (Van Mourik, 2014).

The definition of assets is detailed and normative in nature because this defines the boundaries of what must be recorded as an asset. The definition states that an asset is 'a present economic resource controlled by the entity as a result of past events. An economic resource is a right that has the potential to produce economic benefits' (IASB, 2018, p. F.4.4a). Thus, an asset has specific characteristics: first, it is controlled by the entity. The entity assets that are recordable under the IASB's GAAP are only those controlled by the entity itself. The requirement of being controlled excludes any other assets, such as common pull resources that can be used by the entity but not controlled (i.e., air, natural environment). Second, assets are rights in the legal sense of the term. Third, assets have the potential to produce economic benefits, which, under GAAP, means that they are measurable in monetary terms. Again, this definition of benefits excludes other possible benefits that are not measurable in monetary terms.

Liabilities are a mirror concept. A liability is defined as: 'a present obligation of the entity to transfer economic resources as a result of past events' (IASB, 2018, p. F.4.4b).

The definitions of point 4 are the building blocks of the IASB's recording system and act as postulates because, as explained in point 5, from them follow each possible record that can be generated by following the IASB's approach (recognition).

In addition, point 6 adds details on the measurement bases (fair value, value in use, fulfilment value and current cost). This point establishes how to measure, which is the basis for computing accounting values that need to be recorded. This is another key issue that creates substantial differences in the results of accounting measurement systems. Point 7 adds details on the presentation of the values in the statement. Finally, point 8 discusses the concept of capital maintenance. In the IASB framework, this is intended to encompass financial terms defining a notion of value based on this type of capital (Tinker et al., 1982), and it is connected with the double-entry system of record-keeping. The double-entry system constitutes the logic of records and establishes the connection among the postulates of GAAP.

The IASB's conceptual framework is an example of one articulate normative approach to accounting that sets the foundation of such an accounting type. All accounting principles are developed in compliance with the general postulates/axioms that constitute the philosophy of measurement adopted by the IASB's framework.

In sum, the IASB's GAAP has been developed by adopting one normative accounting approach finalized to show enterprises' financial impacts to investors and other lenders, and the resulting numbers should be considered able to satisfy specific informational needs and support investors' choices.

What impacts remain outside of GAAP's boundaries?

The normative foundation of financial accounting based on GAAP, however, is able to track only transactions that show monetary outputs, while all non-financial impacts are excluded by this approach. Likewise, any non-controlled assets are not recorded. However, it is easy to imagine how strong the impact of entities on the environment and society can be (i.e., pollution emissions or employment policies), even when those impacts do not show a direct monetary effect and even if they cannot be defined as controlled by law for any entity.

Consequently, a number of non-financial impacts remain outside the boundaries of measurement systems produced by the existing financial accounting systems. Due to the evident inability of such financial accounting to address the informative needs of stakeholders interested in understanding impacts outside of the monetary sphere, non-financial reporting has been developed.

Non-financial accounting has been developed in an attempt to track all the effects of the existence of enterprises on society and the environment, often referred to as the 'social accounting project' (Gray, 2002; Lamberton, 2005). Social accounting scholars have defined social accounting as the 'universe of all possible accountings' (Gray, 2002, p. 692). In this realm, the notions of sustainable costs (Gray, 1994) and full cost accounting have been developed (Mathews, 1994) in an attempt to enlarge the notion of capital maintenance to natural rather than merely financial capital (Gray, 1992; Lamberton, 2005).

Studies have flourished on how to develop non-financial reporting to increase information to account for other typologies of impacts and to account for stakeholders other than investors (Bebbington, Unerman and O'Dwyer, 2014; KPMG, 2011; Moneva, Archel and Correa, 2006). The result is a constellation of approaches to non-financial accounting that have been investigated under both the normative and positive accounting tradition (De Villiers and Van Staden, 2011; Hřebíček et al., 2015).

To shed light on the usefulness and limitations of this vast constellation of approaches is not an easy task. The following sections describe some authoritative normative approaches to non-financial impacts and related issues in order to outline the need for further investigations regarding non-financial impact measurements and their connection with financial ones.

The Global Reporting Initiative guidelines approach

The Global Reporting Initiative (GRI) provides guidelines for defining the principles, content, quality and boundaries of sustainability reports (Raine and Ulrich, 2009). The GRI guidelines cover the three pillars that are the foundation of the concept of sustainability: social, economic and environmental.

The boundaries of sustainability reports represent an important and highly debated issue among scholars and practitioners because the process of boundaries assessment establishes which information should be included in the reports and which should be left out (Pesci and Andrei, 2011). Such an issue becomes particularly important when the impacts to be tracked do not refer merely to financial impacts generated by assets on which entities exercise control but are extended to society and the natural environment (Antonini and Larrinaga, 2017; Archel, Fernández and Larrinaga, 2008).

The mission of the GRI helps in understanding its ambition of satisfying a number of informational needs: 'to empower decisions that create social, environmental and economic benefits for everyone' (GRI, 2020). This mission is translated into four focus areas for the future: (1) creating standards to advance sustainable development; (2) harmonizing sustainability standards; (3) leading effective and efficient sustainability reporting; and (4) driving useful sustainability information to improve performance (ibid.).

In the GRI's guidelines, disclosure on the three sustainability pillars is based on the following indicators:

- social performance indicators that address labour conditions, quality and human rights;
- economic performance indicators that address economic impacts on employees, suppliers and customers; and
- environmental performance indicators that address waste management, environmental and health risk, biodiversity and waste management.

Notably, the latest draft of GRI guidelines is structured in two main blocks:

- universal standards (GRI 101, 102 and 103); and
- topic-specific standards (GRI 201–206, 301–307, and 401–419).

GRI 101 is particularly worthy of attention for the purpose of this chapter because it serves as normative foundation of the GRI's non-financial accounting approach (GRI, 2016). In other words, GRI 101 acts as a conceptual framework that establishes the foundation of GRI's (2016) approach in normative terms.

The basic GRI postulates contained in GRI 101 are stakeholder inclusiveness, sustainability, context, materiality, completeness, accuracy, balance, clarity, comparability, reliability and timeliness (ibid.). Out of these postulates, materiality, stakeholder inclusiveness and context represent the most relevant ones in the GRI's view.

Materiality assessment is an essential component of the process of sustainability reporting using GRI standards. Given the wide range of sustainability topics on which the organization could report on, materiality assists the organization in prioritizing all the possible topics in order to allow the organization to decide which ones are sufficiently important for them to be reported on (ibid.).

Stakeholder inclusiveness is considered key in the GRI reporting process line. The reasonable expectations and interests of stakeholders should be taken into account by the organization when determining the materiality of each different topic (ibid.). The complex process of gathering, understanding and balancing stakeholders' different views is crucial in 'making decisions about [the organization's] reporting' and results in ongoing learning within the organization that increases accountability to the widest range of stakeholders (ibid., p. 8). GRI's ultimate ambition is to satisfy the informational needs of a plethora of stakeholders interested in the entity's activity.

The structure of GRI clearly shows how this normative approach leads to differences in comparison to the financial GAAP approach, such as that of the IASB. The GRI is normative in the sense that it prescribes what impacts should be tracked and how, but it leaves more freedom in terms of adoption and provides less articulated definitions in relation to the basic elements that should compose the disclosure. The GRI approach is considered one of the most reliable and detailed sources of information for sustainability issues (Daub, 2007; Fuente, García-Sánchez and Lozano, 2017; KPMG, 2011; Moneva et al., 2006).

Nevertheless, GRI's approach has been criticized both for its conceptualization and for its possible inability to deliver the expected results. In particular, some authors are convinced that the structure of GRI's guidelines is not designed well enough to deliver the promised informational support. In this critical view of the reporting standard, the GRI represents a means for the camouflaging of corporate unsustainability, rather than a way to communicate the actual corporate performance on sustainability issues (Moneva et al., 2006).

Raine and Ulrich (2009) argued that the structure of sustainability reports drafted according to GRI standards results in very long documents, adding complexity in delivering information to all stakeholders (ibid.). Furthermore, the complex structure of GRI reports prevents smaller enterprises from drafting sustainability reports, leaving a relevant part of the market's sustainability assessment needs unaddressed (Brown, de Jong and Lessidrenska, 2009). Finally, according to Boiral and Henri (2017), comparability among different companies using the GRI guidelines is currently not possible, even if the structure and form of such reports are the same.

The integrated reporting approach

The integrated reporting (IR) approach can be considered another normative approach due to its ambitions to standardize reporting on the overall impacts of organizational activities. The name itself recalls the need for and the idea of integrating financial and non-financial disclosure. In this regard, it is important to achieve an understanding of the meaning of the adjective 'integrated' under this approach.

IR proposes an integration process, the result of which is a single document in which economic, social and environmental issues are reported together (Jensen and Berg, 2012). This document is intended to be a concise and complete communication about the way an organization's performance leads to value creation over time (IIRC, 2013; Lee and Yeo, 2016; Stubbs, Higgins and Milne, 2020). The IR approach's aim is described as follows: 'an integrated report benefits all stakeholders interested in an organization's ability to create value over time' (IIRC, 2013, p. 5). Nevertheless, many scholars contend that IR's principal aim is to serve investors' informative needs with a single, high-quality (in terms of information), balanced and integrated report about the overall performance of an organization (Adams, 2015; Brown and Dillard, 2014; Eccles and Krzus, 2010; IIRC, 2013; Kim, Maas and Perego, 2018).

Consistent with its normative approach, IR also contains general principles that shape its philosophy of reporting. The general guiding principles supporting this approach are strategic focus and future orientation, connectivity of information, stakeholder relationships, materiality, conciseness, reliability and completeness, consistency and comparability (IIRC, 2013).

According to the IR framework (ibid.), every organization comprises six different forms of capital and, through ordinary operations and activities, they can be enriched or depleted over time. In this sense, the drafting of an integrated report should include the estimated amounts for these six forms of capital, showing the change of each in the period of time covered by the disclosure. These six forms of capital are as follows (Adams et al., 2016; IIRC, 2013):

1. Financial capital: represents the pool of funds available to the organization for use and obtained through operations or external financing.
2. Manufactured capital: physical objects available to the organization for its activities (buildings, equipment, infrastructures, etc.).
3. Intellectual capital: the knowledge-based intangible assets of the organization – for example, intellectual property, software, patents, rights, and

so on – and 'organizational capital', represented by the tacit knowledge, culture, and so forth.

4. Human capital: people's capabilities, competencies and experience that, in alignment with an organization's governance, improve process and services.

5. Social and relationship capital: shared norms and values in order to manage stakeholder and institutions relationships.

6. Natural capital: renewable and non-renewable natural resources that support the prosperity of the organization (includes air, water, land, forests, etc.).

The normative IR approach attempts to integrate financial normative GAAP by providing stakeholders and shareholders in particular with a system of measurement for non-financial impacts that follows similar logics, with which stakeholders skilled in financial accounting are familiar (notions of capital).

In academia, the IR approach has been the object of an animated debate since its conception in 2010 (Rinaldi, Unerman and De Villiers, 2018). On the one hand, some scholars have praised the adoption of IR prescriptions and its consequences on the quality of corporate reports and organizational activities (Atkins and Maroun, 2015; Bernardi and Stark, 2018; De Villiers and Maroun, 2018; De Villiers, Venter and Hsiao, 2017; Dumay et al., 2016; Kim et al., 2018). On the other hand, many academics and professionals have pointed out potential limitations and drawbacks related to the implementation of IR guidelines (Brown and Dillard, 2014; Flower, 2015; Haji and Hossain, 2016; Humphrey, O'Dwyer and Unerman, 2017; Rinaldi et al., 2018).

Some authors criticize the IR approach for its inability to provide truly informative and transparent sustainability reports (Flower, 2015; Humphrey et al., 2017; Stubbs et al., 2020). Furthermore, Brown and Dillard (2014) believe that IR does not properly serve all stakeholders but, on the contrary, seems to be designed to address the company's economic evaluation issues for the benefit of shareholders only (ibid.).

Regulation on non-financial disclosure

In an attempt to reach a level of harmonization regarding non-financial accounting metrics, many countries have progressively introduced regulations to ensure that at least the most influential companies communicate information about both their financial and their non-financial impacts

(Baboukardos and Rimmel, 2016; Jackson et al., 2019; Mion and Adaui, 2019). The European Union (EU), for example, through the intervention of the European Commission (EC), published an innovative directive (Directive 2014/95EU) aimed at large European companies[1] to push them to develop a more comprehensive reporting system, including non-financial impacts (European Commission, n.d.; Jackson et al., 2019; European Union, 2014).

This approach, shaped by the EU regulation, is referred to as non-financial disclosure (NFD). The directive explicitly states that 'disclosure of non-financial information helps the measuring, monitoring and managing of undertakings' performance and their impact on society [with] a sufficient level of comparability to meet the needs of investors and other stakeholders as well as the need to provide consumers with easy access to information on the impact of businesses' (European Union, 2014, p. 1). Consequently, the aim of the novel EU 2014/95 regulation is 'to provide investors and other stakeholders with a more complete picture of an organization's financial and non-financial, as well as social, environmental and economic performance' (Busco, Izzo and Grana, 2019, p. 45). This objective enlarges the scope of the disclosure to stakeholders other than investors and lenders of capital, meeting the exigency of accounting for non-financial impacts.

The non-financial impacts explicitly mentioned by the regulation are connected to the following topics: environment, social and employees, respect for human rights, anti-corruption and bribery, diversity, and business model (Carini et al., 2017; European Union, 2014). For each topic, the reporting organization should provide a description of the policies (including due diligence) implemented, highlighting the outcomes; the organization's risk evaluation and management policies; and sector-specific non-financial key performance indicators.

The general principle for any foreseen information requirement is to 'comply or explain' (Carini et al., 2017; European Union, 2014). Furthermore, the EC guidelines refer to 'materiality' as a crucial concept of the directive and, consequently, 'the non-financial statement is expected to…avoid immaterial information' (European Commission, 2017).

EU Directive 2014/95 does not prescribe a specific form or structure for mandatory non-financial reports (European Union, 2014; Jackson et al., 2019), allowing companies to opt for the sustainability report structure that better serves the sector-specific features and peculiarities (Carini et al., 2017). However, EU Directive 2014/95 and the EC encourage companies to rely on already existing recognized normative frameworks. The adoption of either

GRI's Sustainability Reporting Guidelines, the UN Global Compact, the OECD Guidelines for Multinational Enterprises, or ISO 26000 is recommended.

The prescriptions of the directive on mandatory non-financial reporting seem to stand somewhere between granting full company-level discretion on the structure of the report on the one hand, and nudging companies toward the use of existent normative standards on the other. This evident ambivalence in the directive's prescriptions suggests the possibility of perpetuating the adoption of previously used frameworks and does not offer guidance in the choice of the most appropriate one.

The approach in the US to non-financial reports is different from that adopted within the EU. In the US, sustainability reports are not yet mandatory for companies; however, the Senate and the House of Representatives have released clear signals of political attention on the theme. The H.R.4329 – ESG Disclosure Simplification Act adopted in 2019 has spurred interest in this regard (Robinson et al., 2019). Notably, large public companies in the US have recently independently developed sustainability reports and, in 2018, 86 per cent of the S&P 500 companies had a sustainability reporting system, compared to only 20 per cent in 2011 (ibid.).

Beneath the evident normative direction taken by governments on mandatory non-financial reporting, the debate on its effectiveness and impacts continues among policy makers and scholars. In particular, a trade-off between government regulation and business self-regulation arises.

Self-regulation should provide more flexible, tailored and sector-specific sustainability reports that can depict the actual nature and performance of the reporting company. On the other hand, this allows companies too much freedom, and the lack of external pressure can lead to poor and self-interested practices (Jackson et al., 2019).

Some studies have investigated whether companies are positively affected by mandatory sustainability reporting policies. Jackson et al. (2019) found that firms operating in countries that require NFD tend to adopt significantly more CSR practices (ibid.). Similarly, Mion and Adaui (2019) found that mandatory NFD had a positive effect on the quality of sustainability reporting in the studied companies. On the other hand, advocates of self-regulation believe that it can offer greater flexibility over the three dimensions of sustainability (economic, social and environmental), leading to the consolidation of best practices while adjusting for the specific needs of individual companies (Dhaliwal et al., 2011, 2014; Gregory, 2000).

However, an effective middle ground between government intervention and self-regulation may exist. The research by Fox, Ward and Howard (2002) proposes a balance in the trade-off between government intervention and self-regulation, suggesting four government undertakings in order to effectively implement regulation on non-financial issues. In the authors' view, governments should be mandating (defining standards); facilitating (giving incentives); partnering with industries and businesses; and endorsing (through special awards). By following these prescriptions, governments can effectively lead businesses toward a true and informative non-financial reporting system.

Not-for-profit arena and stakeholder-driven approaches

In the not-for-profit setting where the mission is not driven by the profit-maximization paradigm, measuring financial impacts is merely a constraint because financial results do not show whether organizations are able to pursue their true mission (Ebrahim and Rangan, 2010; Nicholls, 2009). To measure the fulfilment of social aims, a plethora of alternatives is available (Arena, Azzone and Bengo, 2015; Arvidson et al., 2013; Dillenburg, Greene and Erekson, 2003; Gibbon and Dey, 2011; McLoughlin et al., 2009).

In this regard, the main issue has long been choosing the best normative alternative for shaping a meaningful accounting system capable of capturing both financial and non-financial impacts. The normative approaches available are numerous, and to orient the decision toward one single measurement system is not an easy task. In 2015, the Organisation for Economic Co-operation and Development (OECD) shifted the normative problem to a different level. Instead of promoting one single normative accounting approach, it promoted a normative path for choosing among different available options (Costa and Pesci, 2016; OECD, 2015). In other words, the proposed framework shapes the process of choosing, which is tailored to the informative needs of stakeholders. Some academic studies promote this view, due to the objective impossibility of finding a common set of impact measurements that can satisfy the numerous involved stakeholders (Groupe d'Experts de la Commission sur l'Entrepreuriat Social [GECES], 2014). This approach is underpinned by the definition of stakeholder and by the following involvement of each stakeholder's category in the process of defining and providing information (Costa and Pesci, 2016).

By being based on a process of definition and negotiation with stakeholders regarding informative needs, this normative approach shows advantages connected with the provision of specific and tailored information. However, the main negative side is the risk of producing non-comparable information, which can be connected with camouflaging the real situation due to the difficulties in establishing benchmarking (GECES, 2014). The continuous involvement of stakeholders in the process of information provision becomes a key issue potentially capable of feeding a virtuous cycle.

Issues and future trajectories at the intersection of financial and non-financial impact measurement

Following the brief overview of the topic of normative approaches to financial and non-financial accounting provided in the previous sections, the first point that should be considered worthy of attention by scholars and students is the importance of refreshing the meaning and usefulness of normative approaches in accounting (Mattessich, 2002). The normative stance of accounting measurement systems embodies the potentialities and limitations of measurement systems themselves. Bearing in mind the objective and the postulates of each system helps in achieving an understanding of the system and in imagining how to overcome the current limitations that each system shows.

Normative accounting systems based on GAAP are affected by limitations regarding the boundaries to which they refer: (1) in terms of objectives, they aim to satisfy only investors and lenders of money; (2) in terms of postulates, they are anchored to the notion of control in defining the main postulates, such as assets (Gray, 2002; Lamberton, 2005; Tinker et al., 1982).

The GRI approach overcomes the limitation of being devoted to satisfying only stakeholders who own a monetary interest in the entity's activity by enlarging the objective to satisfy the informative needs of a plethora of stakeholders. Nevertheless, the boundaries of such reporting systems are again anchored to some extent to the notion of control. In addition, the GRI guidelines have been criticized for not allowing real comparability due to the fact that they abandon the double-entry logic and tend to propose the use of indicators that can be drafted in several ways (Boiral and Henri, 2017),

The IR claims to be integrated as it offers the possibility of evaluating an entity by referring to six different notions of capital (Adams et al., 2016). This approach, however, has been criticized because of its claims to be useful to all stakeholders while the aforementioned capitals have been designed to add details to the traditional information shaped by the needs of investors (Brown and Dillard, 2014). Furthermore, this approach is affected by the same limitations as the previously mentioned approaches, which provide information on controlled assets and liabilities.

Attempts through regulation to adopt a normative approach able to account both for financial and non-financial impacts seem naive because they merely suggest or impose the adoption of one of the already existing approaches (Jackson et al., 2019).

Finally, the growing not-for profit normative tendency in guiding the disclosure of social impacts has shifted the norm to another level – that is, the level of the stakeholders' engagement. This approach can potentially satisfy stakeholders' informative needs, but leaves the potential for camouflaging the real situation (Michelon et al., 2016) and does not address the problem of comparability.

Future trajectories in the studies of how to account for non-financial impacts and how to integrate social, environmental and economic information can progress based on several considerations outlined in this chapter, including the following:

1. Revisit notions of capital and their connections with accounting and social impact measurements. The notion of capital adopted, indeed, is a key issue that cannot merely be accepted as already defined in terms of financial capital. To further investigate possible alternative notions, such as that of capital maintenance expanded to natural rather than merely financial capital, is an issue that cannot be abandoned in the realm of accounting impact measurements (Gray, 2002; Lamberton, 2005; Tinker et al., 1982).
2. Start from the main issues of reframing the objectives and postulates of existing standards and guidelines (Peasnell, 1982). Objectives and postulates of existing GAAP are taken for granted and not sufficiently discussed and problematized in the light of expanding accounting towards considering non-financial impacts. Accounting postulates should be reframed in order to include non-financial impacts and two main issues should be faced: how to measure and what to measure? These questions are worthy of further investigation.
3. Investigate the issues regarding a real integration of different perspectives (Brown and Dillard, 2014). The terms 'integration' or 'integrated' are often connected with the IR approach. There is a lack of understanding of these words and connected concepts in the direction of a true integration of financial and non-financial information. Scholars could further investigate the issue of integration by proposing new integrated approaches.
4. Investigate potentialities for proper tailored approaches that can satisfy specific informational needs (Costa and Pesci, 2016). Tailored approaches

addressed to satisfy specific informative needs are based on the standardization of processes instead of content. This normative level connected with
processes could be more fruitful for matching informative needs of stakeholders. Future research could investigate the potentialities of accounting
systems whose normative level entails the processes.

5. Investigate the balance between the exigency of comparability and the
   exigency of tailored information for satisfying particular informational
   needs (Boiral and Henri, 2017; Michelon et al., 2016; OECD, 2015).
   Comparability is an issue that cannot be overlooked. It is true that each
   organization needs to satisfy informative needs that to some extent are different, but to abandon the idea that accounting should be comparable is an
   error. Accounting needs comparisons; consequently, there is the urgency
   to understand how to balance the exigency of comparability and the fact
   that organizations needs to track peculiar non financial impacts.

6. Add to the debate on the notions concerning the boundaries of financial
   and non-financial reporting (Antonini and Larrinaga, 2017). The debate
   around how and where to track the boundaries of non-financial impacts is
   far from arriving at a conclusion. Scholars could study practical and theoretical approaches for understanding how and where to track the boundaries of non-financial impacts without excluding relevant issues, while also
   allowing them to find a proper measurement of such impacts.

7. Highlight the role of positive and normative theories in accounting by
   recognizing the inevitable normative feature of the discipline (Mattessich,
   2002). Debates regarding the nature of accounting should not be abandoned
   by scholars. In particular, the structures of normative approaches need to
   be constantly investigated and debated. In the arena of non-financial
   impact measurements, a proactive attitude toward developing effective
   normative approaches should guide scholars in future.

8. Investigate the notion of negotiation among stakeholders as substitution
   for or in support of the notion of inclusiveness. The GRI's principle of
   inclusiveness needs to be complemented with further notions such as negotiation. Scholars could study complementary or substitute principles that
   can be used in practice by organizations in implementing non-financial
   impact measurements.

9. Direct the existing criticism toward non-financial impact measurements
   toward more practical and affordable solutions. Scholars need to investigate how to arrive at more practical and affordable solutions for measuring
   non-financial impacts.

10. Investigate, debate and develop the regulation on non-financial impact
    measurements. The concrete effectiveness of regulation should be the
    object of constant debate by scholars in the direction of an improvement of

the existing practices but also in the direction of improving the regulation itself. Current regulation, indeed, seems to be only an initial attempt in the direction of including non-financial impacts measurements in reporting practices.

The majority of these issues, as explained in previous paragraphs, have been already addressed to some extent, but the constellation of different proposals, positions and approaches has not helped to shed light on these debates; on the contrary, it has often obfuscated the search for better solutions to satisfy real and new informational needs.

The idea is not to arrive at a static notion of financial and non-financial impact measurements, because they depend on the informational needs of society, which, by nature, are evolving; however, continuous work to develop a better understanding of current systems and to dramatically alter the status quo is essential.

Finally, social and environmental impacts should be the object of further investigation and further reflection by scholars and students because the need to measure such impacts is directly connected with the possibility of controlling the phenomena that are connected with the survival of our planet.

Note

1. The definition of large companies, in the context of the EC, is connected with the notion of 'public interest' acquired by certain relevant companies. In particular, EU Directive 2014/95 identifies large public-interest companies as those organizations that employ more than 500 people, listed companies, insurance companies, banks and strategic companies as indicated by national authorities (European Commission, n.d.; Robinson et al., 2019). Companies with these features account for more than 6000 companies throughout Europe (European Commission, n.d.).

References

Abela, M., Barker, R. and Sommer, R. et al. (2014). Towards a new conceptual framework: presentations at the *Accounting in Europe* and European Accounting Association Financial Reporting Standards Committee symposium. *Accounting in Europe*, 11(2), 259–71.
Adams, C.A. (2015). The International Integrated Reporting Council: a call to action. *Critical Perspectives on Accounting*, 27, 23–8.

Adams, C.A., Potter, B., Singh, P.J. and York, J. (2016). Exploring the implications of integrated reporting for social investment (disclosures). *British Accounting Review*, 48(3), 283–96.

Alexander, D. and Nobes, C. (1994). *A European Introduction to Financial Accounting*. New York: Prentice Hall.

Antonini, C. and Larrinaga, C. (2017). Planetary boundaries and sustainability indicators: a survey of corporate reporting boundaries. *Sustainable Development*, 25(2), 123–37.

Archel, P., Fernández, M. and Larrinaga, C. (2008). The organizational and operational boundaries of triple bottom line reporting: a survey. *Environmental Management*, 41(1), 106–17.

Arena, M., Azzone, G. and Bengo, I. (2015). Performance measurement for social enterprises. *International Journal of Voluntary and Nonprofit Organizations*, 26(2), 649–72.

Arvidson, M., Lyon, F., McKay, S. and Moro, D. (2013), Valuing the social? The nature and controversies of measuring social return on Investment (SROI). *Voluntary Sector Review*, 4(1), 3–18.

Atkins, J. and Maroun, W. (2015). Integrated reporting in South Africa in 2012. *Meditari Accountancy Research*, 23(2), 197–221.

Baboukardos, D. and Rimmel, G. (2016). Value relevance of accounting information under an integrated reporting approach: a research note. *Journal of Accounting and Public Policy*, 35(4), 437–52.

Ball, R. and Brown, P. (1968). An empirical evaluation of accounting income numbers. *Journal of Accounting Research*, 6(2), 159–78.

Bebbington, J., Unerman, J. and O'Dwyer, B. (2014). *Sustainability Accounting and Accountability*. Abingdon: Routledge.

Bernardi, C. and Stark, A.W. (2018). Environmental, social and governance disclosure, integrated reporting, and the accuracy of analyst forecasts. *The British Accounting Review*, 50(1), 16–31.

Boiral, O. and Henri, J.F. (2017). Is sustainability performance comparable? A study of GRI reports of mining organizations. *Business and Society*, 56(2), 283–317.

Brown, H.S., de Jong, M. and Lessidrenska, T. (2009). The rise of the Global Reporting Initiative: a case of institutional entrepreneurship. *Environmental Politics*, 18(2), 182–200.

Brown, J. and Dillard, J. (2014). Integrated reporting: on the need for broadening out and opening up. *Accounting, Auditing and Accountability Journal*, 27(7), 1120–56.

Bryer, R.A. (1993). The late nineteenth-century revolution in financial reporting: accounting for the rise of investor or managerial capitalism? *Accounting, Organizations and Society*, 18(7), 649–90.

Busco, F., Izzo, M.F. and Grana, C. (2019). *Sustainable Development Goals and Integrated Reporting*. Abingdon: Routledge.

Carini, C., Rocca, L., Veneziani, M. and Teodori, C. (2017). The regulation of sustainability information – the contribution of Directive 2014/95. Preprint, https://doi.org/10.20944/preprints201707.0025.v1.

Costa, E. and Pesci, C. (2016). Social impact measurement: why do stakeholders matter? *Sustainability Accounting, Management and Policy Journal*, 7(1), 99–124.

Daub, C.H. (2007). Assessing the quality of sustainability reporting: an alternative methodological approach. *Journal of Cleaner Production*, 15(1), 75–85.

De Villiers, C. and Maroun, W. (2018). *Sustainability Accounting and Integrated Reporting*. Abingdon: Routledge.

De Villiers, C. and Van Staden, C.J. (2011). Where firms choose to disclose voluntary environmental information. *Journal of Accounting and Public Policy*, 30(6), 504–25.

De Villiers, C., Venter, E.R. and Hsiao, P.C.K. (2017). Integrated reporting: background, measurement issues, approaches and an agenda for future research. *Accounting and Finance*, 54(4), 937–59.

Dhaliwal, D.S., Li, O.Z., Tsang, A. and Yang, Y.G. (2011). Voluntary nonfinancial disclosure and the cost of equity capital: the initiation of corporate social responsibility reporting. *The Accounting Review*, 86(1), 59–100.

Dhaliwal, D., Li, O.Z., Tsang, A. and Yang, Y.G. (2014). Corporate social responsibility disclosure and the cost of equity capital: the roles of stakeholder orientation and financial transparency. *Journal of Accounting and Public Policy*, 33(4), 328–55.

Dillenburg, S., Greene, T. and Erekson, O.H. (2003). Approaching socially responsible investment with a comprehensive ratings scheme: total social impact. *Journal of Business Ethics*, 43(3), 167–77.

Dumay, J., Bernardi, C., Guthrie, J. and Demartini, P. (2016). Integrated reporting: a structured literature review. *Accounting Forum*, 40(3), 166–85.

Ebrahim, A. and Rangan, V.K. (2010). The limits of non-profit impact: a contingency framework for measuring social performance. *Harvard Business School Working Paper, No. 10-099*. Accessed 12 April 2020 at https://hbswk.hbs.edu/item/the-limits-of-nonprofit-impact-a-contingency-framework-for-measuring-social-performance.

Eccles, R.G. and Krzus, M.P. (2010). *One Report: Integrated Reporting for a Sustainable Strategy*. Hoboken, NJ: John Wiley & Sons.

European Commission (n.d.). Non-financial reporting: EU rules require large companies to publish regular reports on the social and environmental impacts of their activities. Accessed 20 February 2020 at https://ec.europa.eu/info/business-economy-euro/company-reporting-and-auditing/company-reporting/non-financial-reporting_en.

European Commission (2017). Commission guidelines on non-financial reporting. Accessed 25 March 2020 at https://ec.europa.eu/info/publications/non-financial-reporting-guidelines_en.

European Union (2014, 15 November). Directive 2014/95/EU. *Official Journal of the European Union*, L 330/1.

Flower, J. (2015). The international integrated reporting council: a story of failure. *Critical Perspectives on Accounting*, 27, 1–17.

Fox, T., Ward, H. and Howard, B. (2002). Public sector roles in strengthening corporate social responsibility: a baseline study. *The World Bank – Corporate Social Responsibility Practice, No. 34655*. Accessed 12 January 2020 at https://www.semanticscholar.org/paper/Public-sector-roles-in-strengthening-corporate-a-Fox-Ward/574c617d14a77b85a1a9f5619e07042acc7e6f03.

Frank, W.G. (1979). An empirical analysis of international accounting principles. *Journal of Accounting Research*, 17(2), 593–605.

Fuente, J.A., García-Sánchez, I.M. and Lozano, M.B. (2017). The role of the board of directors in the adoption of GRI guidelines for the disclosure of CSR information. *Journal of Cleaner Production*, 141, 737–50.

Gibbon, J. and Dey, C. (2011). Developments in social impact measurement in the third sector: scaling up or dumbing down? *Social and Environmental Accountability Journal*, 31(1), 63–72.

Global Reporting Initiative (GRI) (2016). *GRI Standards: GRI 101: Foundation 2016*. Amsterdam: GRI.

Global Reporting Initiative (GRI) (2020). About GRI. Accessed 12 February 2020 at https://www.globalreporting.org.

Gray, R.H. (1992). Accounting and environmentalism: an exploration of the challenge of gently accounting for accountability, transparency and sustainability. *Accounting, Organizations and Society*, 17(5), 399–425.

Gray, R.H. (1994). Social and environmental accounting, accountability and reporting: new wine in old skins or silk purses from sows' ears? Paper presented at the Accounting Forum Dundee, Scotland.

Gray, R.H. (2002). The social accounting project and *Accounting, Organizations and Society*: privileging engagement, imaginings, new accountings and pragmatism over critique? *Accounting, Organizations and Society*, 27(7), 687–708.

Gregory, H.J. (2000). *International Comparison of Corporate Governance Guidelines and Codes of Best Practice*. New York: Weil, Gotshal & Manges LLP.

Groupe d'Experts de la Commission sur l'Entrepreuriat Social [GECES] Sub-group on Impact Measurement (2014). *Proposed Approaches to Social Impact Measurement in European Commission Legislation and in Practice Relating to EuSEFs and the EaSI*. Accessed 20 January 2020 at https://op.europa.eu/en/publication-detail/-/publication/0c0b5d38-4ac8-43d1-a7af-32f7b6fcf1cc.

Haji, A.A. and Hossain, D.M. (2016). Exploring the implications of integrated reporting on organisational reporting practice: evidence from highly regarded integrated reporters. *Qualitative Research in Accounting and Management*, 13(4), 415–44.

Haller, A., Ernstberger, J. and Froschhammer, M. (2009). Implications of the mandatory transition from national GAAP to IFRS – empirical evidence from Germany. *Advances in Accounting*, 25(2), 226–36.

Hřebíček, J., Faldík, O., Kasem, E. and Trenz, O. (2015). Determinants of sustainability reporting in food and agriculture sectors. *Acta Universitatis Agriculturae et Silviculturae Mendelianae Brunensis*, 63(2), 539–52.

Humphrey, C., O'Dwyer, B. and Unerman, J. (2017). Re-theorizing the configuration of organizational fields: the IIRC and the pursuit of 'enlightened' corporate reporting. *Accounting and Business Research*, 47(1), 30–63.

International Accounting Standards Board (IASB) (2018). *Conceptual Framework for Financial Reporting*. Norwalk, CT: IASB.

International Integrated Reporting Council (IIRC) (2013). *The International Integrated Reporting Framework*. Accessed 10 January 2020 at https://integratedreporting.org/wp-content/uploads/2013/12/13-12-08-THE-INTERNATIONAL-IR-FRAMEWORK-2-1.pdf.

Jackson, G., Bartosch, J. and Avetisyan, E. et al. (2019). Mandatory non-financial disclosure and its influence on CSR: an international comparison. *Journal of Business Ethics*, 162(2), 323–42.

Jensen, J.C. and Berg, N. (2012). Determinants of traditional sustainability reporting versus integrated reporting: an institutionalist approach. *Business Strategy and the Environment*, 21(5), 299–316.

Jones, S. and Wolnizer, P.W. (2003). Harmonization and the conceptual framework: an international perspective. *Abacus*, 39(3), 375–87.

Kaplan, S.E. and Ruland, R.G. (1991). Positive theory, rationality and accounting regulation. *Critical Perspectives on Accounting*, 2(4), 361–74.

Kim, S., Maas, K. and Perego, P. (2018). The effect of publication, format and content of Integrated Reports on analysts' earnings forecasts. In S. Boubaker, D. Cumming and D. Kuuong Nguyen (eds), *Research Handbook of Finance and*

Sustainability (pp. 550–86). Cheltenham, UK and Northampton, MA, USA: Edward Elgar Publishing.

KPMG (2011). *International Survey of Corporate Responsibility Reporting 2011.* Accessed 19 January 2020 at https://www.eticanews.it/wp-content/uploads/2011/12/CR_Report_2011_v10.pdf.

Lamberton, G. (2005). Sustainability accounting – a brief history and conceptual framework. *Accounting Forum*, 29(1), 7–26.

Lee, K.-W. and Yeo, G.H.-H. (2016). The association between integrated reporting and firm valuation. *Review of Quantitative Finance and Accounting*, 47(4), 1221–50.

Mathews, M.R. (1994). *Socially Responsible Accounting.* London: Chapman & Hall.

Mattessich, R. (1995). Conditional-normative accounting methodology: incorporating value judgments and means–end relations of an applied science. *Accounting, Organizations and Society*, 20(4), 259–84.

Mattessich, R. (2002). *Two Hundred Years of Accounting Research.* Abingdon: Routledge.

McLoughlin, J., Kaminski, J. and Sodagar et al. (2009). A strategic approach to social impact measurement of social enterprises. *Social Enterprise Journal*, 5(2), 154–78.

Michelon, G., Pilonato, S., Ricceri, F. and Roberts, R.W. (2016). Behind camouflaging: traditional and innovative theoretical perspectives in social and environmental accounting research. *Sustainability Accounting, Management and Policy Journal*, 7(1), 1–33.

Milne, M.J. (2002). Positive accounting theory, political costs and social disclosure analyses: a critical look. *Critical Perspectives on Accounting*, 13(3), 369–95.

Mion, G. and Adaui, C.R.L. (2019). Mandatory non-financial disclosure and its consequences on the sustainability reporting quality of Italian and German companies. *Sustainability*, 11(17), 1–28.

Moneva, J.M., Archel, P. and Correa, C. (2006). GRI and the camouflaging of corporate unsustainability. *Accounting Forum*, 30(2), 121–37.

Moonitz, M. (1961). Basic postulates of accounting. *Accounting Research Study No. 01.* University of Mississippi eGrove. Accessed 12 March 2020 at https://egrove.olemiss.edu/cgi/viewcontent.cgi?article=1140&context=aicpa_guides.

Nicholls, A. (2009). 'We do good things, don't we?': 'blended value accounting' in social entrepreneurship. *Accounting, Organizations and Society*, 34(6–7), 755–69.

Organisation for Economic Co-operation and Development (OECD) (2015). Policy brief on social impact measurement for social enterprises: policies for social entrepreneurship. Accessed 14 February 2020 at https://www.euricse.eu/wp-content/uploads/2015/07/PB-SIM-Web_FINAL.pdf.

Peasnell, K.V. (1982). The function of a conceptual framework for corporate financial reporting. *Accounting and Business Research*, 12(48), 243–56.

Pesci, C. and Andrei, P. (2011). An empirical investigation into the boundary of corporate social reports and consolidated financial statements. *Social and Environmental Accountability Journal*, 31(1), 73–84.

Riahi-Belkaoui, A. (2004). *Accounting Theory.* London: Thomson.

Raine, I. and Ulrich, S. (2009). What does GRI-reporting tell us about corporate sustainability? *The TQM Journal*, 21(2), 168–81.

Rinaldi, L., Unerman, J. and De Villiers, C. (2018). Evaluating the integrated reporting journey: insights, gaps and agendas for future research. *Accounting, Auditing and Accountability Journal*, 31(5), 1294–318.

Robinson, C., Vodovoz, I., Sullivan, K. and Burns, J. (2019). #DeloitteESGnow: Sustainability disclosure goes mainstream. *Heads Up*, 26(21), 1–8.

Schipper, K. and Trombetta, M. (2010). Measurement issues in financial reporting. *European Accounting Review*, 19(3), 425–8.

Sprouse, R.T. and Moonitz, M. (1962). Tentative set of broad accounting principles for business enterprises. *Accounting Research Study No. 03.* University of Mississippi eGrove.

Stubbs, W., Higgins, C.P. and Milne, M.J. (2020). Empty vessels: integrated reporting and non-financial stakeholders. Working paper.

Tinker, A.M., Merino, B.D. and Neimark, M.D. (1982). The normative origins of positive theories: ideology and accounting thought. *Accounting, Organizations and Society*, 7(2), 167–200.

Tsalavoutas, I., André, P. and Evans, L. (2012). The transition to IFRS and the value relevance of financial statements in Greece. *The British Accounting Review*, 44(4), 262–77.

Van Mourik, C. (2014). The equity theories and the IASB conceptual framework. *Accounting in Europe*, 11(2), 219–33.

Watts, R.L. and Zimmerman, J.L. (1978). Towards a positive theory of the determination of accounting standards. *Accounting Review*, 53, 112–34.

Watts, R.L. and Zimmerman, J.L. (1990). Positive accounting theory: a ten year perspective. *Accounting Review*, 65(1), 131–56.

Whittington, G. (2005). The adoption of international accounting standards in the European Union. *European Accounting Review*, 14(1), 127–53.

Whittington, G. (2008). Harmonisation or discord? The critical role of the IASB conceptual framework review. *Journal of Accounting and Public Policy*, 27(6), 495–502.

8. The banking sector and the SDGs: interconnections and future directions[1]

Olaf Weber

Introduction

Although estimates of the amount required vary, there is no doubt that financing is needed to achieve the Sustainable Development Goals (SDGs) adopted by the United Nations in 2016. On the other hand, the SDGs might be a huge market opportunity for businesses (Elkington, 2018). This chapter will first describe the financing needs of sustainable development and the SDGs in order to achieve the goals until 2030. Second, it will contrast the SDGs with the banking industry's current sustainability approaches. Finally, it will present some policy recommendations to guarantee the financing needed to achieve the SDGs.

The Sustainable Development Goals (SDGs)

The SDGs, approved by the United Nations in 2016 (Sachs, 2012), are the successor to the Millennium Development Goals (MDGs). The MDGs mainly addressed development issues, such as poverty and hunger, education, gender equality, child mortality, maternal health and global diseases (such as HIV and malaria), while ensuring environmental sustainability. They were founded in 2000 and were more focused on individual problems than on integrating different goals. Furthermore, the MDGs missed addressing the triple bottom line and the need to stay in the safe operating space for the global environment (ibid.).

The SDGs combine major social and environmental goals to achieve sustainable development and address environmental issues much more prominently to protect the life support systems necessary for sustainable development. Furthermore, they connect sustainable development and sustainable business issues, such as responsible production and consumption, while still promoting economic growth to create decent workplaces. As Jeffrey D. Sachs (2012) described it, the SDGs focus on the triple bottom line plus good governance. Hence, the new definition of sustainable development based on the SDGs is the following: 'Development that meets the needs of the present, while safeguarding Earth's life-support system, on which the welfare of current and future generations depends' (Griggs et al., 2013, p. 305).

The primary reason for addressing environmental issues is the finding that global development might exceed global environmental limits if it is conducted without taking planetary boundaries into account. Recent publications suggest that planetary boundaries for genetic biodiversity and nitrogen flows are already crossed.

Furthermore, land-system changes and climatic change are likely to cross those boundaries (Griggs et al., 2013; Rockström et al., 2009; Steffen et al., 2015). Losing life-support systems, such as land and biodiversity, however, meant that many other goals could not be achieved or will be harder to achieve. One example is climate change. Climate change might affect the alleviation of hunger because of extreme weather events that might increase the risk of floods and droughts, which might have a negative impact on the agriculture required to provide food. Therefore, Goal 7 of the MDGs, 'Ensure environmental sustainability', has been split into four goals addressing the environment (SDG 7, 13, 14 and 15).

Finally, the SDGs address the impact of the economy on the environment through SDG 12, 'Responsible consumption and production'. The SDGs accept that the main pillars of economic growth – namely, consumption and production – must be conducted responsibly.

There is a continuing discussion whether some of the goals, such as climate action, must be achieved to enable other goals to be attainable. However, what is clear is that partnerships (SDG 17) are needed to achieve the goals. These partnerships include businesses, non-governmental organizations (NGOs) and public institutions. Furthermore, as described in more detail below, substantial financial inputs are needed to achieve the goals. A part of the necessary funding might come from non-governmental funders, such as businesses.

A recent report shows that businesses seem to address the SDGs in their corporate social responsibility strategies, mostly SDG 8, 'Decent work and economic growth'; SDG 12, 'Responsible consumption and production'; and SDG 13, 'Climate action' (PWC, 2018). Also, the financial industry mainly addresses SDG 8 and SDG 12 but focuses on SDG 4, 'Quality education', as the third main goal. In contrast, citizens want to address SDG 1, SDG 2 and SDG 4 (ibid.). Differences between businesses and the financial sector on the one side and citizens on the other might be a risk or could be an opportunity. There is a risk that businesses only address SDGs that are beneficial for their bottom line; however, it is possible that the business sector addresses goals that are less likely to be addressed by public institutions.

Financing the SDGs

Without doubt, financing will be needed to achieve the SDGs. The United Nations Conference on Trade and Development (UNCTAD, 2015) estimated an investment gap for developing countries of $2.5 trillion.[2] Overall, $5–7 trillion will be needed annually until 2030 to achieve the SDGs. The World Bank estimated that domestic governments would provide between 50 and 80 percent of the funding for the SDGs (Niculescu, 2017). Some of the biggest institutional funds, however, such as the Norwegian Sovereign Wealth Funds or the California Public Employees' Retirement System, manage assets of about US$1 trillion and the value of global financial assets is more than US$290 trillion, with a growth rate of 5 percent per year (du Toit, Shah and Wilson, 2017). Compared to these figures, the $5–7 trillion needed for the SDGs does not look that big. Financing the SDGs should be possible if there is a willingness to do so.

Traditionally, a crucial part of the funding for international development is official development assistance (ODA). However, only a few countries have achieved the UN target to use 0.7 percent of their gross national income for ODA (Lebada, 2017). According to the Organisation for Economic Co-operation and Development (OECD),[3] ODA was $142.6 billion in 2016 (Niculescu, 2017), while private sector direct foreign investment was $523.3 billion and personal remittance was $383.2 billion in 2015. These amounts, however, do not add up to the $5–7 trillion needed to address the SDGs (ibid.). Therefore, private investment might be needed to complement public assistance.

It is also important to mention that funds for, and investments in, the least developed countries (LDCs) are on the decline (Lebada, 2017). The world's 31 LDCs only received $18 billion in investment in 2016. Since the SDGs also address LDCs, this could have a major impact on achieving the SDGs. Consequently, the Financing for Development Forum encourages multilateral development banks (MDBs) and financial institutions to collaborate with private sector investment and to address investor needs. Furthermore, the forum encourages private sector efforts to align internal incentives with long-term investment goals supporting the SDGs and sustainable development (ibid.) instead of only rewarding managers for the achievement of short-term success.

Furthermore, countries must create financeable and bankable projects in food and agriculture, energy and materials, health and well being, and other sectors to attract investments in addition to funding. Maria Niculescu (2017) estimates that addressing the SDGs through investments in these fields could create 380 million jobs by 2030. Impact investment, a new form of investment that will be described below, could invest in these fields as well as conventional finance.

Finally, as described above, some of the SDGs are more attractive to private investments than others. It will be easier to find private investment for SDG 8, 'Decent work and economic growth'; SDG 12, 'Responsible consumption and production'; and SDG 13, 'Climate action', than for SDG 1, 'No poverty'; and SDG 2, 'Zero hunger'. As mentioned above, the latter three goals have been prioritized by citizens but not by businesses (PWC, 2018), while the first two goals seem to be more material for businesses.

Sustainability in the banking industry

The following sections mainly discuss the banking industry, including public and multilateral development banks. A discussion of other financial industry players with regard to the SDGs, such as insurance companies, would go beyond the scope of this chapter.

In the early 1990s, banks started to address sustainability issues, primarily by focusing on their internal operations. The goal was to decrease costs by saving energy, water and materials, such as paper, and to be a role model for clients to do the same. The aim of influencing clients has been to enable them to reduce their environmentally induced costs and, therefore, decrease their credit and investment risk (Weber and Feltmate, 2016). The next phase of banking sustainability centred on environmental risks in the credit business. Because of newly implemented environmental regulations, such as the Comprehensive Environmental Response, Compensation, and Liability Act, known also as the Superfund, in the United States, and environmental regulations addressing soil, water and air, environmental risks became material mainly in commercial lending. While before, sites that had been used as collateral could be easily sold in case of credit default, the new regulations established the 'polluter pays principle' and regulated the disclosure of contaminations in the case of a land transfer.

As a result, lenders either had to disclose the contamination of a site used as collateral or had to clean up the site before being able to sell it. In both cases, the value of the site has often been reduced significantly. The reduced value of contaminated sites and changes in environmental regulations that created financial burdens on commercial borrowers motivated banks to integrate environmental and social risk criteria into their credit risk assessment (Weber, Fenchel and Scholz, 2008). As a result, lenders were able to decrease the credit risks caused by sustainability risks (Weber, Scholz and Michalik, 2010) and to retain their reputation as a non-polluting industry.

The banking sector's next step with regard to sustainability has been to address opportunities. The increasing popularity of the topic, among others, pushed forward by the report of the World Commission on Environment and Development, *Our Common Future* (1987, also known as the Brundtland Report), which defined sustainable development, led to the development of sustainable asset management and investment products, such as socially responsible investment funds or green loans. The banking sector became aware of the opportunity to finance the change to more sustainable development instead of just focusing on risks for their lending business. In 1996, Stephan Schmidheiny and Federico J.L. Zorraquin published the prominent book *Financing Change: The Financial Community, Eco-efficiency, and Sustainable Development*. The book presented business opportunities for the financial sector, including banks, that have a positive impact on both sustainable development and the financial bottom line. At the same time, in cooperation with the United Nations, NGOs and public entities, the industry established financial sector codes of conduct focusing on sustainable development, such as the United Nations Environmental Programme Finance Initiative (UNEP FI), the Principles for Responsible Investment (PRI) and the Equator Principles for project finance. These codes of conduct presented guidelines for the financial industry to address sustainable development.

Initially, the activities described mainly addressed conventional financial products and services, and the connection between social and environmental issues on the one side and financial risks and reputation on the other. This changed after 2000. Social banking and impact investing became increasingly prominent (Weber, 2016b, 2016c). This type of banking tries to create a positive impact on sustainability issues through financial products and services (see below) based on the sustainability case of banking (Weber, 2014). For impact investors and social banks, sustainable development is not only a means to increase the business performance, but also a main strategic goal.

Development banks play a major role in financing sustainable development – for example, in climate finance (SDG 13) or in financing eco-system services (Sell et al., 2006). Bhattacharya, Oppenheim and Stern (2015) argue that development banks have an essential role to play to help move nations and regions from 'business-as-usual outcomes', to 'sustainable infrastructure outcomes'. The social and environmental guidelines of the World Bank and the International Finance Corporation (IFC) are a basis for many social and environmental risk assessment schemes, such as the Equator Principles (The Equator Principles, 2020; Weber and Acheta, 2014b). With its standards, the IFC is a de facto norm setter for environmental and social risk assessment in project finance and helped the sector to increase its sustainability performance. Consequently, the World Bank and IFC could be a trendsetter in addressing the SDGs. The Sustainable Banking Network (SBN) conducted under the IFC's umbrella, for instance, could support financial regulators in addressing sustainable finance and help these organizations to address the SDGs.[4]

Furthermore, MDBs, regional and domestic development banks, and green banks issue a major portion of green bonds and climate bonds. They started issuing these types of bonds before domestic government financial institutions and private issuers engaged in green bonds. Green bonds are fixed-income bonds issued to finance sustainability-related projects, such as renewable energy, climate mitigation and adaptation, and water.

Finally, MDBs can help domestic financial institutions to integrate sustainability into their business by making financing dependent on the implementation of social and environmental sustainability guidelines for banks. The IFC is already coordinating the development of financial sector sustainability regulations in some emerging countries, such as Nigeria and Bangladesh, and should continue to do so to support the sustainability case for the financial sector (Oyegunle and Weber, 2015). One consequence has been that, in some countries, financial sector sustainability guidelines currently exist to guide banks in assessing environmental, social and sustainability criteria in financial decision making.

In general, the SDGs explicitly address the role of the private (business) sector in achieving sustainable development (Bebbington and Unerman, 2018). Furthermore, the financial sector might be a major player with regard to achieving sustainable development, but the industry is relatively slow in adopting sustainability principles (Jones, Hillier and Comfort, 2017; Weber, Diaz and Schwegler, 2014). A recent report by the Bank of England (2018, p. 3), for instance, stated that 'many banks have some way to go to identify and measure the financial risks from climate change comprehensively'. Banks are behind in assessing sustainability risks for their business and strong efforts are needed to enable them to create positive impacts on sustainable development.

Hence, the SDGs might be an opportunity for the industry to further establish sustainability principles. According to the United Nations Global Compact and KPMG International (2015), four categories for the financial industry to address the SDGs have been identified. They are financial inclusion; financing renewable energy and sustainable infrastructure; including sustainability risk analyses in financial decision making; and influencing corporate clients to address environmental, social and governance criteria in their businesses. However, although proposals exist on how the financial industry might contribute to sustainable development, there is no coherent definition of financial sector sustainability.

What is sustainable banking?

Recently, the International Network of Financial Centres for Sustainability (FC4S, 2018) of the Group of Seven published a taxonomy on green and sustainable finance to define what sustainable finance is and how it could be assessed. This statement made it quite clear that there is as yet no common definition of sustainable finance, nor is it clear what sustainability means for the banking industry. Even the book *Sustainable Banking* (Bouma, Jeucken and Klinkers, 1999), one of the standard publications in the field, did not define sustainable finance or sustainable banking comprehensively.

Weber and Feltmate (2016) distinguish between the business case for sustainability and the sustainability case for banking. The business case for sustainability approach claims that banks only address sustainability issues, such as environmental and social risks and opportunities, if they contribute to their financial bottom line, either through increasing financial returns or decreasing costs. Jones et al. (2017) claim that this sustainability approach is the dominant one, but that it must be transformed into the sustainability case for banking to better address the SDGs. The sustainability case for banking states that banks start with the main sustainability issues – for instance, by analyzing the importance of different SDGs – and try to develop products and services that can address the issue and are financially attractive at the same time.

Due to the lack of a definition of sustainable finance and banking, different players in the banking industry have different approaches to sustainable finance. While for some institutions sustainability does not play a role at all beyond financial sustainability, others base their products and services on sustainability or consider sustainability criteria in their business decisions. Microfinance organizations, for instance, directly address SDG 1, 'No poverty', as well as SDG 8, 'Decent work and economic growth', or, in the case of microfinance institutions for women, SDG 5, 'Gender equality'.

Climate bonds, which facilitate investing in climate change mitigation and adaptation, address SDG 13, 'Climate action'. Green bonds address environmental issues, such as SDG 14, 'Life below water'; SDG 15, 'Life on land'; and SDG 7, 'Affordable and clean energy'. Some credit unions' business is to finance sustainable cities and communities (SDG 11), and many global banks address SDG 5, 'Gender equality', through their employment policies. Investors following the socially responsible investment (SRI) approach consider the environmental, social and governance criteria in investment decisions (Weber and Feltmate, 2016) and therefore address SDG 12, 'Responsible consumption and production'. Finally, impact investors invest in certain SDGs already. One example is the Bill & Melinda Gates Foundation addressing SDG 3, 'Good health and well-being'. Except for financial institutions and financial products that directly address sustainability issues, such as social banking and impact investing, the integration of sustainability issues into finance decisions is mainly driven by risk management purposes, new business opportunities or cost savings (ibid.). Often, however, sustainable products and services are offered in parallel with conventional products that might even contradict the principles of sustainable development. Also, most of the products and services are niche products and even social banks and impact investors that exclusively address sustainability issues are a very small group inside the banking industry (ibid.).

Types of banking and the SDGs

There are different types of banking as well as financial products and services that might address the SDGs, including conventional banking. These are SRI, impact investing, social banking, green and social impact bonds, development banking, project finance and green lending. Table 8.1 presents a short overview of these types of banking and how they might address sustainable development.

Table 8.1   Types of banking addressing the SDGs

Type of Banking	Addressing Sustainable Development
SRI	Using positive and negative environmental, social and governance criteria in addition to financial criteria to identify investments and risks (Chegut, Schenk and Scholtens, 2011)
Impact investing	Investments that try to create a positive environmental or social impact (Weber, 2016b)
Social impact bonds	Bonds that try to involve private investments in solving social problems (Khovrenkov and Kobayashi, 2018)
Green bonds	Public or company bonds for environmental investments, such as sustainable infrastructure, clean energy, water or ecosystem services (Saravade and Weber, 2020)
Development banks	Lending and investing in projects and other activities addressing sustainable development (Nolet et al., 2014)
Project finance	Applying the Equator Principles (social and environmental criteria as well as standardized processes and reporting) to mitigate the sustainability risks of projects (Weber, 2016a)
Sustainable credit risk assessment	Applying social and environmental risk indicators in credit risk assessment (Weber et al., 2010)
Microfinance	Financing for the poor to start a business to make their living and providing access to finance (Weber, 2014)
Green credit	Loans for commercial borrowers with businesses addressing environmental issues (Cui et al., 2018)

The following sections will describe the types of banking and how they might address the SDGs in detail.

SRI

SRI uses non-financial criteria to screen investments for social, environmental or governance reasons or to pick investments that perform well with regard to both financial and non-financial indicators (Geobey and Weber, 2013). SRI, also called responsible investing, started as a financial niche product but found entrance into mainstream investing because it improves the risk management in investment decisions through the integration of social, environmental and governance criteria (Weber, 2015). It conducts 'social' screening, community investment and shareholder advocacy (O'Rourke, 2003a) to guarantee sustainable financial returns. The main goals of SRI are to achieve attractive financial returns through investments that take long-term sustainability concerns into account (Weber, Mansfeld and Schirrmann, 2011). Furthermore, SRI strives to channel financial capital toward sustainable businesses (Buttle, 2007; Weber, 2006).

Many of the non-financial SRI criteria are taken from sustainability rating systems, such as the Dow Jones Sustainability Index or Sustainability Accounting Standards Board (SASB). These indicators help investors to address the SDGs and channel investments accordingly. Since the share of SRI has increased during the last decade, more funds will be directed into sustainability-related issues. Currently, $22.89 trillion is managed responsibly (Global Sustainable Investment Alliance, 2017). This amount exceeds the $5–7 trillion needed to achieve the SDGs, although it is not specifically aimed at the SDGs. Although not all these investments are directed to the SDGs, there is an opportunity to connect the SDGs with the SRI field in two ways. First, SRI could be directed to finance the SDGs, and second, the SDGs could provide sustainability criteria that could be used by SRI investors to analyze investments. However, the SDGs could provide socially responsible investors with investment criteria and therefore tap into the SRI resources.

In addition to directing investments, SRI also conducts shareholder engagement (O'Rourke, 2003b). Some SRI investors engage with firms they are invested in to convince them to follow a more sustainable business approach. Usually, they table motions at the companies' annual general meetings that ask for certain sustainability activities or the disclosure of sustainability-related activities. With regard to the SDGs, investors might ask companies to disclose how and whether they address the SDGs, and, in cases where they do not address them, ask them to do so.

Impact investing

Impact investing is often seen as the main source of private SDG investment (Niculescu, 2017). It intends to address social or environmental challenges while generating financial returns for investors. Its main goal is to create a positive societal impact through capital investment. The spectrum of financial returns can vary. Some impact investments achieve financial returns that are comparable to conventional investments, while others may not achieve financial returns. Impact investing had its origins in philanthropy and emerged as a result of philanthropists trying to find ways to invest their endowments to support social or environmental issues. Impact investors typically invest in equity of social enterprises or quasi-equity of charitable organizations or non-profits (Weber and Feltmate, 2016). Many of them, however, invest in international sustainable development issues, such as reducing hunger and poverty or eradicating diseases such as malaria (Weber, 2016b). In Europe, impact investing achieved $107 billion in 2016; it has a much bigger share in the United States with more than $4 trillion (Global Sustainable Investment Alliance, 2017). Since impact investment is increasing in all parts of the world, it might become a type of finance that could significantly contribute to the SDGs.

Social impact bonds

Similar to green bonds, social impact bonds (SIBs) strive to achieve a double return – financially and socially. The first SIBs were issued in the United Kingdom in 2010 to attract private investors to solve social problems. In contrast to green bonds, SIBs use a pay-per-performance approach. This means that the interest paid on the bond depends on the outcome of the project financed by the bond (Trotta et al., 2015).

Current SIBs address employment and public safety (SDG 8, SDG 11), reducing reconviction rates of former prisoners (SDG 11), education (SDG 4), health (SDG 3) and housing (SDG 11) (Mulgan et al., 2011; Trotta et al., 2015). In Canada, CA$5 million has been issued in SIBs for education (SDG 4), health (SDG 3) and for workplaces (SDG 8) (Khovrenkov and Kobayashi, 2018).

Although SIBs lost some of their momentum after a powerful start in 2010, they might be a financial product that could address the social components of the SDGs. As described above, the challenge will be to lift SIBs from a mainly regional level to an international level to address the SDGs. Furthermore, it will be crucial to find ways to assess the efficiency of the SIBs (Jackson, 2013).

Currently, it is estimated that the total value of investments in SIBs is about $210 million (Floyd, 2017).

Green bonds

Global issuance of green bonds exceeded $160 billion in 2017 and is estimated to be more than $200 billion in 2018 (Sustainable Banking Network [SBN], 2018). Green bonds address sustainability issues, such as climate change (SDG 13), water (SDG 6), clean energy (SDG 7), industry, innovation and infrastructure (SDG 9), and sustainable cities and communities (SDG 11). According to the SBN, they are an effective financial product to address climate change and the SDGs (ibid.). They enable investors, in particular institutional investors, to direct their investments toward sustainable development while maintaining comparable financial returns compared to conventional bonds. Because many institutional investors today conduct environmental, social and governance (ESG) disclosure (either on a voluntary or mandatory basis), their appetite for green investments that are in line with fiduciary duty increases. Therefore, green bonds are already a way to finance environment-related SDGs and offer an opportunity to further close the SDG financing gap, in particular in emerging countries that might issue bonds to attract private investors. Since currently guidelines for green bonds are developed to increase their transparency, the SDGs could provide an ideal basis for green bond assessments.

Development banks

Overall, MDB climate finance, addressing SDG 13, will be a significant source of all climate finance planned and needed in the future (Westphal et al., 2015). In 2015, after China pledged to infuse $3.2 billion into a developing country fund for climate change, the Asian Development Bank, the World Bank and others began pledging major funds as well. The World Bank pledged to increase climate finance to $29 billion (an increase of one-third) by 2025, and the Inter-American Development Bank pledged to make climate finance 25–30 percent of total lending by that time (Yuan and Gallagher, 2015). All these activities address SDG 13.

Furthermore, domestic development banks, such as the newly founded Canadian FinDev, the European Development Bank and others, are main contributors to development finance and consequently address the SDGs. One main issue of development finance will be to analyze financing activities that might address certain SDGs but contradict others. Financing decent work and economic growth (SDG 8), for instance, might contradict other SDGs that focus on safeguarding the environment, such as SDG 13, SDG 14 and SDG

15. Again, the SDGs could be a guideline for these banks to streamline their portfolio toward sustainable development.

Currently, it is estimated that the MDBs have outstanding loans of about $1.5 trillion (Munir and Gallagher, 2018). This amount does not include grants and contributions of domestic development banks. Therefore, the total loans given by development banks are estimated at about $2 trillion. Because these funds are allocated to development funding, it is assumed that most of it also addresses the SDGs.

Project finance

Project finance is a means of finance for big projects, such as infrastructure, energy and tourism projects. This type of finance addresses SDG 9 directly and other SDGs, such as SDG 6, SDG 7 and SDG 11, indirectly.

After NGOs and affected communities criticized some of the negative impacts of projects on communities and the environment, project financiers founded the Equator Principles in 2003 to provide guidelines for assessing the social and environmental risks of projects (Weber, 2016a). The Equator Principles guidelines are based on the IFC's Performance Standards on Environmental and Social Sustainability (IFC, 2012). The Equator Principles include principles for environmental and social assessment, stakeholder inclusion, grievance mechanisms, independent reviews and reporting guidelines (Weber and Acheta, 2014b). Although the Equator Principles are sometimes criticized for being toothless and because of their focus on risk avoidance instead of on promoting sustainable development (Wright and Rwabizambuga, 2006), they deliver a social and environmental industry standard that might at least help to avoid negative impacts of project finance on sustainable development. About 80 percent of financed projects by value follow this standard (Weber and Acheta, 2014a), representing total project finance of around $200 billion per year, extrapolated to $3 trillion for the 15 years of existence of the Equator Principles. This significant amount might contribute to achieving the SDGs. Because the Equator Principles are updated regularly, the SDGs could provide some input for a future version that also includes the assessment of the positive impacts of projects on sustainable development.

Sustainable credit risk assessment

To date, commercial lenders conduct environmental and social credit risk assessments regularly (Weber et al., 2014). Studies suggest that sustainable credit risk assessment reduces credit defaults because it analyzes risks that could be material for the borrower. If conducted seriously, sustainable credit risk assessment could lead to channelling loans to greener and more social clients, as studies on green lending in China (Cui et al., 2018), North America (Gracer, 2009; Robbins and Bisset, 1994), South America (Zeidan, Boechat and Fleury, 2015), Europe (Weber et al., 2010) and Bangladesh (Weber, Hoque and Islam, 2015) suggest.

Hence, lenders are able to integrate sustainability indicators into their credit risk assessment systems. Consequently, they might also be able to integrate criteria based on the SDGs. To incentivize them, however, the materiality of addressing the SDGs should be analyzed. If analysis could demonstrate that it makes sense to integrate the SDGs into credit risk assessments from a credit risk point of view, lenders will do so.

Microfinance

Microfinance has been a means of development finance for many decades. It has been growing at a rate of about 9 percent per year. In 2017, microfinance reached about 139 million low-income clients and had a loan portfolio of about $114 billion (Convergences, 2018). The focus of microfinance is on South Asia and South America. In general, microfinance institutions are profitable, making investments in microfinance profitable as well.

Microfinance mainly addresses SDG 8, 'Decent work and economic growth', by offering loans to start a small business. It has additional impacts, however, on SDG 5, 'Gender equality', because microfinance often addresses women who do not have access to conventional loans (Weber and Ahmad, 2014). Furthermore, microfinance addresses SDG 18, 'Reduced inequalities', through offering inclusive finance. United Nations Capital Development Fund (UNCDF) even states that inclusive finance additionally affects SDG 1, 'No poverty'; SDG 2, 'Zero hunger'; SDG 3, 'Good health and well-being'; SDG 9, 'Industry, innovation, and infrastructure'; and SDG 10, 'Reduced inequalities'.

As a profitable financial approach that has a record of a positive cost–benefit and outreach, microfinance has been able to influence sustainable development positively and to attract investors at the same time (Khanam et al., 2018). Therefore, there is a high likelihood that it will continue to contribute to financing the SDGs.

Green credit

Green credit is a form of credit that is promoted by the Chinese Green Credit Policy (China Banking Regulatory Commission, 2014; IFC, n.d.; Zhang, Yang and Bi, 2011). With this policy, the People's Bank of China promotes lending to green industries and tries to decrease lending to polluting industries. Chinese banks must disclose key performance indicators about the amount of green lending to the financial supervisor. Green lending addresses diverse environmental impacts, such as air (SDG 3) and water pollution (SDG 8, SDG 14), waste, climate change and environmentally efficient production (SDG 12). The Chinese Banking Regulator estimates that 9 percent of all loans from the major Chinese banks are green loans. This equals a total amount of about $1 trillion of green loans (Stanway, 2016).

Amount of SDG finance by different types of banking

The section above has demonstrated that a crucial amount of banking sector funding is already allocated to sustainable development. These figures, however, do not include conventional banking that might also deliver funds to the SDGs. Table 8.2 presents an estimation of the funds that different types of banking invest in sustainable development.

Although the estimation in Table 8.2 only refers to particular green or sustainable financial products and services and is a very rough estimation, it suggests that there is some funding already directed to the SDGs. Furthermore, the figures show that there is some potential to tap in for further finance, for instance, with regard to SRI. It is estimated that about $60–84 trillion is needed until 2013 to achieve the SDGs. Funding by the banking sector through specialized green and sustainable financial products seems to be able to address a crucial part of the funding needed.

Table 8.2   Potential amount of investment in sustainable development by type of banking

Type of Banking	Amount	Comment
SRI	$18 trillion	Based on Global Sustainable Investment Alliance (2017). Total SRI minus the impact investment part
Impact investing	$4.6 trillion	Based on Global Sustainable Investment Alliance (2017)
Social impact bonds	$210 million	Based on Floyd (2017)
Green bonds	$160 billion	Based on Sustainable Banking Network (2010)
Development banks	$2 trillion	Only loans of major MDBs and estimation for domestic development banks. Based on Munir and Gallagher (2018)
Project finance	$3 trillion	Projects financed by Equator Principles members. Based on Weber and Acheta (2014b)
Sustainable credit risk assessment	–	Cannot be estimated because of missing data
Microfinance	$114 billion	Based on Convergences (2018)
Green loans	$1 trillion	Only China; based on Stanway (2016)
Total	$29.084 trillion	

Controversies between the financial industry and sustainable development

As this chapter has demonstrated, there are some approaches in the banking industry that address sustainable development and the SDGs. The role of the financial sector, however, is ambivalent, as investors contribute, sometimes even at the same time, both to the causes of sustainability problems and to the solution to these problems through a variety of investment and lending practices (Wiek and Weber, 2014). The same financial institutions, for instance, might finance green energy projects addressing SDG 13, 'Climate action', and polluting coal power plants at the same time. Even MDBs are criticized for financing climate change mitigation and climate change adaptation projects at the same time as they finance coal power plants (Ghio, 2015; Yang and Cui, 2012).

In addition, indirect links between finance and the SDGs exist. The banking industry finances all industries and some of them might have negative effects on the SDGs – for instance, through offering poor job conditions (SDG 8) or through negative impacts on the environment (SDG 14, SDG 15). Through financing global processed food producers, banks might negatively contribute to SDG 14, 'Life below water', because of the increasing amount of plastic used in the food and beverage sector that has negative impacts on rivers, lakes and oceans. Risk assessment systems, such as those used in credit risk management or project finance, could be improved to address these negative impacts on sustainable development.

SDG strategies for the banking sector

Current initiatives, such as UNEP FI Positive Impact[5] or the FC4S,[6] work on concepts to better define sustainable finance and to better address the SDGs. The UNEP FI, for instance, states that the financial industry should take an integrated approach to sustainable finance instead of addressing sustainability issues individually and disconnected from other financial products and services. Also, FC4S tries to define sustainable finance to increase the transparency with regard to financial impacts on sustainable development. A better definition will help stakeholders to analyze the sustainability performance of banks and will support the management in the industry to align their business strategy with the SDGs.

Banks can explore how they can engage with sustainable development issues by channelling financial capital and creating innovative products, services and strategies based on an analysis of sustainable development needs. The SDGs are an ideal way to identify the most important sustainability needs. Banks can focus on the 17 goals instead of addressing rather opaque definitions, such as 'meeting the needs of the current generations without limiting the opportunities of future generations to meet their needs' in the Brundtland Report (WCED, 1987) which offers a comprehensive but less practical guideline for addressing sustainable development. As the UNEP FI Positive Impact Manifesto states, this includes holistic and disruptive approaches to finance the SDGs (UNEP Finance Initiative, 2016) based on a comprehensive analysis of what sustainable finance means.

A way to make this process transparent is standardized reporting. With a few exceptions, sustainability reporting to date has been decoupled from financial reporting and is based on major guidelines, such as the Global Reporting

Initiative (GRI, 2013), including a financial sector supplement (GRI, 2011). Standards such as the GRI have already started to integrate the SDGs into their reporting guidelines. Therefore, it can be expected that banks will also integrate the SDGs into their sustainability reporting. If the SDG reporting is conducted in an integrated way, it will connect impacts on the SDGs with financial figures and will be able to report about the benefits and risks of addressing the SDGs through financial products and services (Eccles, Cheng and Saltzmann, 2010) for both the banks and the SDGs.

Conclusions: a research agenda for SDG finance

The banking sector can play a crucial role in financing the SDGs. Financial institutions can help to close the financing gap and enhance their business at the same time. In addition to enhancing current strategies, products and services that already address sustainable development, the industry might start to develop additional innovative financial products to address the SDGs. Governments and regulators could support the industry through establishing risk-mitigating mechanisms and through the integration of sustainability aspects into supervisory activities.

The question remains, however, what future research is needed to support SDG finance. Five areas have been identified:

- the analysis of negative impacts of banking on the SDGs;
- understanding the net gain of banking on the SDGs;
- researching the additionality of SDG finance;
- understanding financial risk and opportunity of SDG banking for individual SDGs;
- exploring types of SDG finance products and services.

First, research is needed about the negative impacts of financial activities on the SDGs (Arnsperger, 2014). As a first step, it is necessary to know what the financial industry should avoid doing if it strives to support the SDGs. So far, most of the research in impact finance addresses positive impacts. However, research on negative impacts is needed as well.

Second, research that analyzes the net gain of financing with regard to sustainability must be conducted (Jones et al., 2017). Currently, we do not know whether, for instance, banks that also engage in social finance have an overall positive or negative societal and environmental impact. Therefore, we need research and research methods to analyze questions about net benefits and net losses.

Third, similar to research on the additionality of climate finance (Dutschke and Michaelowa, 2006), research is needed to analyze the additionality of SDG financing. There is the risk that standard financing will be labelled as SDG finance. For instance, general infrastructure finance might be labelled as SDG 9, 'Industry, innovation and infrastructure'. Though this is not negative per se, it might bias analyses about actual SDG finance compared to other types of finance.

Fourth, more research is needed to analyze financing risks and opportunities for individual SDGs (Schramade, 2017). There might be some SDGs, such as SDG 9 or SDG 7, that are attractive for financiers and others that might be less attractive from an investment perspective but need finance as well. Hence, research might contribute to identifying financing opportunities for SDGs that are not yet in the focus of investors.

Fifth, research is needed to explore which types of banking products and services can be used for SDG financing. Possible products and services are impact investing (Niculescu, 2017), SDG bonds (Tolliver, Keeley and Managi, 2019), and SDG-related loans (Chirambo, 2018). However, a better understanding about the benefits and drawbacks of the different financial products and services is needed.

To conclude, it is clear that more SDG financing by banks is needed, but that SDG financing can also be an opportunity for banks to enhance their businesses. This also offers opportunities for research as described above.

Notes

1. This chapter is based on the paper 'The financial sector and the SDGs: interconnections and future directions', published by the Centre for International Governance Innovation, Canada, copyright 2018.
2. Unless otherwise stated, all figures are in US dollars.
3. See www.oecd.org/dac/stats/beyond-oda.htm#dataviz; accessed 23 September 2020.
4. See www.ifc.org/wps/wcm/connect/topics_ext_content/ifc_external_corporate _site/sustainability-at-ifc/company-resources/sustainable-finance/sbn; accessed 23 September 2020.
5. See www.unepfi.org/positive-impact/positive-impact/; accessed 23 September 2020.
6. See www.fc4s.org; accessed 23 September 2020.

References

Arnsperger, C. (2014). On the politics of social and sustainable banking. *Global Social Policy*, 14(2), 279–81.

Bank of England (2018). *Transition in Thinking: The Impact of Climate Change on the UK Banking Sector*. London: Bank of England.

Bebbington, J. and Unerman, J. (2018). Achieving the United Nations Sustainable Development Goals: an enabling role for accounting research. *Accounting, Auditing & Accountability Journal*, 31(1), 2–24.

Bhattacharya, A., Oppenheim, J. and Stern, N. (2015). Driving sustainable development through better infrastructure: key elements of a transformation program. *Global Economy & Development Working Paper, 91*. Brookings Institution.

Bouma, J.J., Jeucken, M.H.A. and Klinkers, L. (eds) (1999). *Sustainable Banking: The Greening of Finance*. Sheffield: Greenleaf Publishing.

Buttle, M. (2007). 'I'm not in it for the money': constructing and mediating ethical reconnections in UK social banking. *Geoforum*, 38(6), 1076–88.

Chegut, A., Schenk, H. and Scholtens, B. (2011). Assessing SRI fund performance research: best practices in empirical analysis. *Sustainable Development*, 19(2), 77–9.

China Banking Regulatory Commission (2014). *Notice on Green Credit Key Performance Indicators* (No. 186). Green Finance Platform.

Chirambo, D. (2018). Towards the achievement of SDG 7 in sub-Saharan Africa: creating synergies between Power Africa, Sustainable Energy for All and climate finance in order to achieve universal energy access before 2030. *Renewable and Sustainable Energy Reviews*, 94, 600–608.

Convergences (2018). *Microfinance Barometer 2018*. Accessed 23 January 2021 at https://www.european-microfinance.org/publication/microfinance-barometer -2018.

Cui, Y., Geobey, S., Weber, O. and Lin, H. (2018). The impact of green lending on credit risk in China. *Sustainability*, 10(6), 1–16.

du Toit, H., A. Shah and Wilson, M. (2017). Ideas for action for a long-term and sustainable financial system. Paper commissioned by the Business and Sustainable Development Commission.

Dutschke, M. and Michaelowa, A. (2006). Development assistance and the CDM – how to interpret 'financial additionality'. *Environment and Development Economics*, 11(2), 235–46.

Eccles, R.G., Cheng, B. and Saltzmann, D. (eds) (2010). *The Landscape of Integrated Reporting Reflections and Next Steps*. Cambridge, MA: Harvard Business School Press.

Elkington, J. (2018). 25 years ago I coined the phrase 'triple bottom line.' Here's why it's time to rethink it. *Harvard Business Review*, June.

Floyd, D. (2017). *Social Impact Bonds: An Overview of the Global Market for Commissioners and Policymakers*. London: SocialSpider.

Geobey, S. and Weber, O. (2013). Lessons in operationalizing social finance: the case of Vancouver City Savings Credit Union. *Journal of Sustainable Finance & Investment*, 3(2), 124–37.

Ghio, N. (2015, 29 January). New report once again shows danger of MDB financing for large fossil fuel projects. *Huffington Post*. Accessed 23 September 2020 at http://www .huffingtonpost.com/nicole-ghio/new-report-once-again-sho_b_7102638.html.

Global Reporting Initiative (GRI) (2011). *Sustainability Reporting Guidelines & Financial Services Sector Supplement*. Amsterdam: GRI.

Global Reporting Initiative (GRI) (2013). *G4 Sustainability Reporting Guidelines*. Amsterdam: GRI.

Global Sustainable Investment Alliance (2017). *2016 Global Sustainable Investment Review*. Accessed 21 January 2021 at http://www.gsi-alliance.org/members-resources/trends-report-2016/.

Gracer, J.B. (2009). Buyers, creditors, and counterparties beware: managing environmental risk in U.S. bankruptcies. *Environmental Claims Journal*, 21(1), 82–7.

Griggs, D., Stafford-Smith, M. and Gaffney, O. et al. (2013). Policy: sustainable development goals for people and planet. *Nature*, 495(7441), 305–7.

International Finance Corporation (IFC) (n.d.). *Green Credit Guidelines*. Washington, DC: International Finance Corporation.

International Finance Corporation (IFC) (2012). *IFC Performance Standards on Environmental and Social Sustainability*. Washington, DC: International Finance Corporation. Accessed 23 September 2020 at http://www.ifc.org/wps/wcm/connect/topics_ext_content/ifc_external_corporate_site/ifc+sustainability/publications/publications_handbook_pps.

International Network of Financial Centres for Sustainability (FC4S) (2018). *Building Shared Language for Green and Sustainable Finance – Guiding Principles for the Development of Taxonomies*.

Jackson, E.T. (2013). Evaluating social impact bonds: questions, challenges, innovations, and possibilities in measuring outcomes in impact investing. *Community Development*, 44(5), 608–16.

Jones, P., Hillier, D. and Comfort, D. (2017). The Sustainable Development Goals and the financial services industry. *Athens Journal of Business and Economics*, 3(1), 37–50.

Khanam, D., Mohiuddin, M., Hoque, A. and Weber, O. (2018). Financing micro-entrepreneurs for poverty alleviation: a performance analysis of microfinance services offered by BRAC, ASA, and Proshika from Bangladesh. *Journal of Global Entrepreneurship Research*, 8(27), 1–17.

Khovrenkov, I. and Kobayashi, C. (2018, 19 January). Assessing social impact bonds in Canada. Johnson Shoyama Graduate School of Public Policy.

Lebada, A.M. (2017, 11 July). Where are we in financing the SDGs? International Institute for Sustainable Development. Accessed 13 December 2013 at http://sdg.iisd.org/commentary/policy-briefs/where-are-we-in-financing-the-sdgs/.

Mulgan, G., Reeder, N., Aylott, M. and Bo'sher, L. (2011). *Social Impact Investment: The Challenge and Opportunity of Social Impact Bonds*. London: The Young Foundation.

Munir, W. and Gallagher, K.P. (2018). Scaling up lending at the multi-lateral development banks: benefits and costs of expanding and optimizing MDB balance sheets. *GEGI Working Paper, 013*. Boston University Global Development Policy Center.

Niculescu, M. (2017). Impact investment to close the SDG funding gap. United Nations Development Programme. Accessed 20 January 2021 at https://www.undp.org/content/undp/en/home/blog/2017/7/13/What-kind-of-blender-do-we-need-to-finance-the-SDGs-.html.

Nolet, G., Vosmer, W., de Bruijn, M. and Braly-Cartillier, I. (2014). *Managing Environmental and Social Risks: A Roadmap for National Development Banks in Latin America and the Caribbean*. Inter-American Development Bank. Accessed 23 September 2020 at http://publications.iadb.org/bitstream/handle/11319/6437/

CMF%20MON%20Managing%20Environmental%20and%20Social%20Risks.pdf ?sequence=1.

O'Rourke, A. (2003a). The message and methods of ethical investment. *Journal of Cleaner Production*, 11(6), 683–93.

O'Rourke, A. (2003b). A new politics of engagement: shareholder activism for corporate social responsibility. *Business Strategy and the Environment*, 12(4), 227–39.

Oyegunle, A. and Weber, O. (2015). Development of sustainability and green banking regulations: existing codes and practices. *CIGI Papers, No. 65*. Centre for International Governance Innovation.

PWC (2018). *SDG Reporting Challenge 2017: Exploring Business Communication on the Global Goals*. London: PWC.

Robbins, L. and Bisset, D.M. (1994). The role of environmental risk management in the credit process. *The Journal of Commercial Lending*, 76(10), 18–25.

Rockström, J., Steffen, W. and Noone, K. et al. (2009). Planetary boundaries: exploring the safe operating space for humanity. *Ecology and Society*, 14(2), Article 32.

Sachs, J.D. (2012). From millennium development goals to sustainable development goals. *The Lancet*, 379(9832), 2206–11.

Saravade, V. and Weber, O. (2020). An institutional pressure and adaptive capacity framework for green bonds: insights from India's emerging green bond market. *World*, 1(3), 239–63.

Schmidheiny, S. and Zorraquin, F.J.L. with the World Business Council for Sustainable Development (1996). *Financing Change: The Financial Community, Eco-efficiency, and Sustainable Development*. Cambridge, MA: MIT Press.

Schramade, W. (2017). Investing in the UN Sustainable Development Goals: opportunities for companies and investors. *Journal of Applied Corporate Finance*, 29(2), 87–99.

Sell, J., Koellner, T. and Weber, O. et al. (2006). Decision criteria of European and Latin American market actors for tropical forestry projects providing environmental services. *Ecological Economics*, 58, 17–36.

Stanway, D. (2016, 2 September). China provides $1 trillion in 'green credit'. *Scientific American*. Accessed 23 September 2020 at https://www.scientificamerican.com/article/china-provides-1-trillion-in-green-credit/.

Steffen, W., Richardson, K. and Rockström, J. et al. (2015). Planetary boundaries: guiding human development on a changing planet. *Science*, 347(6223), Article 1259855.

Sustainable Banking Network (2018). *Creating Green Bond Markets – Insights, Innovations, and Tools from Emerging Markets*. Washington, DC: Sustainable Banking Network.

The Equator Principles (2020). *The Equator Principles July 2020*. Geneva: The Equator Principles Association.

Tolliver, C., Keeley, A.R. and Managi, S. (2019). Green bonds for the Paris agreement and sustainable development goals. *Environmental Research Letters*, 14(6), Article 064009.

Trotta, A., Caré, R. and Severino, R. et al. (2015). Mobilizing private finance for public good: challenges and opportunities of social impact bonds. *European Scientific Journal*, 11(10), 259–79.

United Nations Conference on Trade and Development (UNCTAD) (2015). *Investing in Sustainable Development Goals – Action Plan for Private Investments in SDGs*. Accessed 23 September 2020 at http://unctad.org/en/PublicationsLibrary/osg2015d3_en.pdf.

United Nations Environment Programme Finance Initiative (UNEP FI) (2016). *Positive Impact Manifesto*. Accessed 21 January 2021 at https://www.unepfi.org/wordpress/wp-content/uploads/2017/01/POSITIVE-IMPACT-MANIFESTO-NEW-1.pdf.

United Nations Global Compact and KPMG International (2015). *SDG Industry Matrix: Financial Services*.

Weber, O. (2006). Investment and environmental management: the interaction between environmentally responsible investment and environmental management practices. *International Journal of Sustainable Development*, 9(4), 336–54.

Weber, O. (2014). The financial sector's impact on sustainable development. *Journal of Sustainable Finance & Investment*, 4(1), 1–8.

Weber, O. (2015). Sustainable finance. In H. Heinrichs, P. Martens, G. Michelsen and A. Wiek (eds), *Sustainability Science Handbook* (pp. 119–27). Heidelberg: Springer.

Weber, O. (2016a). Equator Principles reporting: factors influencing the quality of reports. *International Journal of Corporate Strategy and Social Responsibility*, 1(2), 141–60.

Weber, O. (2016b). Impact investing. In O.M. Lehner (ed.), *Routledge Handbook on Social and Sustainable Finance* (pp. 85–101). Abingdon: Routledge.

Weber, O. (2016c). Social banks mission and finance. In O.M. Lehner (ed.), *Routledge Handbook on Social and Sustainable Finance* (pp. 467–79). Abingdon: Routledge.

Weber, O. and Acheta, E. (2014a, 18 December). The Equator Principles: a tool for a sustainable financial sector? Centre for International Governance Innovation.

Weber, O. and Acheta, E. (2014b). The Equator Principles: ten teenage years of implementation and a search for outcome. *CIGI Papers, No. 24*. Centre for International Governance Innovation.

Weber, O. and Ahmad, A. (2014). Empowerment through microfinance: the relation between loan cycle and level of empowerment. *World Development*, 62(C), 75–87.

Weber, O., Diaz, M. and Schwegler, R. (2014). Corporate social responsibility of the financial sector – strengths, weaknesses and the impact on sustainable development. *Sustainable Development*, 22, 321–35.

Weber, O. and Feltmate, B. (2016). *Sustainable Banking and Finance: Managing the Social and Environmental Impact of Financial Institutions*. Toronto, ON: University of Toronto Press.

Weber, O., Fenchel, M. and Scholz, R.W. (2008). Empirical analysis of the integration of environmental risks into the credit risk management process of European banks. *Business Strategy and the Environment*, 17, 149–59.

Weber, O., Hoque, A. and Islam, A.M. (2015). Incorporating environmental criteria into credit risk management in Bangladeshi banks. *Journal of Sustainable Finance & Investment*, 5(1–2), 1–15.

Weber, O., Mansfeld, M. and Schirrmann, E. (2011). The financial performance of RI funds after 2000. In W. Vandekerckhove, J. Leys and K. Alm et al. (eds), *Responsible Investment in Times of Turmoil* (pp. 75–91). Berlin: Springer.

Weber, O., Scholz, R.W. and Michalik, G. (2010). Incorporating sustainability criteria into credit risk management. *Business Strategy and the Environment*, 19(1), 39–50.

Westphal, M.I., Canfin, P., Ballesteros, A. and Morgan, J. (2015). Getting to $100 billion: climate finance scenarios and projections to 2020. Working paper. World Resources Institute.

Wiek, A. and Weber, O. (2014). Sustainability challenges and the ambivalent role of the financial sector. *Journal of Sustainable Finance & Investment*, 4(1), 9–20.

World Commission on Environment and Development (WCED) (1987). *Our Common Future* [Brundtland Report]. Oxford: Oxford University Press.

Wright, C. and Rwabizambuga, A. (2006). Institutional pressures, corporate reputation, and voluntary codes of conduct: an examination of the Equator Principles. *Business and Society Review*, 111(1), 89–117.

Yang, A. and Cui, Y. (2012). *Global Coal Risk Assessment: Data Analysis and Market Research*. Washington, DC: World Resources Institute.

Yuan, F. and Gallagher, K.P. (2015). *Greening Development Finance in the Americas*. Boston University Global Economic Governance Initiative.

Zeidan, R., Boechat, C. and Fleury, A. (2015). Developing a sustainability credit score system. *Journal of Business Ethics*, 127(2), 283–96.

Zhang, B., Yang, Y. and Bi, J. (2011). Tracking the implementation of green credit policy in China: top-down perspective and bottom-up reform. *Journal of Environmental Management*, 92(4), 1321–7.

9. Financial sustainability conscientiousness

Julia M. Puaschunder[1]

Sustainability implementation

Sustainability research has been proliferating in recent decades. Given what is at stake in our common environmental well-being and the broad applications of sustainability, its real-world relevant implementation should embrace public and private sector forces concertedly. Harvesting technological advantages and social innovations provides future opportunities for accelerated economic growth within the limits of our natural resources and the common boundaries of our ecological limits. This chapter covers the interplay of top-down and bottom-up efforts to implement sustainability and ultimately ensure intergenerational equity.

As a top-down approach, taxes are the ultimate driver of revenue creation, granting fiscal space for states to enact sustainability. In a long history of taxation as a financial force for change, this chapter addresses a fairly innovative attempt to ensure tax compliance and fiscal discipline from a societal and psychological view of tax ethics. This creative influence of voluntary, self-chosen tax ethics is novel and opens up opportunities to tap into easily implementable, long-lasting behavioral adjustments and broader cultural changes.

As an integration of top-down and bottom-up sustainability implementation efforts, public–private partnerships (PPPs) are addressed as a feature of contemporary governance that embraces a wide variety of stakeholders. Together with trends to open up our concept of shareholder responsibility to a wider range of stakeholders in every corporate layer, PPPs have spearheaded multi-stakeholder engagement and imbued the broadest sense of responsibility in the corporate and financial worlds. In recent decades, PPPs have thus been leveraged as the ultimate driver of corporate social responsibility (CSR) and socially responsible investment (SRI) (Puaschunder, 2010, 2011).

As a more bottom-up effort by the corporate world, CSR has become a vital part of corporate culture that lives in harmony with the values of and respect for the wider society. Companies now strive to contribute to the 'triple bottom line' to harmoniously consider social, environmental and economic sustainability in everyday corporate decision making (Elkington, 1997). Respect for 'people, planet and profits' in line with UN mandates and societal directives has become a corporate necessity and industrial imperative.

Financial social responsibility primarily comes to life in SRIs, which integrate social, ethical and environmental concerns into portfolio choices and financial management. Enacted by public and private sector solutions, ethical, environmental, social and governance (ESG)-oriented investments are key to sustainable prosperity. Thereby, in a bottom-up endeavor, conscientious investors pursue both economic and social value maximization in social screenings,[2] shareholder advocacy and community investing (Puaschunder, 2017d).

One of the most recent finance advancements that integrates top-down with bottom-up sustainability is the so-called tax-and-transfer-bonds strategy. In the realm of climate change, climate justice is thereby being enacted through taxation and bonds alike. Thereby, taxation and bond financing solutions actively and viably fund mitigation and adaptation strategies. In the future, countries with positive economic growth prospects are advised to use taxation to raise revenues to offset the losses incurred by climate change. Those countries that will clearly face large-scale economic losses due to global warming could raise funds by issuing bonds that must be paid back by taxing future generations. This strategic diversification is also favorable in terms of Pareto efficiency over time.

All these novel and innovative financial sustainability conscientiousness approaches may help to conserve scarce environmental resources for this generation and those following.

Financial sustainability approaches in the twenty-first century

Sustainability endeavors are complex and their solutions interdependent. The global challenges of a warming earth that cannot be solved at the national level require international leadership that facilitates and structures public engagement in common concerns. In top-down approaches, global consortia concertedly solve internationally interconnected common goods problems and work towards a common vision of global justice throughout the world. Top-down directives have recently been successfully coupled or even surpassed by bottom-up sustainability in action approaches.

Sustainability implementation requires a multi-stakeholder approach in which public and private sector forces concertedly increase productivity through technological advantages and social innovations. Equality of merit-based access to opportunity accelerates economic growth that should be attuned to sustainability goals and social integration. Intergenerational justice on the operative bottom-up level features foresight and socially responsible policies (Puaschunder, 2016d). Age-diversified juries, well-balanced investigation panels and generational partnerships foster information exchange and resource transfers between young and old. Through voting, the young partake in societal decision making. Youth coalitions advocate for long-term decision making in parliamentary circles. In participatory democracy, in which decisions are made publicly and discussed openly, with people having a say in the solution, citizens are better able to decide the needs of their children. The political communication on intergenerational equity implementation strategies should focus on easily understandable, personal examples that help to bring the present into the future to help people to think in terms of their own children and imagine the sustainability of their welfare (Chichilnisky, Heal and Vercelli, 1998). Political advocacy should be accompanied by peaceful democracy-in-action protests to allow people to think and give beyond their own lives.

Bottom-up discussion platforms ingrain intergenerational perspectives in current decision making. Generations coming together will enable the discussion of problems with social consent found in the intergenerational dialogue. Open debates about commonly shared values and goals will solidify environmental responsibility for future generations and leverage intergenerational equity into a uniting, politically driven issue (Brandstetter and Lehner, 2015). General discussions nurture consensus on societal problems of all age groups. Combining the old and young's perspectives in dialogues between generations helps to focus attention on future generations' needs and creates a balance between the young, who strive for novel change, and the old, who pass on the wisdom of their experience. New media technologies help bridge the gap between the young and old by granting access to information on the needs of all age groups. The current interconnectedness of the world becomes a tool with which to embrace older people and include them in society so that they are more willing to save for their children, invest in youth, and pass on wealth rather than spending it on their current consumption. A harmonious representation of diversified viewpoints is gained in a dialogue between generations that integrates viewpoints of the young and the old and represents all societal groups. Beyond legal and regulatory boundaries, partnerships between the young and the old encourage a culture of voluntary intergenerational fairness. Transfers of wisdom from the old to the young increase solidarity in the intergenerational dialogue and grant stability for the community whilst fostering positive social development and societal welfare.

Intergenerational equity as a natural behavioral law serves as an ethical anchor from which to steer behavior towards future orientation and societal responsibility (Puaschunder, 2019). Beyond legal contracts, family bonds and responsible education form pro-social, intergenerationally conscientious norms as a basis for a favorable societal climate. Education will lead people to feel obliged to invest in the young and see future allocations as societal progress.

Ecologically, with regard to natural resource consumption and climate change, we must not live at the expense of future generations. As the market by itself is not future oriented, ecological problems demand a political governance frame to implement foresight and governmental will to find well-balanced resource distribution over time. Climate conscientiousness will require a modern, multi-cultural, multi-factual and urgent response to climate fragility in the future. International consensus must ensure that large, emerging economies – such as China and India – undertake systems of monitoring, reporting and verification of emission reduction. Legislation backing intergenerational equity will leverage climate justice as a human right in order to alleviate global emergent risks of resource scarcity.

Tax ethics

Within society, the most prominent form of revenue creation for public causes is taxes. Taxation is codified in all major societies and is a hallmark of democracy. Aimed at redistributing assets to provide public goods and ensure societal harmony, taxation improves societal welfare.

Tax compliance is a universal phenomenon based on cooperation in the desire to improve the intergenerational dialogue. When considering parting with personal funds for the sake of contributing to common causes, taxpayers voluntarily decide to what extent to pay or avoid tax that limits their personal freedom. In a social dilemma, individual interests are in conflict with collective goals. From a myopic economic perspective, the optimal strategy of rational individuals would be not to cooperate and thus evade tax. Short term, the single civilian tax contribution does not make a significant difference in the overall maintenance of public goods – if only a few taxpayers evade tax, public goods will not disappear or be reduced. However, if a considerable number of taxpayers do not contribute to tax over time, common goods are not guaranteed and ultimately everyone will suffer from suboptimal societal conditions (Puaschunder, 2015c).

Contemporary economic research has focused on the costs and risks of tax evasion. Coercive means – such as audits and fines – have been found to crowd out tax morale and result in greater non-compliance as people feel controlled and not trusted. In the last decade, researchers have begun to recognize the importance of incorporating morals and social dynamics in economic theory on tax behavior (Kirchler, 2007).

When analyzing tax behavior, insights from behavioral economics research have drawn attention to social influences (ibid.). Tax psychologists widen the lens for a socio-psychological understanding of tax compliance. In order to derive realistic models of tax compliance, social dilemmas have been replicated in laboratory settings that capture participants' decisions to cooperate or defect on common-pool goods (Puaschunder, 2012). Social nudge theories apply the insights of behavioral economics to change people's tax behavior. Apart from governmental control and sanction mechanisms, social situations were found to determine tax cooperation. Social setting directly influences tax compliance. In social dilemma experiments, participants' cooperation increases if their behavior is publicly known, if they are allowed to communicate with each other, and mutual empathy is established.

Behavioral approaches towards public administration have recently covered voluntary, self-chosen tax ethics influenced by situational cues. In general, social norms define internalized standards on how to behave. Internalized social norms are based on comparisons with others, which may determine tax morale. Social norms elicit concurring behavior when taxpayers identify with the goals of a group but also if they feel they are treated fairly within that group. Social fairness in a tax reference group may thus be essential for taxpayer compliance. Fairness is believed to decrease egoistic utility maximization. Perceptions of social fairness underlying social norms are therefore potential tax ethics nudges. Tax morale may only emerge if individuals compare themselves with other groups and feel that the tax burden is distributed in a fair and just manner. Taxation non-compliance may stem from the notion of unfairness in how the tax burden is weighted more heavily towards some parts of society.

How to breed a perception of fairness in taxation throughout society? Emotions were recently found to influence social responsibility – prerequisites for inter-temporal foresight to discount and care for future lives (Horberg, Oveis and Keltner, 2011). Emotionally laden intergenerational values appear as windows of opportunity from which to steer tax ethicality. Trust – as a concept related to emotionality – could be an additional intergenerational ethicality nudge to overcome the lack of identification with future beneficiaries (Ostrom, 2009).

Fairness in the wake of reciprocity perceived in tax contributions may stem from the feeling of being treated in a respectful way by the government. People tend to adhere to a social contract in their relationship with the government. According to this psychological bonding with the community and perceived good relationship with the government, taxpayers feel a self-imposed obligation and willingness to comply with tax requirements if governmental actions are favorable to ensure tax compliance. In a tit-for-tat strategy, taxpayers' compliance may depend on public goods provided by the government but also on the procedural and distributive justice perceived within society. Based on the interaction between tax authorities and taxpayers, taxpayers see themselves as members of a social group; following its social norms is a source of pride and contributing to the group feels right if the members perceive they are being offered a fair deal. Convincing the public that taxes are fair and lead to a public good appears to require a multi-dimensional conception of tax as a dynamic social phenomenon.

In the emergent field of tax psychology, behavioral decision-making experiments, in which 256 participants played an economic trust game followed by a common goods game, found evidence that trust and reciprocity lead to individuals contributing to common goals (Puaschunder, 2015c). The more that trust and reciprocity were practiced and experienced, the more common goals were supported, thus leveraging trust and reciprocity as interesting tax compliance antecedents. The results have widespread implications for government–citizen relations. Based on the findings, institutional technocrats are able to design social contexts that automatically raise social conscientiousness and help implement institutional models that motivate citizens to contribute to common goals. Policy makers and public servants are advised to establish trust and reciprocity with citizens in order to reach common societal goals.

Understanding the socio-dynamics of tax ethicality follows from the greater goal of finding strategies to steer a pro-social society. Deriving information on circumstances under which decision makers are likely to deviate from rational profit maximization in common goods allocations helps to model individual tax ethics. Elucidating the role of social forces in economic tax allocation decisions opens up ways to foster civic duties based on a cooperative relationship within society. Finding tax ethics nudges provides strategies to elicit taxpayers' voluntary compliance. Identifying tax ethics triggers is aimed at modeling day-to-day societal decision making.

Outlining the importance of trust and fairness for collective decision making is an innovative attempt to help policy makers improve tax ethicality in the absence of legal enforcement and governmental control (Ostrom, 2009). As taxpayers' trust in the government is preferable, their experience with tax authorities appears to be a key driver of tax compliance. Determining trust and reciprocity as the basis of socially favorable tax allocation outcomes helps governmental officials to reach common goals and establish justice. Overall, underlining the role of trust and reciprocity as a means to implement tax compliance fosters the greater goal of ensuring a sustainable and fair society.

Finding evidence for the importance of the government–citizen relationship for tax compliance thus implies that tax authorities are advised to treat taxpayers respectfully. Rather than responding to tax non-compliance with intrusive audits and severe punishment, supportive communication and collective interaction inspiring trust and reciprocity promises to encourage tax compliance. Replacing cops-and-robbers strategies featuring control and sanctions with developing trust and reciprocity in a service-oriented tax ethics approach will help foster tax compliance within future societies.

New cultures of customer relations orientation can create a cooperative tax climate. A cooperative contractual relationship and psychological contract, rather than control and punishment, should feature respectful client-oriented interactions in order to build trust and improve fiscal conscientiousness. Tax authorities are advised to consider taxpayers as customers. A new culture of customer relationship orientation appears more promising for enhancing cooperation and voluntary compliance without governmental oversight. In a service and client approach, taxpayers and tax authorities should create a climate of mutual trust and reciprocity based on clear and understandable regulations, transparency of procedures, as well as respect and politeness for citizens. Taxpayers are more likely to report honestly if they feel that they are being treated courteously by the tax agency. If tax authorities and officers treat taxpayers equally, in a respectful and responsible way, trust in the institution and cooperation increase. Tax authorities should also communicate to enhance a feeling of civic duty. Community responsiveness and citizen communication will mean that the norms of contribution to the public good will become a landmark of national stability and societal wealth.

For the future, cooperative strategies of self-regulation and education will help to gain tax compliance. The training of tax officers and improving organizations to offer effective advice and problem resolution will foster good public relations, resulting in enhanced tax compliance. Educating taxpayers to be cooperative citizens and a service–client atmosphere will lead to their voluntary compliance and will help them to understand the necessity of contributing to common goals. Trust and reciprocity could also be enabled through positive rewards and raising awareness of social obligations. Fostering relations of trust and reciprocity will establish a psychological contract between governmental officials and citizens. Tax contributions practiced in an atmosphere of mutual trust and reciprocity will breed a positive tax morale and voluntary compliance. Avenues for future research may consider procedural fairness as an additional driver of tax responsibility. Personal identification with friends, occupational groups or the nation could also be investigated as tax compliance moderators.

Public-private partnerships (PPPs)

Globalization, with its concomitant societal problems out of the reach of nation state control, has transformed the demand for global governance. An emerging global governance trend features PPP social service provision. Under the guidance of international organizations, PPPs connect the corporate world with governments on societal concerns. Global governance PPPs reduce social deficiencies and foster international development. As flexible governance structures, PPPs ingrain multi-stakeholder expertise and resources in public management. For corporations, innovative PPPs allow first-mover advantages and public relations management. With continuing globalization and worldwide corporate expansion, international organizations are believed to increasingly view PPPs as a means for enhancing societal prosperity – foremost in CSR and SRIs (Puaschunder, 2010, 2011).

Corporate social responsibility (CSR)

Globalization has also shifted national governments' sustainability implementation to international governance solutions in the corporate world (Panitch and Gindin, 2012). Currently pressing dilemmas beyond the control of single nation states call for attention to intergenerational fairness and corporate social activities to back governmental crisis mitigation (Centeno et al., 2013). In the light of growing environmental challenges, heightened stakeholder concern has increased the attention of global stakeholders to corporate environmental conduct. Heightened transparency and greater accessibility in the digital age make corporate conduct and governmental actions more visible to a broad range of constituents, and local communities, customers, employees and non-governmental organizations as well as shareholders are increasingly monitoring ethical behavior. Amidst the surge of the positive organizational scholarship movement, the corporate world is now more than ever being urged to consider the needs of a wider range of stakeholders in their decision making, to go beyond ethical requirements and outperform responsibility expectations. Crowdfunding for the social causes of these stakeholder groups has become the most vibrant social finance solution (Lehner, 2015).

Given the pressing demand for attention to climate change mitigation, there is a blatant need for intergenerational equity conscientiousness in the corporate world. In a climate of corporate governance and global challenges beyond the control of single nation states, the idea of promoting intergenerational equity in the corporate world has reached unprecedented momentum. Departing from narrow-minded, outdated views of responsibilities of corporations only looking to making profit for shareholders and abiding by the law (Friedman, 1970), corporate executives are now more prone to act responsibly in meeting the needs of a wide range of constituents. Corporate executives proactively engage in corporate governance practice with a wider constituency outlook, including the needs of future generations.

As a multi-layered economic system is structured by the strategic coordination of international corporate entities, corporate multinationals have now turned to solving global societal crises beyond the control of single nation states. International trade, global capitalism and economic hegemony of corporations have led to a strategic coordination of public and private actors' awareness of intergenerational imbalances (Binder et al., 2014). Intergenerational equity deficiencies are subsequently tackled with bottom-up approaches to shed light on the rights of youth, voice the needs of the unborn, and lobby for favorable future conditions.

Increasing and expanding CSR initiatives indicate that increasing numbers of business leaders are committing their companies to contribute to the 'triple bottom line' to harmoniously consider social, environmental and economic sustainability in everyday corporate decision making (Elkington, 1997). Corporate sustainability and social responsibility have thus emerged to unprecedented momentum in academia and practitioners' discourse (Lehner, 2017). In the international arena, the UN Global Compact has gained over 10 000 members since its foundation in 2000, including over 7000 businesses in 145 countries around the world. Today, business leaders contribute to the creation of economic and societal progress in a globally responsible and sustainable way never before experienced.

Today's conceptualization of sustainable and responsible managerial behavior may embrace the wider constituency and extend the concept of corporate responsibility to voluntary sustainability for future generations. An extended stakeholder view considers a broader set of constituencies, including future generations, in corporate decision making with impact on the social performance and long-term viability of their organizations (Chichilnisky and Heal, 2000). A broader, social contract between business and future society may be enacted by discretionary activities that are not expected of corporations and their leaders in a moral or legal sense but directly contribute to societal welfare and the well-being of future generations (Chichilnisky and Sheeran, 2018). This suggests that there is a need for a broader definition of corporate responsibility that goes beyond compliance and encompasses the obligation to contribute to societal progress in a responsible and sustainable way.

Intergenerationally responsible leadership is called for that steers intentional corporate executive actions to benefit the stakeholders of the company as well as society, including future generations (Puaschunder, 2018b). Intergenerational corporate leadership imbues 'should do' care for future generations alongside concerns about future society. By adopting a positive and proactive ethics lens, intergenerationally responsible leadership is an 'überethical' drive to consider the interests of a wider range of stakeholders (Puaschunder, 2017b). Concerns for intergenerational justice of the corporate world thereby directly reach out to future world inhabitants.

Incorporating intergenerational equity into contemporary CSR models serves the idea of 'positive CSR' – that is, outdoing legal and ethical expectations – with respect for future constituents. Going beyond mere compliance involves actions that proactively promote social good beyond what is required by law. Intergenerational corporate responsibility extends CSR as a broader social contract between business and society over time. Intergenerational equity leadership of the corporate sector defines social responsibility beyond compliance and encompasses the wider obligation to contribute to societal progress in a responsible and sustainable way. Stretching constituency attention to future generations is based on voluntary sustainability with respect for future generations' needs to ensure the long-term viability of society.

Corporate leaders thereby proactively outperform legal and ethical expectations regarding the rights and needs of future generations. This positive CSR drive refers to an 'überethical' enhancement of societal welfare beyond the narrow scope of the current generation (Puaschunder, 2017b). As a broader definition of corporate responsibility beyond avoidance of negative outcomes, the call for intergenerational responsible leadership in the corporate world encompasses the obligation to contribute to societal progress with respect for the needs of future generations (Chichilnisky and Bal, 2019). Defining novel responsibilities with a broader social contract between business and society embraces discretionary activities that contribute to sustainable societal welfare and thereby provides a broad range of corporate, social and societal advantages.

If the corporate world adopts intergenerational equity in current CSR endeavors, it could help governmental officials in very many different ways, ranging from tax ethics to 'first-aid' global governance support.[3] For society, acknowledging intergenerational equity in CSR practices promises to alleviate currently pressing environmental threats. Investigating the possibilities of integrating a temporal dimension in contemporary CSR thus innovatively guides the implementation of environmental protection. Corporate attention to intergenerational concerns would thereby embrace future climate change prevention. Besides averting negative impacts of managerial unethical corporate conduct, corporate intergenerational ethicality would also build business reputation, attract talent and raise customer confidence, as well as sustainable employee and citizenry welfare. Within academia, integrating the notion of intergenerational fairness in corporate governance models fills an as yet undiscovered research gap that spearheads interdisciplinary behavioral law and economic models.

Overall, enhancing intergenerational social conscientiousness in the corporate world is an innovative way to unprecedentedly leverage untapped potentials to implement social welfare and environmental protection through future-oriented and socially responsible economic market approaches. Averting future predictable economic, social and environmental crises thereby serves the greater goal to ensure a future sustainable and temporally harmonious humankind.

Finance sector solutions

Financing climate justice through a tax-and-transfer-bonds strategy

Puaschunder (2020) outlines the macroeconomic gains and losses from a warming earth by country. A macroeconomic cost–benefit analysis thereby helps to find the optimum solution as to how to distribute climate change benefits and burden within society. When unidimensionally focusing on estimated gross domestic product (GDP) growth, given a warmer temperature to the year 2100, over all calculated models, assuming linear, prospect or hyperbolic gains and losses, the world will be gaining more than losing from a warming earth. Based on a Winner–Loser (WL) index of 188 countries of the world, fewer countries ($n = 78$) will gain from global warming to 2100 than more countries ($n = 111$) will lose from a warming earth. Based on the overall WL index factored by GDP per inhabitant, global warming benefits need to be redistributed in a fair way to offset the costs of climate change-losing countries for climate change mitigation and adaptation efforts and to instigate a transition into renewable energy. Shedding light on the gains of a warming earth allows for the redistribution of climate change benefits to those areas of the world that will lose from a warming earth. In the implementation, climate change bonds but also taxation strategies are recommended (Puaschunder, 2017d, 2020).

Adding to contemporary climate fund-raising strategies ranging from emissions trading schemes (ETS) and carbon tax policies, as well as financing climate justice through bonds as viable mitigation and adaptation strategies, the concept of climate justice is introduced, comprising fairness between countries but also over generations in a unique and unprecedented tax-and-transfer-bonds climate change gains and losses distribution strategy (Chichilnisky, 1996; Puaschunder, 2020). Climate change-winning countries are advised to use taxation to raise revenues to offset the losses incurred by climate change. Climate change losers could raise revenues by issuing bonds that must be paid back by taxing future generations. Within the winning countries, the gaining GDP sectors should be taxed. Climate justice within a country should also pay tribute to the fact that low- and high-income households share the same burden proportional to their dispensable income, enabled, for instance, through a progressive carbon taxation. Those who caused climate change could be regulated to bear a higher cost through carbon tax in combination with retroactive billing through inheritance tax to map benefits from past wealth accumulation that potentially contributed to global warming. Deriving respective policy recommendations for the wider climate change community in the discussion of the results aims to ensure that not only the burden but also the benefits of climate change are shared within society in an economically efficient, legally equitable and practically feasible way.

In order to avoid governmental expenditure on climate change hindering economic growth (Barro, 1990), the climate transfers should be enacted through bonds and taxes. The 'climate change in the 21st century' idea (Puaschunder, 2017d) takes these insights into account in order to offer a new way of funding climate change mitigation and adaptation policies but also the transition to renewable energy through a broad-based climate stability bonds-and-taxation mix that also involves future generations (Puaschunder, 2020; World Bank, 2015).

To finance climate change abatement, a climate bonds financing mix could subsidize the current world industry for transitioning to green solutions. Sharing the costs of climate stabilization between and across generations is a Pareto-optimal strategy to immediately instigate climate action without curbing today's economic growth potentials (Chichilnisky, 2007).

Jeffrey Sachs (2014) presented an overlapping-generations model of burden sharing through fiscal policy with bond issuing in order to reflect the implementation of contemporary finance and growth models with respect to maximizing utility of the model. In an overlapping-generations-type model, future research should elucidate climate change abatement and mitigation policies to lead to a fairer solution across generations. The current generation mitigates climate change and provides infrastructure against climate risk financed through climate bonds to be paid by future generations. Since for future generations the currently created externalities from economic activities – the effects of CO_2 emissions – are removed, this entails that the current generations remain financially as well off as without mitigation while improving environmental well-being of future generations. As Sachs (2014) shows, this intergenerational tax-and-transfer-bonds policy turns climate change mitigation and adaptation policy into a Pareto-improving strategy. Countries that are on the climate change economic winning side should only engage in actions they want to be done for themselves (Kant [1783] 1993; Puaschunder, 2017f, 2017g; Rawls, 1971). This implies that climate change-winning territories must also strive for climate change mitigation and adaptation as they see the problem of global warming from a rounded perspective that shows empathy and compassion for the climate change losers (Puaschunder, 2017f). Shifting the costs for climate abatement to the recipients of the benefits of climate stability appears a novel, feasible and easily implementable solution to nudge many overlapping generations towards future-oriented loss aversion in the sustainability domain (Puaschunder, 2016c).

The respective bonds-and-taxation climate stability financing strategy therefore proposes that the burden of climate change is shared in a right, just and fair way around the globe. In the climate change-winning countries, taxation should become the main driver over financing climate stability strategies. Foremost, the industries winning from a warming climate should be taxed. The WL index is based on the cardinal temperatures for all GDP-contributing sectors. Based on the cardinal temperatures for the three GDP components, agriculture, industry and service, the taxation should be enacted for those sectors with most time ahead. The rationale is that these sectors will be gaining the most from a warming earth and will therefore be flourishing.

The taxation models should help to share the burden of climate change within society in a fair way. Regarding concrete climate taxation strategies, a carbon tax on top of the existing tax system should be used to reduce the burden of climate change and encourage economic growth through subsidies (Chancel and Piketty, 2015). Within a country, high- and low-income households should face the same burden of climate stabilization adjusted for their disposable income. First, climate justice within a country should pay tribute to the fact that low- and high-income households share the same burden proportional to their dispensable income – for instance, through a progressive carbon taxation. Those who caused climate change could be regulated to bear a higher cost through carbon tax in combination with retroactive billing through inheritance tax. However, developed and underdeveloped countries as well as various overlapping generations are affected differently. Besides progressive taxation schemes to imbue a sense of fairness in climate change burden sharing, inheritance taxation is also a flexible means to reap past wealth accumulation that potentially caused environmental damage. The burden of climate change mitigation and adaptation could also be allocated in a fair way within society through contemporary corporate inheritance tax in order to reap benefits of past wealth accumulation. But in order to determine a fair corporate inheritance for tax grantors and beneficiaries, one needs information on what countries and what sectors of the economy have a rising or declining economic prospect in light of climate change.

In addition, finding the optimum balance between consumption tax adjusted for disposable income through a progressive tax scheme will help to unravel drivers of tax compliance in the sustainability domain. If climate taxation is perceived as a fair and just allocation of the climate burden, this could convince taxpayers to pay their share. A novel 'service-and-client' atmosphere could promote taxpayers as cooperative citizens who are willing to comply if they feel their share is a fair contribution to the environment (Puaschunder, 2015a). Taxpayers as cooperative citizens would then be willing to comply voluntarily following the greater goal to promote taxpayer collaboration and enhance tax morale in the environmental domain. International comparisons of tax behavior also reveal tax norms as being related to different stages of institutional development of the government, which is an essential considera-tion in sharing the climate change burden in a fair manner between countries. A completely novel approach is to shed light on the benefits of a warming earth in order to derive fair climate gains distribution strategies around the world (Puaschunder, 2016e, 2017a, 2017e).

To conclude, climate change-winning countries are advised to use taxation of the gaining GDP sectors to raise revenues to offset the losses incurred by climate change (Chichilnisky, 2010; Rolle, 2016). Climate change losers should issue bonds to be paid back by taxing future generations. Tax-and-transfer-bonds could be used to subsidize industry actors for choosing clean energy in order to shift the general race-to-the-bottom price-cutting behavior to a race-to-the-top hunt for subsidies for going into clean energy.

Ethical, ESG-oriented investments

As mentioned in the first section, ethical, ESG-oriented investments are key to sustainable prosperity. As for an investment philosophy that combines profit maximization with social endeavors, socially conscientious investors pursue economic and social value maximization alike in social screenings, shareholder advocacy and community investing (Puaschunder, 2017b, 2017e).

As part of human nature, social responsibility guides corporate activities and financial considerations (Puaschunder, 2011, 2018a). Socially conscien-tious asset allocation styles add to expected yield and volatility of securities' social, environmental and institutional considerations (Puaschunder, 2017a). Altruism, need for innovation and entrepreneurial zest alongside utility derived from social status enhancement prospects and transparency steer investors' social conscientiousness. Self-enhancement and social expression of future-oriented SRI options supplement profit-maximization goals. As for these intrinsic motivational factors, SRI is an extraordinarily crises-robust sustainable market alternative (Puaschunder, 2017e).

Originating from religious and moral considerations, SRI evolved in the wake of sociopolitical deficiencies, legislative compulsion and CSR. In recent decades, financial social responsibility boomed in the wake of globalization and political trends (Puaschunder, 2016c, 2016f). An unprecedented intercon-nectivity of globalized financial markets strengthened the societal role of finan-cial institutions. Political libertarianism implicitly shifted social responsibility to the private sector (Puaschunder, 2021). Deregulation and liberalization attributed a rising share of global governance to financial markets. With these market trends, financial social considerations leveraged into an implicit fiduciary responsibility (Puaschunder, 2017e).

As social global governance has increasingly entered financial markets since the turn of the millennium, a growing proportion of investment firms and governmental agencies around the world have adopted a more socially conscientious investment philosophy (Puaschunder, 2016c). Information disclosure on corporate social conduct in combination with benchmarking of corporate social engagement and governmental encouragement of trustees' social conscientiousness propelled SRI (ibid.). Institutional investors increasingly used their power to influence corporate conduct and actively demanded corporate governance reforms to act on societal and intergenerational concerns (Puaschunder, 2015a, 2015b, 2017e).

The advanced consideration of financial social responsibility by major institutional investors helped SRI to mature from being a niche market option to becoming a more mainstream asset allocation style (Puaschunder, 2010). SRI reached unprecedented diversity, featuring a wide range of social engagement possibilities. As SRI gained in prominence and broadened in size, scale and scope, practitioners and academics started documenting state-of-the-art financial social responsibility practices (Puaschunder, 2016b). Business professionals reported and analysts monitored social, ethical and environmental corporate performance (ibid.). Social and environmental stock exchange rating agencies and certifications measured SRI impacts.

In the aftermath of the 2008/09 global recession, ethical investing blossomed as a crisis-robust market opportunity to re-establish trust in the economy (Puaschunder, 2016c). Financial social responsibility was meant to strengthen a more sustainable, inclusive and equitable society. Recent concerns about the strength and conduct of individual foreign investors have brought foreign investment in general under scrutiny (United Nations Conference on Trade and Development [UNCTAD], 2015). Increasingly, investment behavior is assessed on whether it complies with international standards, such as the UN Guiding Principles on Business and Human Rights, the revised Organisation for Economic Co-operation (OECD) Guidelines on Multinational Enterprises, and the Food and Agriculture Organization (FAO)/World Bank/UNCTAD/ International Fund for Agricultural Development Principles on Responsible Agricultural Investment (IFAD PRAI). In addition to standards developed by international organizations, investors are expected to report on their consideration of CSR in their portfolio choice.

North American Free Trade Agreement (NAFTA) investment agreements require that investment protection and liberalization objectives must not be pursued at the expense of the protection of health, safety, the environment and the promotion of internationally recognized human rights standards (UNCTAD, 2015). Worldwide regulatory standards are aimed at improving the investment climate by promoting the rule of law and enhancing good governance in finance. Canada and the United States have incorporated proceedings such as open hearings, publication of related legal documentation and the possibility for related stakeholders to submit *amicus curiae* briefs to tribunals (ibid.). The 2015 Sustainable Development Goals advanced the idea of socially conscientious market alternatives that offer a stable investment option combating global economic and environmental fragilities (Puaschunder, 2017e).

Today the range of shareholder engagement possibilities is more sophisticated than ever. In the international arena, various SRI practices emerged concurrently as national rules and legal jurisdictions shape corporate and financial social conduct (Puaschunder, 2010). Legal boundaries guide financial considerations and institutional frameworks predestine financial social responsibility practices.

Crisis-robust ethical financial considerations hold untapped opportunities in the age of climate change. In the current post-COP 21 Paris agreement climate change mitigation and adaptation efforts, the financialization of the ambitious goals has leveraged into an internationally challenging demand (World Bank, 2015). Problematic is that curbing carbon emissions was traditionally related to lowering economic activity and growth. Current generations are thereby seen to sacrifice for future generations' uncertain living conditions (Puaschunder, 2017e). Economic growth versus environmental protection predicaments in light of climate stabilization demands insights on how to align economic with greater societal goals (Puaschunder, 2013, 2016e).

Political divestiture forces political change by imposing financial constraints on politically incorrect regimes that stray from international law. Removing stocks from a portfolio to screen out socially irresponsible corporations based on social, ethical and religious objections follows the greater goal of accomplishing social and political change (McWilliams and Siegel, 2000). In the case of political divestiture, investments are withdrawn from politically incorrect markets in the wake of stakeholder pressure and global governance sanctions economically pressuring coercive regimes and governments that depart from international law and human rights standards. Cultural and diplomatic consequences as well as economic trade restrictions – such as tariffs – are common sanctions imposed for the greater goal of triggering positive and societal change.

Historically, political divestiture shareholder action grew as an anti-war alternative to steer governmental reforms that evolved in the wake of stakeholder activism against socio-political inhumanities (Alperson et al., 1991; Bekefi, 2006; Kanter, 2003; McWilliams and Siegel, 2000). First discussed in the case of the Angolan repressive regime, political divestiture has been practiced to undermine warfare (e.g., the Israel–Palestine conflict), terrorism (e.g., Afghanistan), nuclear proliferation and power accumulation (e.g., Iran), social infringements and human rights violations, such as genocide in the Sudanese Darfur region (Schueth, 2008; Starr, 2008). One of the most powerful and visible political divestiture acts in history was the capital flight from South Africa during apartheid. Additional cases are foreign direct investment withdrawals in the wake of governmental human rights violations in Burma as well as the current humanitarian crises in Sudan's Darfur region. Most recently, political divestiture has evolved, banning carbon-footprint-heavy industries (see, for example, Howard, 2015).

At the 3rd Conference on Financing for Development in July 2015 in Addis Ababa, and at the global summit on the Sustainable Development Goals in New York City in September 2015, external financing for development was proven as a key driver for developing economies. In the wake of the 2015 UN Sustainable Development Goals, a report was published by the United Nations Conference on Trade and Development (UNCTAD, 2015) that aims to elucidate debates surrounding ESG issues in the light of fiduciary duty. The report is meant to foster investors' understanding and consideration of ESG issues in their investment decision making. The research stresses that a failure to consider long-term investment value drivers, which include ESG issues, in investment practices is a failure of fiduciary duty. The report also touches on the implementation of sustainable finance and impact investment in order to propose practical action for institutional investors, financial professionals and policy makers to embrace sustainable development. All these endeavors are aimed at fostering ESG-oriented investments as a future guarantor of economic stability and sustainable social progress throughout the world.

Conclusion and future research outlook

This chapter reflected on financial sustainability conscientiousness from legal, economic and governance perspectives. Different novel strategies were presented as attempts to ensure a sustainable future for this generation and those following.

Sustainability comes to life in tax ethics that generate the necessary fiscal space to be responsible when it comes to natural resources and in order to embrace future generations in today's planning (Puaschunder, 2015b, 2015c). PPPs and CSR were outlined as essential corporate world remedies to make sustainability happen (Puaschunder, 2010). Behavioral insights offer easily implementable governance tools to nudge citizens into sustainable choices (Puaschunder, 2015a, 2017b). Proposed intergenerational equity implementation solutions in the climate justice domain featured the idea of sharing the benefits and burdens of a warming globe via a tax-and-bonds-transfer policy mix (Puaschunder, 2011, 2012, 2016a). The presented innovative approaches still must stand the test of time and proof of feasibility and practicability in enacting sustainability by concerted public and private forces.

Future research to improve sustainability is recommended to be coupled with science-grounded concerted action in the public and private sectors. In terms of tax ethics, cooperative strategies of self-regulation and education will help to gain tax compliance (Puaschunder, 2016e). But for this to be effective, we need a further understanding of the socio-psychological motives of tax honesty and voluntary social contributions (Lehner, 2017; Puaschunder, 2013, 2016c). CSR has been one of the most vibrantly growing areas of corporate advancement in recent decades (Puaschunder, 2010). Qualitative and quantitative advancement of CSR efforts attest to this trend overtaking the corporate world (Puaschunder, 2010). Yet, to this day, there is not a great understanding of intergenerational equity as part of standard CSR efforts (Puaschunder, 2018b).

Behavioral insights research that applies behavioral economics to public choices is still at an early stage. Future studies comprising field and laboratory experiments may unravel more nudges and winks towards how to steer people into a more sustainable choice in their individual lives and within groups, but also promise to imbue a future-oriented conscientiousness for others still to come (Puaschunder, 2016b, 2016f, 2017b, 2017e).

Studies on global responsible intergenerational leadership have recently begun, yet we require more time and data to understand the political economy of intergenerational equity (Puaschunder, 2016e, 2017c). Future research and implementation advocacy may aim to innovatively integrate those most vulnerable segments of the population of future generations (Puaschunder, 2017c, 2018b). Individual choices but also collective efforts should align to make sustainability happen for this generation and those of the future.

In the finance domain, we may also want to address financial social responsibility under the wing of the Green New Deal and continue searching for the most innovative tools and techniques for how to nurture our financial and our greater social and environment benefits concurrently and in harmony (Lehner, 2015; Puaschunder, 2013). Recent advancements in how to bundle market power with financial impetus in fintech solutions demand more attention and should be further explored (Lehner, 2015).

The presented PPP efforts should be enhanced and coupled with brand-new artificial intelligence (AI) developments to answer how public and private sector forces can partner in digitalization efforts (Puaschunder, 2017a). Here again, tax ethics could help in understanding how tax revenues from AI leaders in the field could be obtained in order to fund public sector endeavors. Sustainability could also be extended most innovatively to AI solutions of the future – for instance, when it comes to sustainability concerns of overpopulation in the light of robotics and 24/7 energy-consuming devices. Sustainability definitions may also address AI and robotics ethics on an already overcrowded planet with exhausted resources.

Finally, with the currently ongoing COVID-19 crisis, sustainability may receive the greatest attention in the healthcare domain. Public and private sector entities may already now address what impact COVID will have on health, well-being and financial means in the years to come. Social finance efforts may seek out creative new ways to align our needs for a healthy populace with financial sustainability (Nicholls, Paton and Emerson, 2015).

Financial sustainability conscientiousness strives for ensuring financial market stability with attention to higher environmental long-term goals. All the presented recommendations are work-in-progress endeavors aimed at sharing benefits and burdens of sustainability protection within society in an economically efficient, legally equitable and practically feasible way now and also between generations in an economically interdependent, politically diverse and environmentally fragile world.

Notes

1.   The author most gratefully acknowledges the August Harvard University community's ennobling spirit, the Harvard University Faculty of Arts and Sciences and the Center for the Environment's kind hospitality, the Max Kade Foundation New York in cooperation with the Austrian Academy of Sciences' generous financial

support, the University of Vienna's noble gift of public education, the European Forum Alpbach's access to elite insights, and the Harvard Decision Science Laboratory, enabling empirical endeavors. The financial support of the American Academic Research Conference on Global Business, Economics, Finance and Social Sciences, Austrian Academy of Sciences, European Parliament, Fritz Thyssen Foundation, George Washington University, Max Kade Foundation, New School (Dean's Office, Department of Economics, Eugene Lang College, Fee Board, The New School for Social Research, The New School for Public Affairs), Research Association for Interdisciplinary Studies, The New School Dean's Office, The New School Department of Economics, The New School Fee Board, The New School for Social Research, The New School Eugene Lang College, the University of Vienna, Vernon Arts and Science, and the Vienna University of Economics and Business, is gratefully acknowledged. The author declares no conflict of interest. All omissions, errors and misunderstandings in this piece are solely the author's.

2. Social screenings are the practice of excluding or including investments from portfolios based on social performance criteria. By excluding non-social market performance through political divestiture (e.g., of harmful and ethically questionable behavior such as smoking or warfare), social performance of the overall markets is enhanced. In fostering social market options via funding streams, the overall social performance of markets and socially favorable positive externalities are targeted (Little, 2008).

3. For instance, green bonds to fund climate change mitigation and adaptation or in PPP solutions for social investments.

References

Alperson, M., Tepper-Marlin, A.T., Schorsch, J. and Wil, R. for the Council on Economic Priorities (1991). *The Better World Investment Guide.* Upper Saddle River, NJ: Prentice Hall.

Barro, Robert J. (1990). Government spending in a simple model of endogenous growth. *Journal of Political Economy*, 98(5), 103–25.

Bekefi, T. (2006). *Business as a Partner in Tackling Micronutrient Deficiency: Lessons in Multisector Partnership.* Corporate Responsibility Initiative, Harvard University.

Binder, C., Kriebaum, U. and Marboe, I. et al. (2014). Völkerrecht [study guide]. Vienna: University of Vienna Faculty of Law Juridicum.

Brandstetter, L. and Lehner, O.M. (2015). Opening the market for impact investments: the need for adapted portfolio tools. *Entrepreneurship Research Journal*, 5(2), 87–107.

Centeno, M.A., Cinlar, E. and Cloud, D. et al. (2013). Global systemic risk. Unpublished manuscript. Princeton Institute for International and Regional Studies, Princeton University.

Chancel, L. and Piketty, T. (2015). Carbon and inequality: from Kyoto to Paris. Paris School of Economics.

Chichilnisky, G. (1996). Development and global finance: the case for an international bank for environmental settlements. Discussion paper. Office of Development Studies, United Nations Development Programme.

Chichilnisky, G. (2007). *The Economics of Global Environment: Catastrophic Risks in Theory and Policy.* Cham, Switzerland: Springer International.

Chichilnisky, G. (2010). *The Economics of Climate Change*. Cheltenham, UK and Northampton, MA, USA: Edward Elgar Publishing.

Chichilnisky, G. and Bal, P. (2019). *Reversing Climate Change: How Carbon Removals Can Resolve Climate Change and Fix the Economy*. Singapore: World Scientific Publishing.

Chichilnisky, G. and Heal, G. (2000). *Environmental Markets: Equity and Efficiency*. New York: Columbia University Press.

Chichilnisky, G., Heal, G. and Vercelli, A. (1998). *Sustainability: Dynamics and Uncertainty*. Dordrecht: Kluwer.

Chichilnisky, G. and Sheeran, K. (2018). *Handbook on the Economics of Climate Change*. Cheltenham, UK and Northampton, MA, USA: Edward Elgar Publishing.

Elkington, J. (1997). *Cannibals With Forks: The Triple Bottom Line of Twenty-First Century Business*. Oxford: Capstone.

Friedman, M. (1970, 13 September). The social responsibility of business is to increase its profits. *The New York Times*.

Horberg, E.J., Oveis, C. and Keltner, D. (2011). Emotions as moral amplifiers: an appraisal tendency approach to the influences of distinct emotions upon moral judgment. *Emotion Review*, 3, 237–44.

Howard, E. (2015, 25 March). Keep it in the ground campaign: six things we have learned. *The Guardian*.

Kant, I. ([1783] 1993). *Grounding for the Metaphysics of Morals*. Cambridge, MA: Hackett.

Kanter, R.M. (2003, May-June). From spare change to real change. *Harvard Business Review*.

Kirchler, E.M. (2007). *The Economic Psychology of Tax Behaviour*. Cambridge, UK: Cambridge University Press.

Lehner, O.M. (2015). Crowdfunding in social finance. In A. Nicholls, R. Paton and J. Emerson (eds), *Social Finance* (pp. 521–42). Oxford: Oxford University Press.

Lehner, O.M. (2017). *Routledge Handbook of Social and Sustainable Finance*. Abingdon: Routledge.

Little, K. (2008). *Socially Responsible Investing: Put Your Money Where Your Values Are*. New York: Penguin.

McWilliams, A. and Siegel, D. (2000). Corporate social responsibility and financial performance: correlation or mis-specification? *Strategic Management Journal*, 21, 603–9.

Nicholls, A., Paton, R. and Emerson, J. (2015). *Social Finance*. Oxford: Oxford University Press.

Ostrom, E. (2009). Beyond markets and states: polycentric governance of complex economic systems. Prize lecture at The Sveriges Riksbank Prize in Economic Sciences in Memory of Alfred Nobel Laureate 2009.

Panitch, L. and Gindin, S. (2012). *The Making of Global Capitalism: The Political Economy of American Empire*. London: Verso.

Puaschunder, J.M. (2010). On corporate and financial social responsibility. Unpublished doctoral thesis. Faculty of Psychology, University of Vienna.

Puaschunder, J.M. (2011). Intergenerational equity as a natural behavioral law. Copyright Office of the United States Congress Record TXu1-743-422. Library of Congress of the United States.

Puaschunder, J.M. (2012). On the social representations of intergenerational equity. Copyright Office of the United States Congress Record TXu001798159/2012–02–26. Library of Congress of the United States.

Puaschunder, J.M. (2013). Ethical investing and socially responsible investing. In K.H. Baker and V. Ricciardi (eds), *Investor Behavior* (pp. 515–32). New York: John Wiley & Sons.

Puaschunder, J.M. (2015a). On eternal equity in the fin-de-millénaire. *Journal of Leadership, Accountability and Ethics*, 13(2), 1–24.

Puaschunder, J.M. (2015b). On the social representations of intergenerational equity. *Oxford Journal of Finance and Risk Perspectives*, 4(4), 78–99.

Puaschunder, J.M. (2015c). Trust and reciprocity drive social common goods allocation norms. Paper presented at the Cambridge Business and Economics Conference, Cambridge University, UK and the 6th International Conference of the Association of Global Management Studies at Columbia University, USA.

Puaschunder, J.M. (2016a). Intergenerational climate change burden sharing: an economics of climate stability research agenda proposal. *Global Journal of Management and Business Research: Economics and Commerce*, 16(3), 31–8.

Puaschunder, J.M. (2016b). Mapping climate justice. Paper presented at the 2016 Young Scientists Summer Program Conference, International Institute for Applied Systems Analysis (IIASA), Lanburg, Austria.

Puaschunder, J.M. (2016c). Socially responsible investment as emergent risk prevention and means to imbue trust in the post-2008/2009 world financial crisis economy. In O. Lehner (ed.), *Routledge Handbook of Social and Sustainable Finance* (pp. 222–38), Abingdon: Routledge.

Puaschunder, J.M. (2016d). The beauty of ivy: when inequality meets equality. *Global Journal of Management and Business Research: Economics and Commerce*, 16(3), 1–11.

Puaschunder, J.M. (2016e). The call for global responsible intergenerational leadership in the corporate world: the quest for an integration of intergenerational equity in contemporary corporate social responsibility (CSR) models. In D. Jamali (ed.), *Comparative Perspectives in Global Corporate Social Responsibility* (pp. 275–88). Hershey, PA: IGI Global.

Puaschunder, J.M. (2016f). The role of political divestiture for sustainable development. *Journal of Management and Sustainability*, 6(1), 76–91.

Puaschunder, J.M. (2017a). Cross-sectoral solution-finding and policy dialogue on information and communication technologies for sustainable development. In M. Gudic, T.K. Tan and P.M. Flynn (eds), *Beyond the Bottom Line: Integrating the UN Global Compact into Management Practices* (pp. 32–46). Sheffield: Greenleaf Publishing.

Puaschunder, J.M. (2017b). Ethical decision making under social uncertainty: an introduction to überethicality. *Sustainable Production and Consumption*, 12, 78–89.

Puaschunder, J.M. (2017c). *Global Responsible Intergenerational Leadership.* Wilmington, DE: Vernon Art and Science.

Puaschunder, J.M. (2017d). Mapping climate in the 21st century. *Development*, 59(3), 211–16.

Puaschunder, J.M. (2017e). Socio-psychological motives of socially responsible investors. *Advances in Financial Economics*, 19(1), 209–47.

Puaschunder, J.M. (2017f). The climatorial imperative. *Agriculture Research and Technology*, 7(4), 1–2.

Puaschunder, J.M. (2017g). Sunny side up! From climate change burden sharing to fair global warming benefits distribution: groundwork on the metaphysics of the gains of global warming and the climatorial imperative. Paper presented to the

Administrative Sciences Association of Canada Annual Conference, HEC Montreal, Quebec, Canada.

Puaschunder, J.M. (2018a). Nachhaltigkeit und Investment: Psychologische Aspekte von nachhaltigkeitsorientiertem Investitionsverhalten. In C.T. Schmitt and E. Bamberg (eds), *Psychologie und Nachhaltigkeit: Konzeptionelle Grundlagen, Anwendungsbeispiele und Zukunftsperspektiven* (pp. 127–34). Wiesbaden: Springer.

Puaschunder, J.M. (2018b). *Intergenerational Responsibility in the 21st Century.* Wilmington, DE: Vernon Press.

Puaschunder, J.M. (2019). *Intergenerational Equity: Corporate and Financial Social Responsibility.* Cheltenham, UK and Northampton, MA, USA: Edward Elgar Publishing.

Puaschunder, J.M. (2020). *Governance & Climate Justice: Global South & Developing Nations.* Cham, Switzerland: Springer Nature/Palgrave Macmillan.

Puaschunder, J.M. (2021). *Verhaltensökonomie und Verhaltensfinanzökonomie: Ein Vergleich europäischer und nordamerikanischer Modelle.* Cham, Switzerland: Springer Gabler.

Rawls, J. (1971). *A Theory of Justice.* Cambridge, MA: Harvard University Press.

Rolle, M. (2016, 1 September). Reversing climate change: interview with Graciela Chichilnisky. *Global Policy.* Accessed 21 January 2021 at https://www .globalpolicyjournal.com/blog/01/09/2016/reversing-climate-change-interview -graciela-chichilnisky.

Sachs, J.D. (2014). Climate change and intergenerational well-being. In L. Bernard and W. Semmler (eds), *The Oxford Handbook of the Macroeconomics of Global Warming* (pp. 248–59). Oxford: Oxford University Press.

Schueth, S. (2008). Socially responsible investing in the United States. *Journal of Business Ethics,* 4, 189–94.

Starr, M. (2008). Socially responsible investment and pro-social change. *Journal of Economic Issues,* 42(1), 51–73.

United Nations Conference on Trade and Development (UNCTAD) (2015). *World Investment Report 2015: Reforming International Investment Governance.* New York: United Nations.

World Bank (2015). Green bonds attract private sector climate finance. World Bank Brief.

10. Social impact bonds: challenges and success

Eleonora Broccardo and Maria Mazzuca

Introduction to social impact bonds

Social impact bonds (SIBs) are schemes that involve a contract between public or non-profit service providers and private investors, and they provide upfront funding for interventions designed to improve specific social outcomes (Warner, 2013). Investors' returns depend on the impact of the project and whether its outcomes are achieved.

In July 2020, the SIB market consisted of 194 impact bonds in 33 countries, including 11 development impact bonds (DIBs) with a total upfront capital of $420.77 million and an average upfront capital of $3.16 million. Most SIBs were contracted in high-income countries (with the United States and United Kingdom in the lead) and in employment and social welfare sectors (Brookings Institution Global Impact Bond Database, 2020).

As the numbers indicate, SIBs have been increasingly employed since their inception in 2010, when they were first applied to the UK prison sector. The literature on SIBs is very fragmented, and the perspectives employed to study these schemes are multitudinous (Broccardo, Mazzuca and Ruggirello, 2019). The literature suggests the emergence of some challenges that need to be met in order for SIBs to spread and develop. These challenges include the need to develop a theoretical framework and remedy the lack of empirical data on the bonds' effectiveness (Broccardo, Mazzuca and Frigotto, 2020). Furthermore, as the market for SIBs is still limited, some factors might represent an impediment to their application and diffusion. From a financial perspective, we argue that one factor that could potentially limit the application of these schemes is the lack of interest from mainstream investors and blended investors – that is, investors interested in both financial and social returns.

This chapter aims to enrich the ongoing debate on SIBs by facing the above-mentioned emergent challenges, and we will answer the following research questions:

- What are the starting points for developing a theoretical framework for SIBs?
- Which SIB characteristics positively contribute to their effectiveness and success?
- Which factors contribute to enhancing SIBs' financial returns?

To answer these questions, we first describe SIBs and discuss how a related and robust theoretical framework is missing. Then we use financial lenses to focus on SIBs. First, we argue that SIBs' financial aspects could represent one of their potential strengths, especially with respect to other complex solutions that typically aim to address social problems. We enrich the discussion by arguing that some financial characteristics could positively contribute to SIBs' success. Finally, we try to design an analysis that investigates in depth the determinants to SIBs' returns, starting with the underlying hypothesis that high returns could attract mainstream investors.

This chapter contributes to the research on SIBs in several ways as we use financial lenses to consider some open issues on SIBs. First, as the literature on SIBs is fragmented and contains multiple perspectives, some challenges need to be met for SIBs to spread and develop: by focusing on investors' role, we propose some suggestions for a theoretical framework for SIBs. We argue that policy makers need to carefully consider focusing on investors. Second, we highlight the problems that emerge when an empirical analysis is conducted on SIBs from a financial point of view by questioning to what extent a quantitative approach is adequate in conducting research on SIBs.

This chapter is structured as follows. In the next section, we discuss SIBs' nature and functioning. In the third section, we discuss starting points for developing a theoretical framework for SIBs. In the fourth and fifth sections we discuss which factors could impact SIBs' success and which characteristics could affect their financial returns. In the final section we present our conclusions.

The functions of SIBs

Defining the technical and financial characteristics of an impact investment instrument in a timely and exhaustive way is not easy. We believe that it is crucial to identify the peculiarity that, when traced in the context of any financial instrument, allows it to be classified as an investment instrument with a pure impact or as a traditional instrument. The decisive criteria in this attempt are found in the definition of the returns offered to the investor. If the investor is remunerated only and subordinately to the achievement of a specific outcome or on the basis of a verified and measured impact of a social or environmental nature, the investment can be considered an impact investment. We believe that SIBs fully meet these criteria, and therefore they could be the best example of an impact investment instrument.

The first SIB was structured in the United Kingdom in 2010. However, if we consider the nature and purpose of SIBs, we can trace their origin to ten years earlier. It is useful to underline that the concept of bonds is here referenced improperly because SIBs are not structured as bond instruments: they are not standardized financial instruments and are not liquid or traded among investors. The use of the term 'bond' in SIB can be traced back to the intentions of SIBs' creator, the economist Ronnie Horesh, who in 2000 proposed the creation of social policy bonds (SPBs) (Horesh, 2000). SPBs were imagined as new financial instruments created to reward people only when the targeted social goals were achieved. SPBs were to be issued by the public administration and auctioned to the highest bidders. The public administration (PA) would have redeemed SPBs for a fixed sum only if the specified outcomes were achieved. SPBs were to be tradable and, akin to other bonds, their value was imagined to be susceptible to rises and falls. Their differentiating feature (with respect to other bonds issued by the PA) was their uncertain redemption date and the absence of interest. These bonds were to meet the requirements of special investors (called 'active investors') who were strongly interested in the social projects that were to be financed with these bonds. While the proposal was not approved, Horesh's concept was later concretized in the United Kingdom in a model with the same objectives but which does not include the issue of conventional bonds. Ten years later, the first SIB (the Peterborough SIB) appeared and made the SPB proposal concrete.

SIBs are payment-by-results instruments through which public commissioners assign the delivery of public services to service providers. Investors, which are typically non-profit or philanthropic organizations, pay the initial cost of the intervention. The service provider undertakes the commissioned project by delivering the social services. The project's outcomes are monitored and measured by an external evaluator. If the outcomes overcome the predefined trigger point of success, the commissioner will make payments to investors. The underlying assumption is that the payments to investors are motivated

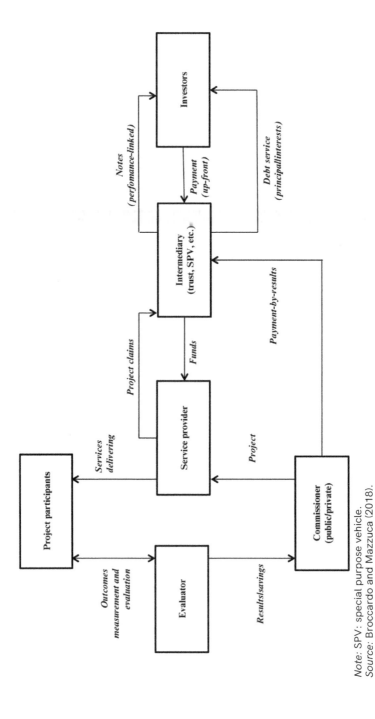

Note: SPV: special purpose vehicle.
Source: Broccardo and Mazzuca (2018).

Figure 10.1   SIBs' basic functioning

and derived from future cost savings that are enabled by the achievement of the project's outcomes. SIBs' basic functions are illustrated in Figure 10.1.

SIBs carry several benefits to project participants. From the commissioner's perspective (the commissioner bears the cost of the impact investment), the benefits are expressed over the long term in the measure of potential future savings. In fact, a social intervention usually aims to intervene in a preventive way to respond to a social need. In the case of no preventive intervention, the underlying social problem could over time reveal further social needs and expenses. However, if the project's outcomes are not achieved, investors lose the invested capital and the commissioner does not bear the costs necessary for the provision of the service. By structuring a SIB, therefore, the public commissioner has the possibility of pursuing specific social objectives without anticipating financial resources and by remunerating investors with a part of the savings achieved.

From the perspective of social enterprise, the main advantage of a SIB is the possibility of being financed ex ante by external investors and therefore being equipped with the stable financial resources necessary to implement a project.

Finally, SIBs allow investors to be involved in the social sector by subscribing to an instrument that remunerates them with a blended value (financial plus social return) and allows them to develop a leverage effect, triggering a virtuous circle of new social financing.

Suggestions for a theoretical framework for SIBs

A complete review of the theoretical literature on SIBs can be found in Broccardo et al. (2020). The authors discussed three groups of studies that covered SIBs' theoretical development. The first group provided theory-based contributions, and these clearly stated the theoretical framework to which the authors referred in the evaluation of SIBs. The second group developed an original interpretative or theoretical framework for the classification or assessment of SIBs.

The third, more interesting and very small group of studies included contributions that can be defined as purely theoretical, as they developed theories on SIBs. They are Wong et al. (2016), Giacomantonio (2017) and Pauly and Swanson (2017). With the aim of understanding why SIBs exist, all these contributions compared them to alternative funding schemes and defined under which conditions they deliver value to stakeholders. Using a decision-tree analysis, Giacomantonio (2017) found that SIBs are a losing proposition for investors unless they are chosen by a risk-averse commissioner and grant-funding agency to maximize grant-making capacities across a portfolio of SIB investments. Wong et al. (2016) theoretically and experimentally showed that SIBs can alleviate the underperformance issue and outperform performance-based contracts because investors can write contracts based on a service provider's performance. According to Pauly and Swanson (2017), a non-profit service provider can obtain funds only through either the issuance of a combination of donations and traditional debt or – jointly with altruistic investors – a SIB contract with the government. The success of SIBs is strictly a function of the involvement of altruistic investors in the service provision. Investors' engagement can be both direct (e.g., through membership with service providers' boards) and indirect (e.g., through participation in project screening based on their ability to assess success probability).

Both Wong et al. (2016) and Pauly and Swanson (2017) offered what we believe is the main theoretical contribution to the existence of SIBs – that is, the central role of investors in their success. However, we believe that much has yet to be done to enhance the understanding of why altruistic investors should select SIBs among the wide and increasing spectrum of socially responsible instruments and to what extent SIBs can balance the participation of different categories of investors who have varying risk–return desiderata. What could shed light on this is empirical evidence within the social responsibility research field. As Brodback, Guenster and Mezger (2019) showed, there is a positive and strong link between the altruistic values of investors and the relative importance of social responsibility. Interestingly, such an effect becomes even stronger when investors believe they can make a positive impact with their investments. In this context, SIBs stand out as the instrument structured to specifically obtain an impact and, as such, could exploit the link between altruistic motivation and social issues. Furthermore, Brodback et al. (2019) demonstrated the role played by the promised financial return: if very altruistic investors associate responsible investments with higher returns, their motivation to invest responsibly decreases. Here, theoretical research on SIBs should make clear whether and how a specific structure (or a flexible one) is effective in attracting investors who have different levels of altruism in order to meet the social goal.

Additionally, we argue that future theoretical research could further focus on comparisons of SIBs with other funding mechanisms to shed light on the role of investors (as so far discussed). However, we do not discount the idea that other issues could be relevant to SIBs' existence. Among these, SIBs' plus features, such as their specifically activated governance, co-production and accountability mechanisms, could play a role in developing a theoretical framework to apply to SIBs.

SIBs' success: which characteristics matter?

With reference to the second and third research questions, in the absence of a complete theory on SIBs and in order to enrich the research agenda, this and the following sections contain ideas to develop the empirical analysis by focusing on SIBs' financial characteristics. Below, we discuss which characteristics could determine their success, and we focus on financial factors. In the next section, we focus on the determinants of financial returns.

Our underlying hypothesis is that the financial characteristics and investors play a key role in SIBs' success. To test this hypothesis, we suggest an empirical strategy in which SIBs' success is measured according to whether the outcome is reached and therefore investors are repaid. An empirical analysis could be developed with a focus on SIBs' financial characteristics, which would be considered key variables. We could also consider other variables that could have an indirect influence on SIBs' attractiveness to investors mainly because they affect the riskiness of the project. Finally, we could control for other characteristics, as suggested by the literature. In Table 10.1, we summarize the variables that an empirical model could include. In column 2, we describe the variables' construction, and in column 3, we indicate the predicted sign of the relations.

The model variables could include the following entities:

- Key variables: these would be indicators aimed at capturing financial characteristics and include the role of investors (number of investors, institutional investors' participation) and other variables that typically signal a scheme's financial profile (internal rate of return, guarantees and maturity).
- Structural variables: these would be factors with a potential indirect influence on the project's attractiveness to investors, such as indicators of the service intervention model (originality, evaluation methodology, costs and success payment to other stakeholders) and other variables that capture the characteristics of the service providers (previous experience in the same type of intervention and non-profit, public or private status).
- Control variables: these would include the size of the intervention/investment, the geographic area and the sectors of intervention.[1]

This analysis is problematic for two main reasons. First, the construction of the data set is very challenging because of the paucity of data in general and of the data publicly disclosed in particular. The second reason is related to the way in which SIBs' success is measured. If we assume that their success is measured according to whether the outcome is reached and investors are therefore repaid, relevant problems arise due to the very small number of SIBs completed so far. Synthesizing the very small number of SIBs contracted and concluded so far does not yield enough data to conduct an unbiased empirical analysis. Below, we discuss these issues and suggest some potential solutions for future research.

To enrich the database, information that is not publicly disclosed could be considered. In other words, several data sources need to be considered to develop a viable database. The starting point could be the Social Finance UK's Impact Bond Global Database. When we look at this database, we discover that it does not make relevant information available. To overcome this problem, we could use the Brookings Institution Global Impact Bond data. However, this information is not publicly disclosed. Other data could be collected by consulting other sources and/or directly from the website of each SIB project. It should be stressed that the manual construction of a data set would expose the researcher to risks related to the consistency of data released from different sources. Furthermore, as always happens in the manual construction of a data set, problems may arise due to errors or the choices of the researcher.

The second problem to overcome is related to how success is measured. First, we emphasize that there are already methodologies that consider the success of a project by integrating different aspects. Among these, the social return on investment (SROI) methodology is noteworthy. It allows for the measuring of the success and impacts of individual SIBs, while it highlights significant limits when an econometric analysis that considers a pool of projects needs to be developed.

To solve the above problems, we must first consider not only the completed projects but also the partially evaluated ones. However, again, the number of SIBs to be considered could be limited. Furthermore, this strategy might not permit the resolution of another problem related to the fact that too few SIBs have concluded with a failure. A different solution could account for the level of success by considering the difference between the outcome trigger point and the actual outcome achieved. This solution is expected to be very interesting. However, developing it would be very challenging because of the difficulty of obtaining necessary data, even in the case in which a researcher tries to collect them manually from the websites of each project.

Table 10.1   Determinants of SIBs' success: descriptions of variables

Variable	Construction	Predicted Sign
Success1	0/1: value of 1 if project is completed (outcome achieved and investors paid)	Dependent variable
Role of investors		
Number of investors	No. of investors	+/-
Institutional investors' participation	Dummy: presence of at least one institutional investor	+
Financial characteristics		
Internal rate of return	IRR (%)	+/-
Guarantees	Dummy: presence of at least one guarantee	+/-
Maturity	No. of years	+/-
Intervention model		
Originality	Dummy: value of 1 if the model is implemented for the first time	-
Evaluation methodology	Type of evaluation	+/-
Cover ratio	Costs not covered by the SIB capital rise/ total costs	+/-
Success payment to other stakeholders	Dummy	+
Service provider		
Service provider experience	Dummy: value of 1 if provider has experience in the same model (or SIBs)	+
Service provider nature	Dummy: value of 1 if public	+/-
Control		
Size of intervention	Capital raised	+/-
Geographic area	Dummy	
Sector of intervention	Dummy	

According to the solutions so far discussed, the analysis could be integrated by conducting robustness tests in which other variables are considered as proxies for SIBs' success or failure (Table 10.2).

Table 10.2   Determinants of SIBs' success: different measures of success

Dependent Variable	Construction
Success1	0/1: value of 1 if project is completed (outcome achieved and investors paid)
Success2	0/1: value of 1 if the project is successfully completed or is partially and positively evaluated
Success3	Level of exceeding the trigger (difference in %)

The limitations that could arise when a researcher decides to develop an econometric analysis of SIBs and the solutions so far discussed perhaps suggest reflections and questions. First, is it correct to approach the issue of the SIBs' success by using a standardized econometric classical analysis such as that suggested in this section? Further, if we focus on investors, other reflections emerge. From investors' perspectives, each SIB is a specific case. If a pool of SIBs could be obtained into which investors could implement a diversification strategy, a quantitative analysis that proposes the consideration of different SIBs as a single data set would be correct. The question we then ask is whether we are sure that an econometric analysis that considers a set of SIBs (which, however, are not accessible) would really help in investigating the phenomenon. Perhaps, a qualitative analysis that permits the detailed observation of individual SIBs could be more useful in designing a model that would be attractive to investors.

To conclude, to properly investigate the determinants of SIBs' success, other hypotheses should be considered. Perhaps success should be measured considering different stakeholders. Perhaps the qualitative analysis, up to now more developed than the quantitative one, would allow the researcher to obtain more interesting results. What does it mean for a SIB to end successfully? Given the fact that SIBs tend to end successfully (so far only one SIB has ended in failure), is an analysis that focuses on measuring their success superfluous? Researchers could examine other issues in the future. For example, distinguishing the perspectives of investors (which we focus on in the next section) from that of the public originator might be of interest. Finally, given the relatively limited number of SIBs carried out so far, researchers might investigate how SIBs can be scaled.

Factors affecting SIBs' financial returns

With reference to the third research question, the suggested analysis aims to verify the factors that impact SIBs' financial returns. A plausible hypothesis is that the higher the financial return, the higher the potential interest of mainstream investors and the greater the potential diffusion of SIBs. As we will discuss in the conclusions section, this is a strong hypothesis that needs to be carefully considered.

Table 10.3   Determinants of MRI: description of variables

Variable	Construction	Predicted Sign of Relation
MRI	%	Dependent variable
Financial risk		
Maturity	No. of years	+
Guarantee	Presence of at least 1 guarantee	–
Guarantee1	Level of guarantee: % of guaranteed capital	–
Intrinsic risk		
Originality	Dummy: value of 1 if the model is implemented for the first time	+
Quality of the service provider	Dummy: value of 1 if provider has experience in SIBs	–
Success payment to other stakeholders	Dummy	+
Governance risk		
Number of participants		+
Level of intermediation	How many intermediaries participate to the project	–
Commissioner nature	Dummy: 1 if public	+/–
Institutional investors' participation	Dummy: presence of at least 1 institutional investor	–
Incentive system	Dummy: 1 if success payment to other stakeholders	–
Control variables		
Geographic area	Dummy	
Sector of intervention	Dummy	

To test which factors affect SIBs' financial returns, we can imagine an empirical strategy that predicts that their financial returns are measured through their maximum return for investors (MRI) – that is, the maximum amount offered to investors that incorporates the repayment of principal plus interest when the outcome is exceeded. It is important to remember that in a SIB, the interest rate can be fixed – that is, predetermined – in the issuance phase. However, in most cases, it is within a certain range and strictly dependent on the level of success, therefore it is dependent on how much outcome the innovative social finance scheme has achieved. This latter aspect highlights how an analysis that only considers MRI could present interesting but only partial results.

To develop the analysis, we could assume a positive risk–return relationship. Therefore, we could focus on the risk factors that may influence the MRI. Risks in a SIB could have several sources, and we should therefore consider different risk proxies (key variables). We could also control for other characteristics, as suggested by the literature. In Table 10.3, we summarize the variables that an empirical model could include.

The model's variables could include the following elements: (1) key variables: these are proxies of financial risk (maturity, presence and level of guarantees), proxies of intrinsic risk (originality and quality/experience of the service provider) and proxies of the governance risk (number of participants, level of intermediation, nature of the commissioner and institutional investors participation, incentive systems); (2) control variables: these are the size of the intervention/investment, the geographic area and the sectors of intervention.

As discussed in the previous section, developing this analysis could create problems in collecting data. In Box 10.1, we report the results of a partial analysis based on the empirical strategy discussed so far but which includes only some of the variables indicated. Additionally, in conducting this analysis, the main challenges were related to constructing the data set. However, the preliminary results of the analysis could be the starting point of future research and could contribute to highlighting the potential challenges of researching SIBs.

Box 10.1 The determinants of SIBs' return: a preliminary analysis

The starting point for constructing the sample was to consider all the SIBs contracted until September 2019[2] – that is, 164 SIBs around the world. Subsequently, 41 were excluded because the data were insufficient in developing the analysis. Of the 123 SIBs left, only 120 were considered after excluding outliers. The final sample included 120 from 25 countries and in seven intervention areas.

As already discussed, to measure the financial return, MRI was considered, and to obtain a simple measure of MRI, two hypotheses were introduced. The first hypothesis was that the SIBs must be assimilated to multi-year zero coupon instruments. The second hypothesis was that the SIBs were unsecured. The first hypothesis appears plausible because the vast majority of the SIBs issued foresaw the payment of the principal plus interest at the end of the implementation period. The second hypothesis was introduced because the available data did not allow researchers to detect, for each SIB, the number of guarantees linked to the repayment of the principal to investors in the event of project failure. Although some SIBs do not have complex guarantee systems, it should be noted that several offer partial capital coverage, and it should be stressed that the issue of guarantees in SIBs is very delicate, as their presence risks undermining some of the fundamental objectives that the participants and, in particular, the originator intend to achieve. Therefore, the guarantees distort SIBs' real nature. Among these objectives, we mention the transfer of risk to investors and the possibility of achieving savings for the public originator.

Given the two hypotheses, the MRI for each SIB was calculated as follows:

$$MaxReturnforInvestors = \sqrt[t]{\left(\frac{MaxOutcomePayment}{CapitalRaised}\right)} - 1$$

where t is the period of the SIB's implementation, and $MaxOutcomePayment$ is the maximum capital payment due to the investors that had to be considered as a cap.

Table 10.4 describes the variables and Table 10.5 presents the descriptive statistics.

The empirical analysis was developed according to the three steps set out below:

1. Construction of a multiple linear regression model on which robustness tests were performed.
2. Assumption of the non-linearity hypothesis and use of the quadratic and cubic regression functions.
3. Verification of the results with a censored regression model, that, is a tobit model.

Table 10.4   A preliminary analysis of the factors affecting SIBs' financial returns: descriptions of variables

Name	Description	Motivation	Sign
Maturity	No. of years (implementation)		+/-
Cohort_size	No. of service beneficiaries (target population)	Complexity increase	+
Central	Value of 1 if the originator is a central government	More money	+
Intermediary	Value of 1 if there is an intermediary (between service provider and investors)	Costs increase Reduction Information asymmetries	-
Launch_year_1-Launch_year_9	Dummies for each year of project launch (no 2011; no SIBs)	Scale effect Economic/political changes	+/-
Area_1-Area_7	Dummies for each area of intervention	Some sectors more critical	+/-
State_1-State_25	Dummies for each country	Developed countries vs. undeveloped	+/-

Table 10.5   A preliminary analysis of the factors affecting SIBs' financial return of the SIBs: descriptive statistics

Variable	Mean	Median	Standard Deviation	Min	Max
Investor_return	0.1839	0.10	0.1852	0.00	0.6994
Maturity	4.1194	4	1.4887	1	10
Cohort_size	1419.6	600	2540.882	11	18 000
Launch_year	2015	2016	2.1133	2010	2019

The main findings of this preliminary analysis can be summarized as follows. First, when the multiple linear regression model was performed, the variable 'Central' seemed to have some relevance. Furthermore, all the launch year dummies signalled a significant increase in returns (due to positive coefficients) compared to 2010 (the reference dummy). Additionally, the dummies aimed at capturing the intervention areas were positively significant, taking the family care as a reference dummy. The country dummies had a negative sign, indicating that, on average, the maximum returns offered in each country were lower than those offered in the reference country, which was Great Britain (where SIBs were born).

Overall, while the results of the preliminary analysis seem to confirm the presence of a non-linear relation and the relevance of the financial profile of the project, it is necessary to approach these findings with caution due to the limitations that affected the analysis: the very limited sample (which made performing an OLS analysis difficult), the presence of too many dummies and the absence of potentially important information on variables that should have been included in the analysis.

Future researchers could try to collect more data to better inform their empirical analyses. This task could become easier as new projects are developed and completed over time. However, we here point out the need for consistent and public information bases. Future researchers may also consider other estimation methods. Among these, a principal component analysis is of interest. Finally, progress in formulating a theory of SIB or of social impact finance could suggest new strategies for empirical analysis.

Conclusions

In this chapter, we discussed SIBs with the objective of enriching the research agenda. Starting from the emerging challenges in the world of SIBs, we focused on three issues: (1) starting points for developing a theoretical framework for SIBs; (2) characteristics of SIBs that positively contribute to their effectiveness/ success; and (3) factors that contribute to the enhancement of SIBs' financial returns.

To examine these issues, we first highlighted the few theoretical contributions to date. Then, using financial lenses, we discussed the factors that could affect the SIBs' success and financial returns. In so doing, we hypothesized a design for an empirical strategy that could be valuable in investigating these issues.

The discussion of the theoretical contributions of SIBs suggests promising theoretical lens for understanding them. With the aim to provide a promising future outlook on SIBs, some future research questions might be the following:

- Under which (market, institutional, legal) conditions could SIBs be superior to other financial schemes in addressing social issues?

- Which category of investors could best contribute within the SIBs' schemes by adding (what) value?
- Which SIBs' features (e.g., from a governance, co-production and accountability perspective) could add insights in developing a theoretical framework for SIBs?

The discussion on the determinants of SIBs' success highlights the relevance of investors and the financial characteristics projects. We also highlighted some of the problems that arise when an empirical analysis is used to test the determinants of the SIBs' success, and these were mainly related to the paucity of available data and the measurement of success. We suggested some solutions to these problems.

We continued the discussion by questioning whether the development of an econometric analysis is an appropriate choice in the case of SIBs and by arguing that a qualitative analysis could reveal some potential strengths, especially when the goal consists of the induction of a model that is attractive to investors. We also suggested some issues that the research agenda could consider, referring to the opportunity to measure success by considering different stakeholders and, most of all, different types of investors as well as the need to measure results using a more nuanced approach. Finally, we discussed how to scale SIBs. Future empirical research might focus on the following research questions:

- How can data on SIBs be collated and shared gain valuable evidence in order to better project future activities through SIBs? In this sense, is the cooperation with (public) institutions, practitioners and research centres vital?
- What could be the best methodology for measuring the success of SIBs? And from the perspective of which stakeholders?
- How can understanding of SIBs by both service providers and investors be strengthened?

The discussion about the determinants of SIBs' financial returns started from the hypothesis that the higher the financial return, the higher the potential interest of mainstream investors and the greater the potential diffusion of SIBs. However, we here argued that in the case of impact investment and, specifically, SIBs, this hypothesis could be too stringent or even wrong. Perhaps, the financial aspects (and, therefore, the return) that represent the main force attracting investors should be investigated.

It should be noted that SIBs' potential could lie in the possibility of differentiating investors. A survey could shed light on this issue by placing potential investors in front of alternatives. The research question could be formulated as follows: 'For the same financial return, how much would you put in one SIB or another?' This would allow the researcher to distinguish among investors sensitive to social issues, those mainly interested in financial returns, blended investors and other types. Ultimately, the question we ask ourselves is: are we sure that as the financial return grows, we can attract an optimal combination of investors? The underlying intuition is that the financial aspect is neither the only nor the main factor investors consider when they contribute to the social agenda.

Notes

1. The proposed analysis relies on the suggestions of the Nonprofit Finance Fund (2019).
2. This analysis was presented at the 3rd Social Impact Investments International Conference (Broccardo et al., 2019).

References

Broccardo, E. and Mazzuca, M. (2018). An alternative way to think of finance: the case of innovative, sustainable financial instruments. In S. Boubaker, D. Cumming and D.K. Nguyen (eds), *Research Handbook of Investing in the Triple Bottom Line*, Cheltenham, UK and Northampton, MA, USA: Edward Elgar Publishing.

Broccardo, E., Mazzuca, M. and Frigotto, M. (2020). Social impact bonds: the evolution of research and a review of the academic literature. *Corporate Social Responsibility and Environmental Management*, 27(3), 1316–32.

Broccardo, E., Mazzuca, M. and Ruggirello, G. (2019). Social impact bonds: challenges and role of investors. Paper presented at 3rd Social Impact Investments International Conference, Sapienza University Rome, 5–6 December.

Brodback, D., Guenster, N. and Mezger, D. (2019). Altruism and egoism in investment decisions. *Review of Financial Economics*, 37(1), 118–48.

Brookings Institution Global Impact Bond Database (2020, 1 July). Brookings impact bonds snapshot. Accessed 1 July 2020 at https://www.brookings.edu/wp-content/uploads/2019/01/Global-Impact-Bonds-Snapshot-July-2020.pdf.

Giacomantonio, C. (2017). Grant-maximizing but not money-making: a simple decision-tree analysis for social impact bonds. *Journal of Social Entrepreneurship*, 8(1), 47–66.

Horesh, R. (2000). Injecting incentives into the solution of social problems: social policy bonds. *Economic Affairs*, 20(3), 39–42.

Nonprofit Finance Fund (2019). *Pay for Success: The First 25. A Comparative Analysis of the First 25 Pay for Success Projects in the United States.* Accessed 1 February 2021 at https://nff.org/report/pay-success-first-25.

Pauly, M.V. and Swanson, A. (2017). Social impact bonds: new product or new package? *The Journal of Law, Economics, and Organization*, 33(4), 718–60.

Warner, M.E. (2013). Private finance for public goods: social impact bonds. *Journal of Economic Policy Reform*, 16(4), 303–19.

Wong, J., Ortmann, A., Motta, A. and Zhang, L. (2016). Understanding social impact bonds and their alternatives: an experimental investigation. *Experiments in Organizational Economics*, 19, 39–83.

Index